Childerley

MORALITY AND SOCIETY
A series edited by Alan Wolfe

CHILDERLEY

Nature and Morality in a Country Village

Michael Mayerfeld Bell

ILLUSTRATED BY
Christian Potter Drury

THE UNIVERSITY OF CHICAGO PRESS
Chicago & London

Michael Bell teaches sociology of the environment at Iowa State University. He is the author of *The Face of Connecticut: People, Geology, and the Land.*

The University of Chicago Press, Chicago 60637
The University of Chicago Press, London
© 1994 by The University of Chicago
All rights reserved. Published 1994
Printed in the United States of America
04 03 02 01 00   99 98 97 96 95 94   5 4 3 2 1

ISBN: 0-226-04197-2 (cloth)
      0-226-04198-0 (paper)

The author gratefully acknowledges permission to reprint portions of chapters 2, 4, and 5, which previously appeared in "The Fruit of Difference: The Rural-Urban Continuum as a System of Identity," *Rural Sociology* 57, no. 1: 65–82.

Library of Congress Cataloging-in-Publication Data

Bell, Michael, 1957–
    Childerley : nature and morality in a country village / Michael
Mayerfeld Bell ; illustrated by Christian Potter Drury.
        p.   cm. — (Morality and society)
    Includes bibliographical references and index.
    1. Hampshire (England)—Social conditions.   2. Hampshire
(England)—Moral conditions.   I. Title.   II. Series.
HN398.E5B45   1994
306'.09422'7—dc20   93-24209
                                                  CIP

*For Sam
and Diane*

CONTENTS

Acknowledgments   ix

ROUNDS

1. The View from Winter Hill   3
2. A Parish on the Fringe   11

CLASS AND COMMUNITY

3. A "Slightly Feudal" Village   27
4. The Front Door and the Back Door   51
5. Country People and City People   85

NATURE AND SELF

6. Finding Nature   119
7. The Natural Conscience   137

REFLECTIONS

8. The Foreground and the Background: Class   161
9. The Pursuit of the Inedible: Politics   182
10. The Mouse in the Sprinkler Pipe: Gender   210

RESONANCE

11. The View from the Bell Tower   227

Methods   243
Notes   251
References   259
Index   269

ACKNOWLEDGMENTS

THE MOST SATISFYING moment in writing a book is writing the acknowledgments. It's an occasion to reflect on something that the very meaning of authorship tries to deny: No work is the product of some singular self singing alone. And that should give us great pleasure. The bright circle of the spotlight, we are often taught, is the place where we should strive to stand. But this ambition seems pale and petty in comparison to the joyous fellowship of the backstage. Let me honor that fellowship (for there is little we should honor more) by welcoming the full crew out for a bow now, before we begin.

My greatest thanks go to the residents of Childerley who so graciously opened their homes and hearts to an American visitor. They are, I sincerely believe, as much authors of this work as I am, and, if credit is due the work, they should get their share. They are authors through the accommodation they made to my stay and my interests through patiently answering my questions, even when I asked awkward ones. But even more, they are the authors of the place I have tried to describe. It is probably not realistic to expect that they will agree with all of my conclusions. I have not written the village history that several residents felt I was working on. And I have failed completely in undertaking the comparative study with an American exurban village that was my initial plan, a plan that especially intrigued a number of Childerleyans. Still, I hope they are pleased with what I have managed to present here, and that they discover in it that critical fondness which the best of friends share.

Perhaps my happiest hours in Childerley were the ones I spent in its bell tower, a poor pupil of the centuries-old art of change-ringing. How patient indeed were my fellow ringers as I tried to grasp the subtleties of rope and sally. How kind they were to embrace me, a passing figure in their lives, as a member of the ringing team. I confess I really never did gain that intuitive sensibility ringers call "rope sight." The best ringing I ever managed was "plain hunting to thirds." But what an exulting feeling that gave! I hope I have been true to the resonant spirit of that moment in what I have written here.

This study began as my doctoral dissertation, jointly in the Department of Sociology and the School of Forestry and Environmental Studies, at Yale University. I carried out most of the fieldwork while a Fulbright Fellow at the Geography Department of University College London. These institutions brought me into contact with teachers who were, on the whole, wise, warm, and giving. I want particularly to mention Wendy Bell, Scott Boorman, Bill Burch, Jacquie Burgess, Kai Erikson, Ram Guha, Peter Jackson, Philip Lowe, David Lowenthal, Richard Munton, Jim Scott, and Garth Voigt. And let me emphasize my gratitude for the special teachings I received (and usually, I think, accepted!) from Garth, Kai, Jim, and Ram.

A great many kind people took the time to read portions of the manuscript as it took shape. A text, Mikhail Bakhtin advised, should strive to be open to, and indeed the product of, dialog. The comments of all these readers have helped me present something that is just that—the product of my conversations with them, as it is with the residents of Childerley.

So let me extend my grateful thanks to Steve Brint, Kevin Rozario, Jim Scott, Kai Erikson, Jonathan Rieder, Bill Burch, Wendy Bell, Ram Guha, David Lowenthal, Carolyn Harrison, Ronald Blythe, Alan Wolfe, Ernie Mayerfeld, Howard Becker, Doug Harper, Jamie Mayerfeld, John Western, William Felstiner, Pete Siegelmen, Sean Redding, and Marilyn Mayerfeld. The title is, in part, the outcome of a delightful dinner conversation with Tom Demske, Connie Mendolia, Chris Evans, and Karyl Evans, all good friends. Margo MacLeod and Jim Bryan asked questions at public presentations that I gave on Childerley that redirected my thinking in significant ways, and for which I would also like to give thanks. Iverson Griffin, bless his huge heart, was my sociological soulmate during the final revisions of the manuscript.

I also had the enormous good fortune of having Doug Mitchell of the University of Chicago Press for my editor. With great effect, he brings the sensibilities of his jazz drumming to his editorial tasks—that is, a kind of solid warmth, infectious drive, and sure sense of a manuscript's fundamental beat. John Grossman, who did the copy editing, went over the manuscript with the finest grade of sand paper, smoothing the writing and, what is more important, bringing out its grain. I am full of admiration and gratitude for what both John and Doug gave to this book.

But Diane Mayerfeld gave the manuscript the closest reading—and the most aggravating, because her many comments were almost always right (although it was often some time before I came to realize it!). She was in a particularly good position to give these comments, for she also accompanied me in the fieldwork. Although she managed to arrange a position in her own field while we were in England, this was no small sacrifice. She has, as well, been my most important teacher. There is only one word that describes the source of all these gifts. That same word applies to what our son Sam gave to the last three and a half of the years in which I worked on this study.

These, then, are my coauthors all.

ROUNDS

O N E

The View from Winter Hill

It is often said that in books like these we paint arcadias that
never did and never could exist on earth. To this I would
answer that there are many such abodes in country places,
if only our minds are such as to realize them.

J. Arthur Gibbs, 1898

I

ACCORDING TO MOST villagers, the best road into Childerley is the
one over Winter Hill. As the narrow, single-lane road emerges
from the dark, sunken passage through the bluebell wood at the
crest of the hill, Childerley's scattered houses can be seen crowning the
ridge beyond, with an apron of green pastures and grain fields below. If
speed or convenience are your interests, take the main road. But for an
introduction to the village as the villagers like to think of it, take the slow
and quiet route over the hill.

Childerley is not a particularly attractive village. Compared against
Hampshire's best-known villages—Selborne, St. Mary Bourne, the Meons,
the Wallops—it's rather too scattered. Nor does it have any particularly
outstanding views, nor any especially noteworthy buildings or historical
associations. But neither has it been "spoilt," as the local people say, by
recent development. Like many similar settlements on the far fringe of
London, Childerley has seen considerable social change in the past thirty
years as new, wealthier people have moved to the village. Yet comparatively few new buildings have gone up. As one older resident expressed
it, "as villages go, this really is still a village."

"As villages go"—a significant qualification, in both senses of the
word. Childerley's fields of rolling, rippling grain, its pleasant pastures
dotted with cows and sheep, its hedgerows and beech copses—all of this
creates a natural frame within which the mind places the village's hundred
and eighty-five households, its church, school, and village hall. The landscape proclaims a pastoral message: This is not a city. But The City,   3

central London, lies a scant two hours away (less, if you drive quickly or catch the fast train from Winford, the closest station). The edge of London's built-up area is something over an hour away; the surrounding satellite cities and market towns, as little as fifteen minutes. Most residents of Childerley work, shop, attend school, see doctors, run errands, and otherwise spend nearly half their waking hours in these faster and noisier realms.

There is even something urban about Childerley's fields, pastures, and copses. Most of the land is managed by large syndicates. The mists seen settling on the fields are often herbicides, insecticides, fungicides, and synthetic fertilizer compounds. The land itself is a kind of factory, the shop floor for a tractor-powered assembly line.

Geographers have a term for places like Childerley: exurbs. A word like *suburb* doesn't seem right for such an open, agricultural landscape. But is this the real country, and are those who live here real country people? These are questions Childerleyans often ponder.

I lived in Childerley for eight months during 1987–88, and again during brief visits in 1990 and 1991. I was there as an ethnographer, studying the lives of the 475 villagers. What drew me to this study was a desire to understand how at least some people in the Western world think about nature and how they use their ideas about it in their everyday lives. I sought nature in its social and moral context. To put it another way, I wanted to explore the *social experience of nature.* I wanted to learn something about how people experience what they regard as nature and how they relate this experience to their necessarily social lives. It could be said that my interest was not in nature, but "nature"—that is, nature as a form of cultural and moral understanding.

Why would a sociologist be interested in nature? Is not nature virtually antithetical to the social, and thus to the domain of sociology? To be sure, nature is a topic that rarely concerns most sociologists. But despite its frequent philosophical opposition to society, the idea of nature permeates social life. For example, there is natural living, natural childbirth, natural food, natural healing, natural talk, natural writing, natural theology, natural philosophy, and natural law (*jus naturae*). There are also natural people, natural feelings, natural desires, natural expressions, natural arts, natural rights, natural sciences, and natural laws (laws of nature). We find "nature" in our understanding of almost all areas of social behavior, among them ethnicity, nationality, gender, family, the life cycle, emotions, and the granting of merit. And as the growing environmental move-

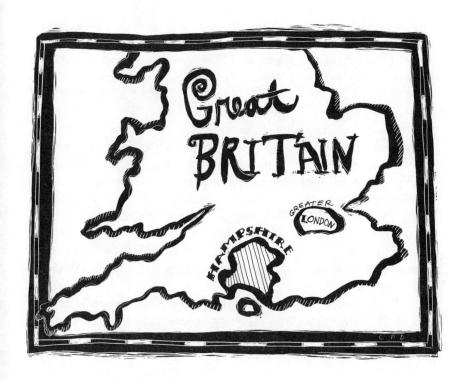

ment attests, we increasingly place a high value on what we regard as "natural."°

The Roman poet Horace once wrote,

Push nature out with a pitchfork, she'll always come back,
And our stupid contempt somehow falls on its face before her.[1]

And indeed, nature is something to which we continually find ourselves returning. The kind of concerns we in the West place in the box we call Nature are among the oldest and most widespread of philosophical issues. It is *ch'i* and *tzu-jan* to the Chinese; *dharma-dhatu* and the Jewel Net of Indra to many Buddhists; and *Tunkashila,* Grandmother, and the *iktomi* to the Lakota Sioux.[2] Nature, as Clarence Glacken observed, "is a grand old word," a powerful mover of human hearts and minds.[3] Nothing could be of greater interest to a sociologist.

I chose not to study nature in the unambiguous setting of a wilderness or a remote rural area. What makes an exurban setting appropriate is that in such a place nature, given its conventional opposition to the city, lies close to its cultural boundaries, and it is at the boundaries that we find the dimensions of our understandings. Concepts need limits and edges. In a place like Childerley, the limits of the city and the edge of nature are constant topics of discussion, for exurbia is a conceptual zone which is neither raw nor cooked. It seems appropriate to study the social experience of nature in a place where people of cultural necessity often discuss this very topic.°°

What I found is that nature is at the heart of Childerleyans' conception of themselves. The main point of this book is to demonstrate the importance in the lives of the villagers of two kinds of moral thinking.

° Although I have done so here and elsewhere, I have chosen not to put quotation marks everywhere around the words *nature* and *natural,* for it is stylistically awkward. As nature is the central problem of this work, the reader should regard these words that way wherever they appear herein. I have added quotation marks only where I felt it necessary to make sure the reader had not forgotten how problematic nature is.

°° Here, as I usually do elsewhere in the book, I write in the present tense. I do so cautiously, for while I think this style of presentation helps give a sense of liveness to the village and its people, it can also give the impression that the author is making claims about eternal truths. History—as any ethnography must immediately, upon publication, become—does not usually allow such confidence. So let the reader keep in mind that I base my writing on what I heard and saw in Childerley during 1987–91, a period whose special characteristics we will, I imagine, come to understand better with time.

One is moral thinking based on ideas the villagers consider to be socially derived. The other is moral thinking based on truths they consider to be above and free from the polluting interests of social life. In a world in which so many traditionally accepted sources of identity and motivation have come to be sharply questioned, in a sea of doubt, this alternative form of thinking gives villagers a moral rock on which to stand, a rock I will be calling the *natural conscience*.

Villagers find that this rock stands firm against a pervasive theme of conversation in Childerley: the materialist critique of social order—the charge that social interest underlies what people say and believe, as well as what they do. This suspicion of interest undermines for them the value of moral thinking derived from what they see as collective beliefs and sentiments, beliefs and sentiments Emile Durkheim long ago called the *collective conscience*.[4] "It is with a view to themselves and their own interest," thought the sophist Callicles twenty-five hundred years ago, "that they make their laws and distribute their praises and censures."[5] It's an old problem of the conscience, one that many people in many places at many times, I imagine, have worried about. One form it takes in contemporary Britain, I believe, is a widespread questioning of that society's major source of conscious group identity: class.

At least in the estimation of Childerleyans, class remains very central to British life and to their own lives, both as a primary source of identity and personal motivation and as a powerful constraint on what motivation and identity can attain. Yet the residents are virtually united in deploring this continuing state of social affairs—even though they themselves knowingly enact it—as we shall hear. The source of the villagers' criticism of class is their suspicion that social interests underlie its continuing force in their society. This *moral ambiguity of class*, as I will call it, leaves Childerleyans searching for an alternative source of social self that can serve as a legitimate basis for motivation.

There are various ways this problem might be resolved. Childerleyans seek to do so by conceiving of themselves and presenting themselves as "country people" and "village people"—people who lead a distinctive way of life characteristic of those who live in the country "closer to nature," as Childerleyans sometimes say. In this way, they find a stable perch for their spirits, a perch in the natural conscience. The nature of the countryside is not the only such perch. By the natural conscience, I mean to include *any* manner of moral thinking conceived as free of social interest, as class itself once was, in more minds than it is today, at least in Childerley. But the perch of class (among others) has been weakened by the erosive power of social critique. Childerleyans now fly toward another roost: country life.

In order to build this roost, one long employed against materialist criticism, Childerleyans have had to arrive at an understanding of nature that adequately resolves the philosophical difficulties that have long beset the concept. As firm and secure as it appears, nature is a singularly variable idea. As Arthur Lovejoy observed, the "semantic fecundity" of the word *nature* is virtually unparalleled.[6] His attempt to catalogue the variety of meanings found sixty-six separate usages and was far from exhaustive.[7] "Nature," said Raymond Williams, "is perhaps the most complex word in the language."[8] Villagers must confront this complexity in order to resolve what might be called the exurban question—the question of whether places like Childerley are the real country, close to nature.

Yet the variability of nature (and here I mean both nature and "nature") allows villagers to make a range of arguments for their right to stand on its moral rock, a range that they can apply to their own varied backgrounds, experiences, and beliefs. Culture, Ann Swidler has suggested, can be described as a kind of "tool kit" we carry about with us.[9] I will suggest the following of Childerleyans: Nature is their wrench, a "spanner" the English would say—an adjustable tool they can fit to the howling machinery of their lives.

My main purpose, then, will be to explore the use of nature as a source of identity and moral understanding by the people of Childerley.

II

WHY AN *English* exurban village? True enough, I probably could have done this study in any Western country, as exurbia is everywhere now. In fact, the wider significance of what I have to say in part depends on this. But I felt that my mind would be clearer, fresher in a setting different from my own native country. As most travelers have likely discovered, a new place tends to summon up the questioning faculty. I hoped thereby I might more easily maintain a sense of wonder—an eye that sees life as strange—that would throw the problem of nature into social relief. This consideration immediately eliminated the United States, where I had lived virtually my whole life. Furthermore, such a study required an easy fluency with the language of the community, a fluency I only have in English.

From the remaining possibilities, I settled on England because the exurban question is particularly developed there. Inhabiting a land that was the first to become truly industrialized and that is still one of the world's most densely populated, the English have long pondered the boundary of nature. If nature exists at all in England, it must be close to human settlement, as people live virtually everywhere in that country. Consequently, the English have come to look for nature not so much in the wilderness they have so little of, but closer to home in the rural hinterlands. As the Australians think of their wild back land, Americans their Rocky Mountain land, and the Canadians their desolate tundra land, so the English think of their "green and pleasant land" of contented ruralia. Such a location for nature, one that already allows for much human settlement and intervention, has made the question of its boundary especially salient and culturally important in England. Virtually the whole of rural England, every hedgerow and tree, is as managed and manipulated as Manchester. Where, then, does nature begin and end? We often show our deepest moral concern over categories with imprecise boundaries. Pastoral nature has been such a concern for the English that the historian Alun Howkins has described the country as adhering to a "cult of the countryside."[10]

Take for example the huge literature on the theme of the changing countryside in England.° In fact, most major English authors of the past three hundred years have dealt heavily with rural matters and rural settings, often showing a near obsession with pastoral nature.°° Or take land

---

° Some of the most compelling and widely read recent works of this genre include Ronald Blythe's *Akenfield* (1969), Howard Newby's *Green and Pleasant Land?* (1979) Richard Mabey's *The Common Ground* (1980), and Marion Shoard's *The Theft of the Countryside* (1981).

°° With the partial (and notable) exception of Dickens, this includes such names as Alexander Pope, Henry Fielding, William Blake, William Cobbett, George Crabbe, John Clare, Jane Austen, William Wordsworth, the Bronte sisters, Thomas Hardy, George Elliot, George Gissing, D. H. Lawrence, Dorothy Sayers, Aldous Huxley, and J. R. R. Tolkien. The stories of Beatrix Potter, Arthur Ransome, E. Nisbit, Francis Hodgson Burnett, A. A. Milne, and C. A. Lewis have delighted children in many countries, and have virtually defined the appropriate genre for children's literature as dominantly rural and natural. There are also the rural remembrances of Mary Russell Mitford, Flora Thompson, Hugh Massingham, Laurie Lee, George Sturt, George Ewart Evans, and James Herriot. Similarly, in art the rural world dominated the imagination of Stubbs, Gainsborough, Constable, Turner, the many English contributors to landscape gardening, the folklorist Cecil Sharpe, and the *sui generis* works of Ruskin and Morris. It is worth speculating as well on the connection of the ambiguity of nature in England to the spectacular history of English contributions to natural history. The world would

planning. From the perspective of the rest of the Anglophone world, the United Kingdom has a stunningly complex and restrictive array of laws which seek to preserve the country's rural character. Although comparable changes have affected the United States, Canada, and Australia, these countries have not produced comparable literatures or planning efforts surrounding the edge of pastoral nature. These countries have their boundary concerns too, of course. As they locate nature more in wilderness, their efforts and literatures emphasize preservation of the boundary of the wild. But I sought to study nature in the most ambiguous setting of all, a community on the exurban edge of the English-speaking world's most exurban country.

Childerley is one such community somewhere in northern Hampshire. Let us now approach it.

---

be a very different place without the work of English natural historians like Gilbert White, William Smith, Thomas Huxley, Alfred Russel Wallace, Charles Lyell, and that other Charles, Charles Darwin.

T W O

A Parish on the Fringe

> this gift of the second life . . . the second, happier childhood
> as it were, the second arrival (but with an adult's perception)
> at a knowledge of natural things, together with the fulfill-
> ment of the child's dream of the safe house in the wood.
>
> V. S. Naipaul, 1987

I

CHILDERLEY SITS HIGH on the knobbed back of the Hampshire Downs, a rolling plateau of Cretaceous chalk, the seventy million or so year-old bed of rock that stretches halfway across southern England. Small hills and valleys ripple across the plateau, and Childerley rests on the crests of three of these topographic waves. The main village is on Church Hill, and several hamlets and outlying farms lie on and between the other two, Winter Hill and Holt Hill.

Saxons settled the area in the sixth and seventh centuries. They were not the first people to live on the plateau. The stone, bronze, and iron axes of earlier folk had already cleared some of the plateau's hillsides, and the Saxons established their settlements in and around the open lands and remaining forest. Yet, as near as we can tell, Childerley owes to the Saxons much more of the basic layout of its several thousand acres of land: the run of many of the roads and lanes, the location of most of the parish boundaries (and even some of the field boundaries), the siting of the hamlets, and possibly even the selection of one hamlet as the dominant one, where the church and manor would be.[1] The Saxons also spoke the language from which most local place names come. To a Saxon, the name "Childerley" would have meant "child's glade."*

A village is supposed to have ancient origins, or so the popular idea of the perfect English village suggests. That misty image also portrays a village of half-timbered thatched cottages, of a grand manor house, and of a pub, church, school, and cricket pitch nestled around a lush green

---

* The actual name *Childerley*, of course, is my invention. (It is pronounced *chill*-der-lee.)

and village pond. Aside from pictures in children's books and the little hand-painted porcelain models of villages sold to tourists, few of these perfect villages exist. And Childerley is not one of them. True, it has the appropriate depth of history, but it does not everywhere look the part. As one Childerley resident described, "It's not the sort of typical quaint English village with the village green and all this. It's not like that, is it? It's more sort of—I don't know. I suspect it's more like the typical English village than that."

Over the centuries, a smallish village grew up around the church and nearby farmland, straggling out along the main roads of Church Hill. Travel guides commonly praise English villages that have the "nucleated" plan thought characteristic of the perfect village. Childerley has its share of thatch and half-timbering, but its form follows a more linear, and there- fore less picturesque, pattern. There is a green, although it is very small, and it does have a pond. The hilltops give a number of fine views of the surrounding pastures, cropland, and woods. The church is very old, at least eight hundred years, and it has a handsome tower with a fine peal of bells and a pleasant and much-visited graveyard. The village has enough attractive features to rate inclusion in one recent list of the "great many really charming villages of Hampshire."[2] But on the whole, its scenery is unremarkable as Hampshire villages go.

Although Childerley is not renowned for its physical charm, older buildings still dominate the parish. The church is the most ancient. There are also more than a dozen cottages and farmhouses from before the 1800s (including some from before 1700) plus several old barns, stables, and granaries. Portions of two buildings even date from the 1300s. Several houses sport the half-timbering and gently rounded caps of thatch of the perfect village. These are intermingled with a fair number of pleasant nineteenth-century and pre–World War II cottages. Almost all the cot- tages were formerly "tied cottages," dwellings "tied" to a local job. With the shrinking of the rural workforce, most are now sold on the open market. As is characteristic of the English countryside, the typical cottage is a semidetached building, joined to another by a common wall.

Childerley also has a handful of "Big Houses," as villagers say, two of which could be properly called manor houses. Neither of these are the twenty-five-bedrooms-and-up type common to many English villages, but they still impress. And there are a number of other large homes, some converted from former farmhouses and, in one case, an old barn.

Many newer buildings stand in Childerley too, but far fewer than in most nearby villages. To the American eye, two groups of the newer

buildings immediately stand out. These are Childerley's two "council estates," what Americans would call "public housing." In the United States,
public housing is a small fraction of the total housing stock, and virtually
none of it exists in the countryside. In Britain, what is probably best
termed "public rented housing" (for it is rarely completely rent-free)
amounts to about a fourth of the housing stock, and about a fifth in rural
areas.[3] There used to be more council properties in the village, but under
the Thatcher government's policy of ending social ownership, a number
of those in Childerley were sold to their tenants.

There are also a dozen or so postwar "tied cottages," some bungalows
built for the retired, and a few grander places built in that somewhat
inflated style real estate advertisements call "well presented." But neither
the British nor the American eye lingers on them. In spite of the glaring
modernity of the newer buildings—and in spite of the cars, the 200-horse-
power tractors dragging pesticide sprayers across the fields, the T.V. aeri-
als which sprout from every roof-top—the village landscape speaks of age,
continuity, and nature.

Like those in other villages in the area, the residents of Childerley
are all white, mainly Tory, entirely Christian, and almost all Protestant.
But within this homogeneity, there is a surprising amount of diversity
along a prominent social axis, the axis of class. Here in exurbia most
employed residents commute out of the village to work. Actually, only a
few work as far away as central London. Most commute to the nearby
satellite cities or the London suburbs. When they get there, many villagers
take up professional, credentialed, white-collar jobs, but many also work
in factories, garages, a nearby airfield, and in the county's booming construction trade.

Although the days when most families derived their income from the
farms and manors are over in Childerley, there is still some employment
in the village. Steady work for fourteen villagers, all men, comes from the
five large farms and half dozen smaller ones. Eleven more work full-time
in the Big Houses, including a chauffeur, two butlers, a gamekeeper, two
gardeners, a handy man, a nanny, and three domestics. Two village women
work full-time in a small craftworks operated by one of the farms. There
is also part-time and occasional work in gardening, cleaning, childcare,
and in the never-ending stream of small construction work required to
keep up village houses and grounds. The school, village shop, and the two
pubs provide a number of other, mainly lower paid, local jobs.

Where in Childerley, which is a very "desirable" village, does this
diversity live? Most houses in the village would have sold for well over

£200,000 at the height of the property market in 1988, and nothing for under £125,000. The least of the Big Houses could not have been bought for less than £400,000. These are stiff prices for a local farm or factory worker making £6,000 to £8,000 a year. Consequently, most Childerleyans come from the "moneyed" classes, as villagers say, including five millionaires and three titled residents. Still, about forty percent of villagers are not moneyed. These residents live in the village's two council estates (some in units they now own), in remaining tied cottages, in a number of houses bought some time ago before prices rose so dramatically, and in a few rented places.

Geographer Sarah Harper has made a statistical study of villages along the urban-to-rural fringe in Hampshire. She notes that they cluster into three types.[4] The smallest she calls "established" villages. Typically, the population numbers about 350. Only about a fourth of the residents commute, as most still work in the village in agriculture or domestic service. About the same percentage own their homes; most villagers live in tied housing. Few services remain—often no shop, possibly no pub, certainly no school, and probably no resident vicar in the parish church. Usually a "lord of the manor" or a wealthy farmer still owns most of the land and buildings.

Others have called this sort of village a "traditional," "occupational," "working class," or "estate" village.[5] The word "hierarchical" also fits. In one such village that borders Childerley, Barringham, the main landowner is still referred to as "the Squire," and worshipers all rise when he enters the parish church for Sunday services.

Another cluster Harper calls "metropolitan" villages. These are the biggest villages, with populations of 3,000 to 4,000. Rates of commuting and home owning are also high—46 percent and 70 percent, on average. There is more money about. Not surprisingly, a metropolitan village typically lies closer to cities, which it bears a closer resemblance to as well. The village center has several shops, a butcher, probably five or six pubs, pavements (sidewalks to Americans), and maybe even a traffic light or two. The church has a vicar in residence, and nonconformists to the Church of England number enough to support a chapel. There are enough children for a school. A direct rail line links the village to the metropolis. It's harder to think of these villages as something other than suburbs, albeit nice ones.[6]

In between is the third village type. Here the typical population is about 650. A third of the inhabitants commute, and slightly over half own their home. There is a more of a balance of social classes. More residents have local or agricultural jobs than those in metropolitan villages, although fewer than in established villages. The proportion of retired people is 15 percent, the highest of all three village types, which brings these villages in line with the age profile of the whole country. (Established and metropolitan villages in Hampshire are actually a bit younger than the age profile of Britain as a whole.) Like established villages, these ones tend to lie in a ring one-and-a-half to two-and-a-half hours commuting time to major urban centers, although often only a few miles from a small city.

Harper calls them "uniform" villages. There are other terms. In his classic study of villages along the urban commuting fringe, Raymond Pahl called such places "two-class villages."[7] Howard Newby, noting the often difficult relations between working-class locals and wealthier newcomers, called them "encapsulated" villages.[8] The Hampshire County Planning Department calls them "high-status villages." (They also use this term for Harper's metropolitan villages).[9]

Childerley is such a village, although somewhat smaller than usual. The population is 475. The working class has a strong presence, but so too do home-owning commuters. About 30 percent of the households still derive significant income (part-time or full-time) from village employment, and 11 percent from agricultural work. Seventeen percent of the villagers are retired. The rest of those who work commute, to both blue collar and white collar jobs.

This makes Childerley a remarkable place.[*] Like most people everywhere, Britons typically live in neighborhoods segregated by wealth (among other attributes). Settings are few where the wealthy live near to people too poor to own their home, or even to rent one without government assistance. Childerley and exurban villages like it are such places.

There is housing segregation in Childerley. The council properties, remaining tied cottages, and done-up former tied cottages occur in

---

[*] American readers mentally searching the outer environs of New York, Chicago, Los Angeles, and Houston for a similar situation of ethnic homogeneity and class diversity in a single village or small town may not find an exact parallel to Childerley and other English "uniform" villages. Tighter planning controls on new construction and the provision of publicly supported housing in small English settlements provide a bulwark against gentrification not found in exurban America. It is my impression that, consequently, the wealthy rapidly overwhelm small exurban American towns, once they become fashionable. There may still be a sizable working-class presence, but the kind of balance found in Childerley will be much less common. My bet is that, were a survey done, American exurban settlements would be more polarized into "established" and "metropolitan" villages and small towns than is the case in Britain. See Powers (1991).

bunches. Still, there are many edges to these little groupings, and the Big Houses are scattered across the parish. The homes of a stockbroker, a retired bank manager, and a London businessman abut directly on the larger council estate. The gracious three-hundred-year-old home of one wealthy woman lies adjacent to the tiny bungalow owned by the school nurse and her husband, a retired working man. The homes of a mechanic, an electrician, and a cleaner look across the road at that of a titled aristocrat. The groupings are small and numerous enough that there is considerably more contact between different social classes than is true of most residential areas in Britain. To some extent, this greater range of social contact is characteristic of most villages on the commuter fringe. But none more so than "uniform," "two-class," "encapsulated," and "high status" places like Childerley.

II

SCENERY AND STATISTICS can only tell so much. One must, of course, meet the people themselves to get a full sense of a place.°

John Bone, 68, is a bit of a loner who lives by himself in a small bungalow on the edge of the village. All his close relatives are dead, and he and his wife were divorced some years ago, without children. Although he has lived in the village for thirty years, most residents do not know him. He was born in a Hampshire village near the coast but raised in Bartley, a parish bordering on Childerley. John recently retired from his position as field representative for a major brewery's chain of pubs. "My life's been one long pub crawl," he jokes. Although he completed his working life in a midlevel service job, John still identifies himself as one of the "ordinary people," just as his father, a local policeman, used to consider himself. John now spends most of his time in "country pursuits": hunting, shooting, fishing, walking, and gardening. "I'm a countryman bred and born," he proudly announces. John also takes great pride in his self-sufficiency. He built his own house, grows much of his own food, makes his own bread, and slaughters his own meat, mainly fish and game that he has caught himself or that friends have given him. There is often a rabbit or a pheasant hanging by the legs in his pantry, waiting to be cleaned. "It's the natural way," he explains. He's a bit gruff on first meeting, but has a twinkle and an easy smile and laugh. John's politics are conservative.

° The following sketches are all as of June 1988. In a few cases, what I say about villagers' politics are guesses—but, I believe, informed ones.

Rachel Wood, 43, is a lively and engaging woman. She has only lived in the village for a year, having recently moved with her husband and two children from a London suburb. They live in a beautiful old cottage, one of the nicest in the village. Rachel is both proud and humbled by living in such a place. As she says, "I feel this house doesn't just belong to me—it belongs to the whole nation, really." Rachel was born into a working class family. Her mother's people were farm workers, and her father was a mechanic. Rachel was raised in a small city in southern England, although she spent all her summers at her grandmother's thatched cottage, the very cottage where her mother was born. Rachel's husband, Robert, is an engineer with a technical degree, and makes a good salary, so she is now considered solidly middle class, especially after purchasing such a sought-after house. Rachel does not have a paid job herself, and her youngest child is now sixteen. This gives her more time to devote to the country activities that occupy a central place in her life. Robert is an avid hunter and shooter, activities that Rachel whole-heartedly supports, and both of them volunteer as beaters for the pheasant shoot maintained by several local land owners. Like John, they catch, clean, and cook much of their own meat. Rachel is a fine dog trainer, and often takes in sick and wounded animals, nursing them back to health. Rachel, I believe, usually votes Conservative.

Audrey Spencer, 39, was born in Winford, the nearby market town, but has family roots in Childerley. She is a slim, pretty woman with a shy friendliness about her. She has lived in Childerley since she moved here at nineteen with her husband, Ted. Audrey works part-time as a cleaner and full-time as a mother of five. Ted works on one of Childerley's larger farms, and he and Audrey live in one of the farm's tied cottages, a semi-detached two-story house built in the early 1960s. Despite the demands of her job and home, Audrey spends a lot of time visiting with neighbors and with her relatives in the village, popping around a couple times a week for tea and a cigarette. Both Audrey and Mary, her eldest daughter, are well-known throughout the village for their hair-styling skills, and they cut for a number of residents, free for close friends. She goes regularly to one of the village's pubs, but never without Ted. Audrey spends some time gardening, but aside from that she engages in no country pursuits. She doesn't walk if she can help it, and is far more likely to be found in high-heels than wellies, the rubber boots by now traditional in rural England, even in the rain. When she votes, Audrey votes Labour.

Margaret Cook, 63, is a close friend and confidant of Audrey's, despite the wide difference in their ages. She was born in a city and has been in the village for only five years. But before that she lived for thirty years in Axworth (a village bordering on Childerley), and has lived in rural areas across Hampshire since her first job on an estate at age fourteen. She lives with her husband, Albert, in a council house next door to Audrey and Ted. The house is small, but it has a spacious garden that she devotes many hours to, three bedrooms, and a flush toilet. Her previous house had only "bucket-and-chuck-it" plumbing, as she says with a laugh. She works part-time as a cook in one of the pubs, and the rest of the time she is to be found about the house, visiting with company, or out seeing their wide circle of friends and family. (They have five children too.) Margaret is also a writer, having put together dozens of short stories on rural themes, as well as having started a novel, all handwritten. She is a warm and sympathetic person, and acquaintances often seek her out for advice and counseling. As an estate worker, Albert never accumulated a substantial pension, and they live on a very tight budget and have no savings. Margaret always votes, sometimes for the Conservatives and sometimes for Labour.

Henry Whithers, 73, is a retired civil servant who has lived in the village since the fifties. He lives with his wife, Sally, in a four-hundred-year-old farmhouse surrounded by spacious and gracious grounds, almost big enough to be considered parkland, such as all true manor houses have. As he says of his house, "It's not as high-brow as some in the village, but it's still one of the oldest." He and Sally do all the work themselves, despite their age, and they have an impressive collection of antique rose varieties and an extensive vegetable garden. Henry was raised in the countryside and is very involved with local politics and with Childerley's church. He has held at one time or another most of the prominent positions in the village, from chair of the Parish Council to chair of the Parochial Church Council and the village-hall committee, a leader of what one villager described as "the village Mafia." Although a bit fierce on the surface, he has a lot of charm and is well liked throughout the village. Henry is very frank about his nationalistic views and adherence to the old conservative values of service, deference, class, and outward distaste for money and display.

Abel Harrowell, 37, is the tractor operator on one of Childerley's farms. He has been in the parish for twelve years, but still keeps close ties with the nearby village where he was born. He is articulate and well informed, although his accent shows little trace of schooling and there is hardly a book in his house. His wife, Lillian, works part-time cleaning village homes, and together they are raising two children in a somewhat run-down tied cottage. Abel is "a bit mad for sports," as he says, and plays for the local cricket club, even though he smokes heavily. He likes walking and sometimes goes out across the farm's fields in the evening with his gun, occasionally bringing home a rabbit. He is devoted to his work and puts in the kind of hours typically associated with a workaholic business executive. He is also devoted to the pub, particularly a real "spit and sawdust pub," as he describes his favorite haunt. He strongly supported Margaret Thatcher and the Conservatives throughout her years as prime minister.

Helen Burton-Collins, 38, lives on the edge of the village in a former manor bought in the midseventies by six couples from London. The house was large enough to divide into six spacious units, each of which is owned separately. The couples own and manage the surrounding parkland and fields jointly, and no couple can sell their unit without the buyer being approved by all households in "the Community," as they call their arrangement. But it's not a commune, Helen says. "I think of communes as having open beds, that sort of thing. We definitely don't have that here." Helen and her husband, Brad, combined their family names with a hyphen when they married. They have two children now, and over the years, the Community has more than doubled in size as all the couples have raised families. Helen used to run a small natural products business, but recently had to give that up. Brad is an architect. They are both dedicated to the efforts of the Community to be as self-sufficient in food as possible. At one time, the couples kept half a dozen cows, a small herd of Jacob sheep, cultivated an extensive garden, and experimented with growing grain, all according to organic methods. They still have the garden and the sheep, but they have had to let the rest of it go. Even with twelve adults, keeping the 25 acres of hayfields and parkland in order is about all they can manage. Helen normally votes Labour or for the Liberals, but recently she has been voting Green when there are Green candidates on the ballot.

Roy Prior, 19, is a foot-press operator in a factory fifteen miles away in Harwinton. Roy is a quiet, good-looking young man and, like his whole family, a devout Methodist. Roy has lived all his life in Childerley, in the same council house with his brother, mother, and father. Mary, his mother, works part-time in the village shop, and Harold, his father, is a mechanic at the airfield in Axworth. Although Roy was born in the village, Mary and Harold were born in Southampton. They came to the village 25 years ago when Harold landed the job at the airfield he has held ever since. Nick, Roy's brother, is an avid fan of "all-wheeling" with a big jacked-up Land Rover, and Roy often accompanies him to rallies and cross-country races. Roy is a hard worker and his company sent him to a special technical institute for a six-week course, from which he recently received a certificate. Roy has never yet voted.

Roger Blunden, 34, is a hardware engineer for a computer firm in London. He has lived in the village for only a year with his wife, Karen, who is a programmer for a software firm in Winford. They live in a much-altered hundred-year-old cottage at the very edge of the village. They have no children and are not planning to have any soon. Except for their immediate neighbors, almost no one in the village knows them. Roger leaves at 7 every morning to catch the first fast train to London out of Winford and doesn't get home until 7:30 in the evening at the earliest. Roger does some gardening, but aside from that he has little time for or interest in the countryside activities important to many other residents—walking, birding, riding, shooting. But Roger relishes the privacy of the countryside and what he describes as the relaxed, uncompetitive flavor of life in the village. He always votes Conservative.

III

WHAT IS IT ABOUT Childerley that such a diverse group of people find so attractive? Why do these nine people and the other residents live in Childerley? Why do they find it worth the long commutes, the isolation from services and, for most newer residents, family and friends as well?

Childerleyans are not alone in wanting to live in a country village. The desire to live in the countryside is widespread, even among those with an urban consciousness, and few Britons today do not share this consciousness—even those who have never lived in a city. Since the fifties, and especially since the midsixties, population and development have been on the rise along the rural fringe of most major urban centers in western Europe and North America. The trend has earlier roots, for even in 1898 advice like that of J. Arthur Gibbs could be heard:

> London is becoming miserably hot and dusty; everybody who can get away is rushing off, north, south, east, and west, some to the seaside, others to pleasant country houses. Who will fly with me westwards to the land of breezy uplands and valleys nestling under limestone hills, where the scream of the railway whistle is seldom heard and the smoke of the factory darkens not the long summer days?[10]

So many have rushed off north, south, east, and west from the miserable heat and dust that cities like London have added another frontier of urban influence: the exurbs. Living further out and further apart than in the suburbs, residents of these areas find a visually rural life still within the economic and cultural glow of city lights. Here computer engineers and factory workers live in the midst of active forestland and farmland. Settlements have clearer edges than they do closer in. Still, development pressures seem ready to burst the fabric of the countryside. The city seems close and distant at the same time.

No hard and fast definition exists for *exurb*. It is a hard line to draw. Indeed, a certain indeterminacy is perhaps central to the definition. There is some farmland and (climate permitting) forestland in many areas most people would recognize as suburbs. And there is at least some urban economic and cultural influence in all rural areas, no matter how peripheral. Yet somewhere in between is a zone where the suburban and the rural grade into each other, a zone where there is plenty of city money to be had but where pastures, fields, and woods clearly dominate the landscape. Exurbs, then, are the kind of place where people likely argue from time to time if this is really still "the country." Ray Pahl once called it the "fringe city." To Sarah Harper, it's the "rural-urban interface." John Fraser Hart calls it the "perimetropolitan bow wave." Anthony Russell describes it as the "accessible countryside."[11] A rose by any other name . . .

Geographers link the growth of exurbs to a phenomenon they call *counterurbanization*. After 1950 or so, the population of Britain's urban cores shrank while that of suburbs, exurbs, and even rural areas expanded. Between 1971 and 1981 Manchester's core lost 17 percent, London's lost 18 percent, and Glasgow's lost 22 percent. These figures are comparable to the steep rate of population decline in rural areas between 1801 and 1939. During these years, the rural share of the population dropped from two-thirds to 18 percent. But after World War II, the percentage of the British population living in rural areas climbed back to almost one fourth and suburbs expanded mightily. Much of the rural and suburban growth was concentrated in exurban counties close in to major cities, particularly the home counties of the southeast, including Hampshire.[12] (As of this writing, the trend is shifting to the north and west due to planning controls and home prices.)

Most Western industrialized countries, from the former West Germany, Denmark, and France to the United States, saw similar changes, with some differences in timing and scale. In the United States, for example, counterurbanization proceeded to the point that during the seventies rural counties were growing at an aggregate rate above that of cities. Rural growth ended in many regions of America during the farm crisis of the eighties, but development pressures continued unabated in exurban areas throughout the country during that decade of metropolitan prosperity.[13]

Counterurbanization is old news now, and explanations for it have been around for a while. Researchers generally agree that there were a number of changes in technology and the economy which facilitated the growth of population in suburban, exurban, and rural settings, settings many people found more satisfactory than cities. Better transportation, rural electrification, electronic media, and the shift away from heavy industry and toward more mobile service work all facilitated the deconcentration of employment opportunities as well as making nonurban living more feasible and, for many, more palatable. Population growth and demographic shifts leading to smaller households also promoted movement out of urban cores by increasing the number of housing units needed for the population. Consequently, population in urban cores declined as smaller households soaked up the existing housing stock with fewer people.[14]

But structural explanations like these only explain what makes a trend possible, not why it happens, for people choose not to do many things that their economy and technology make feasible. For example, entirely new cities could have been built to house a larger population of smaller households. A few new cities were in fact built. Moreover, these technological changes were, in the main, underway or in place since the 1920s when even a village as small as Childerley had its own train station. Travel time from Childerley to London and nearby cities and market towns has, for those able to afford regular train use, increased if anything. (Hundreds of these small rural stations were removed in the 1960s at the order of the now infamous minister of transport of the time, Lord Beeching.) And indeed, there have been commuters in both white and blue collar professions, as well as retirees, in Childerley since the 1930s at least, although their numbers were comparatively small. Closer to London, railroad commuting from villages by manual and professional workers was well underway by the late nineteenth century in Surrey and in Hertfordshire.[15] By 1902, Sir Halford Mackinder could write, "In a manner all southeastern England is a single urban community; for steam and electricity are changing our geographical conceptions."[16]

Furthermore, these structural changes do not explain the actions of those people of equivalent capital and job qualifications who have elected to live in Britain's cities and suburbs rather than the countryside. Of course, people have varying amounts of freedom in choosing where they live, principally depending on their economic resources and the supply of housing. There are particularly severe limitations on housing in Britain's exurban and rural areas. But some people have wrestled with these limitations more than others in equivalent economic situations.

To the extent that people can truly choose where they live, a person's choice of residence depends as well on what Albert Hunter has called "symbolic ecology," the cultural meaning of places.[17] Thus, to account for the great overall increase in enthusiasm for country living, new cultural factors must also be taken into account. In the chapters which follow, I will try to show that, at least in Childerley, among these new factors are an increasingly *positive* outlook on pastoral nature and an increasingly *negative* outlook on class as social norms and as sources of social identity.

CLASS AND COMMUNITY

THREE

A *"Slightly Feudal" Village*

You've got here in this little village the well-to-do
who've bought their status and their land and their
position, and you've got the middle commuter sort of
class, and you've got those who live in the council
houses. . . . And there's a bit of that class feeling left.

Andy Sparrow, 1988

I

SOME VILLAGES ARE famous because of a particularly old and unaltered church, beautiful views, or a fine manor house. Childerley is not particularly famous for anything, but it is best known for the Horse and Hound, a genuine sixteenth-century pub at the end of the village. Visitors come from miles away to take a pint of good ale in front of its huge fireplace, ten feet wide and five feet deep, and to soak in the ambiance of the head-bashingly-low timbered ceiling and the rude board tables and benches. The Horse and Hound is a "free house" (meaning it is not owned by a syndicate) and the publican stocks a wide range of "real ales," the hand-pumped brews which have become popular in recent years. The men's plumbing is still rather primitive, as the pub's faithful love to point out to first-timers—just an outside shed with a trough. The traditional partition between the public bar and lounge bar has been mostly removed, and this has opened up a large dining area for enjoying the output of one of the area's best pub kitchens. Not merely a tourist pub, the "H and H" is a favorite haunt of a good many Childerleyans who come to enjoy its atmosphere and quaint eccentricities. At Sunday lunchtime, you had best arrive early if you want a seat.°

In contrast, many in the village find the Fox, Childerley's other pub, to be "a bit grotty." They see it as "dirty" and "uncongenial," and they hardly ever go. It too is an old building, though not nearly as old as the

---

° In England, the "Sunday pub lunch" is a traditional outing for families and friends, and a place with a good kitchen is likely to fill up minutes after Sunday noon.

Horse and Hound, and it has been a pub for nearly 150 years. (The village once had a third pub, which my imagination tells me was named the Huntsman's Arms, but it disappeared between the wars.) Outside the Fox one seldom sees the Volvos or Land Rovers that pull up to the Horse and Hound; most of the vehicles are Fords, Morrises, delivery vans, and sometimes a tractor. Inside, there is nothing remarkable about the place, despite its age. It's dark, a bit spare, and the tables, chairs, and bar are all new. The food is hearty, but hardly *haute cuisine*, even for a pub. There is a coin-operated pool table, a much-pricked darts board, and a juke box. This is not a sit-down sort of place, and it's usually noisy. On Saturday night, you had better arrive early if you want a place to stand.

Childerley is "a village of haves and have-nots," as villagers often explained to me. The two pubs cater to opposite ends of this social axis that runs through the midst of the village, the axis of *class*. The Horse and Hound is where the "middle bit," the "moneyed people," and the "haves" go. The Fox is for the "ordinary people," the "working man," the "have-nots," where the few remaining "old boys" sometimes hold forth. The same divisions largely dictate who goes to whose house for a coffee or a meal, who goes shopping with whom in the town, and who walks together through the village.

Childerley's residents vote for the same parish council, use the same roads, and often worship in the same church, but circulate socially within fairly homogeneous subcommunities of wealth and associated cultural differences. The villagers know these boundaries well and seldom cross them. Class divisions condition the lives of Childerleyans in a fundamental way, influencing their motivations (their habits, tastes, beliefs, desires, sense of self, and sense of identity) and their realizations (their employment and life chances). Some have argued that class has declined in importance in British society.[1] In Childerley, at least, class continues to pattern both economic and social life.

Although class remains a very significant source of social difference in the lives of villagers, it is, I believe, a morally ambiguous concept for them. On the one hand, class and class mobility remain central social motivations for Childerleyans; yet on the other, villagers routinely deplore that this is so. This contradiction may be said to be a central crack in the moral foundation upon which village—and perhaps British—society currently rests. What results are the conditions for a crisis of identity and legitimation, conditions that a number of sociologists have suggested afflict most Western societies.[2] But Childerleyans are not on the verge of moral collapse. In their own lives, the residents of the village largely resolve this crisis—or perhaps it would be better to say avert it—in a way that is uniquely available to residents of country places close to "nature," as we shall hear from them. But first, let us consider the crack.

II

BOTH AT HOME AND ABROAD, class has long been considered a peculiarly central feature of British society and culture. Particularly in the English-speaking world, the British woman's or man's air of aloof, cultured superiority is one of the staple characterizations of jokes, anecdotes, advertisements, stage, and cinema. The British themselves recognize and largely accept this stereotype as accurate, much as the world often sees Americans—and Americans see themselves—as coming from a classless society. In his book *The English,* J. B. Priestly described his countrymen and countrywomen as having an "inbuilt sense of class, part of their Englishness."[3] The tabloid *Daily Mail* stated in 1990 that "the class system, unbreakable and unshakeable, is ingrained in the British way of life."[4] The Church of England even used to teach its worshipers to sing

The rich man at his castle, the poor man at his gate,
God made them, high or lowly, and order'd their estate.

Class is a characteristic feature of all industrialized societies, not only Britain, and sociologists have questioned the notion of British society as being particularly structured by class. Whether or not the image of Britain (or more accurately, England) as unusually class-ridden is realistic, it is certainly true that over the course of the twentieth century, and especially since about 1940, considerable political will has been directed at creating opportunities for social mobility in the country. Beginning with the Butler Act in 1944, which guaranteed access to secondary education for all, the creation of an "open society" has been, in fits and spurts, one of Britain's principal political goals.[5] A. H. Halsey's statement that "the history of the 20th century is the history of the decline of the values and status system of Victorian Britain" is not pure hyperbole.[6] Not all have supported this goal or agreed on how to get there. And not all agree on how to recognize the goal when it is reached. Yet the desire to break down class barriers (or at least to reformulate them) has guided much of British politics in the postwar period. Even the conservative prime minister John Major declared on his first day in office that he would work for "a genuinely classless society."

Since the war, Britain has grown much wealthier, as have all the countries of the industrialized West. Many born into poor families have gained an education, a high-paying job, and a material standard of living far above what was only recently thought the norm. Many have not. Still, with the advent of Margaret Thatcher's entrepreneurial meritocracy and the decline in the fortunes of the Labour Party throughout the 1980s, observers on both left and right pronounced the death of class in Britain.

On the left, Eric Hobsbawm argued that "the values of consumer-society individualism and the search for private and personal satisfactions above all else" were responsible for the Labour Party's decline. As a result of these cultural changes, said Hobsbawm, most Britons no longer see their interests as lying along class lines, but rather along *sectoral* lines of what is good for consumers and householders.[7] Consequently, people have come to identify more with consumption—the home and leisure pursuits—than production.[8] More toward the political center, Harold Perkin argued that the pattern of social conflict has been changed by the coming of "professional society," in which credentialed workers, sanctioned by professional associations, dominate all the major institutions of state and society, including many blue-collar trades. These hierarchical organizations create vertical solidarities and horizontal conflicts over social and economic resources. Perkin contended that these have "replaced, or more accurately, overlay the horizontal structures and vertical antagonisms of class."[*] Well over to the right, former prime minister Margaret Thatcher declared that "class is a Communist concept." In light of the demise of the Soviet bloc, she suggested, class must no longer exist.[9]

In this intellectual climate, several groups of researchers carried out extensive quantitative surveys of the role of class in contemporary Britain. Best-known is the work of the Oxford Group, which under the direction of John Goldthorpe conducted surveys in the early 1970s and mid-1980s of the life chances of British men born between 1908 and 1947. Social mobility, a person's movement up (or down) the social ladder, is one way to gauge the effect of class. What the Oxford Group found is that there are still strong constraints on social mobility in Britain today—as strong as those of a half century ago.[10]

---

[*]Perkin (1989), xiii. A number of social historians have lately questioned the saliency of class even during Britain's nineteenth century, a time once seen as one

The Oxford Group based their conclusion on a distinction between two forms of social mobility, *absolute* mobility and *relative* mobility. (The latter is often called "social fluidity.") Suppose one morning on your way to work you saw a crew of workers equally distributed on different levels of a vast scaffolding. And suppose that in the evening, on your way home, you saw the following: twice as many workers on the top level, the same number on all the middle levels, and no one remaining on the lowest. That would be a clear case of absolute mobility, for, as a whole, the crew had moved up. Now suppose that your curiosity led you to approach the construction site and to ask the crew how far each member individually had moved that day, and that they told you that each worker had moved up one level, except those at the top, who had no place further up to go. If this were true, then the crew experienced no relative mobility at all, despite ending the day higher up on the scaffolding.

This is essentially what the Oxford Group found for social mobility in Britain. There has indeed been a general upward movement, largely as a result of the expansion of the service sector in the post–World War II economic boom. Britons on the whole make more money than they used to and hold more prestigious jobs. There are now greater percentages of people in the higher levels of the social scaffolding. But most people, over their lifetimes, have moved roughly the same amount. Even today new members of a stratum come mainly from the levels immediately below (and immediately above, for there is much downward mobility too), just as was the case before World War II. So on an absolute basis most people are wealthier and in more prestigious jobs, but the relative rate at which people move up or down during their lives has not changed.

This might seem crudely egalitarian in a way, as nearly everyone in Britain contends with some drag on their social movement. But this drag, this lack of social fluidity, the Oxford Group argues, is in fact what we really mean by social class. Even if this special drag were egalitarian in application—and there is strong evidence that it is not—it is clearly not so in outcome. The child of a farm worker is still far less likely to become a farm owner than the child of a farm owner (and vice versa). In a perfectly fluid society, accidents of origin would have no such effect. That they still do, says the Oxford Group, is surely a fact of class.

I think they are right to say so, and so too does a group of researchers from the University of Essex.[11] The Essex Group also conducted a survey

---

of the principle shapers of class as it exists today. See Cannadine (1992) for a review.

in the mid-1980s, a survey that included women, which the Oxford research had not. They took the unusual step of using four different methods of measuring class. However the Essex Group approached their data, they found that class retains its importance in restricting social fluidity in modern Britain, despite the postwar expansion of the economy. The Essex Group also found that the absolute position of women is considerably lower than that of men—women on the whole work on lower levels of the scaffolding—and their social fluidity is far worse. Despite Thatcherism, consumerism, and generally increased wealth, class still mightily constrains life chances in Britain. Statistics bear out John Goldthorpe's harsh conclusion that "the main function of economic growth can then best be regarded as being not that of facilitating egalitarian reform but rather obscuring its failure."[12]°

Still, the question remains whether, as common wisdom suggests, class is unusually important in Britain. Most studies comparing national mobility rates have in fact found little difference in social fluidity across the Western capitalist democracies.[13] Indeed, the rates in all these countries are remarkably similar. Across the slight range of difference, Britain actually lies about in the middle.[14] Researchers have paid particular attention to contrasting Britain with America, as the opposing images of the two nations make for a vivid comparison. Here again, when studies control for the greater economic expansion of post-1945 America, neither country stands out. Although there has been more absolute mobility in America, social fluidity—the social drag of a person's class origin, independent of economic pull—is the same in the two countries.[15]

Yet there does seem to be something distinctive about the *way* class emerges as a major social influence in Britain. There is a dichotomy, old in social theory, between social status based on *ascription* versus *achievement*, that is, between immutable designations and ones that people attain, between the sense that you-are-what-you-are and you-are-what-you-make-of-yourself. Applying this dichotomy, Seymour Martin Lipset once argued that social standing in Britain depended more on ascribed characteristics, locking one into a social class from birth, than the achieved status system of America, the land of the self-made man and woman.[16]

Work by Alan Kerckhoff and his associates supports Lipset's analysis. Despite the overall similarities found by comparative studies of social

---

° Marshall et al. (1988: 253) also found that "class remains an important factor closely allied with voting intentions." The misfortunes of the Labour Party during the 1980s, they conclude, are due more to problems in the party's platform and presentation than to any sea-change in Britain's social structure.

fluidity, Kerckhoff and company have found that the results depend on how one measures class.[17] Class scales based on skill and income levels within the two countries show little difference, while scales based on occupational prestige show considerably less fluidity in Britain. The British public apparently tends more to perceive as appropriate whatever the occupations of succeeding generations are, regardless of income. In other words, whatever the children of higher or lower classes wind up doing will tend in Britain to be labeled as high or low status. The same process is probably at work in the United States as well, but apparently to a lesser degree.[18]

III

MOST RESIDENTS OF Childerley would agree with the results of these surveys, should they read them—that is, they would agree both that class remains very important and that ascription plays an important role in it. I often talked with the villagers about class, particularly in the early months of my stay in the village. Sometimes I asked about it, and sometimes people made a special point of bringing it up. I occasionally had the sense that villagers wanted to make sure I understood this aspect of life in Childerley, which they felt an American, especially one as young in looks as myself, might not notice. In their eyes, I believe, I appeared first as an American, and only secondarily as the upper-middle-class person I am in my own country, and usually as only the former. As I came from elsewhere, I did not fit easily into local categories. Nor could I be expected to know them myself—especially coming from a reputedly classless society. Consequently, villagers sometimes were not sure I would recognize this essential part of the context of their remarks. By no means were all the villagers so forward in discussing class, and these little offers of words-to-the-wise became less frequent as the residents came to know me and got the sense (I'm not sure how) that I was beginning to understand these matters. A few villagers who knew me well, however, continued to make regular observations about class when they realized that I had become especially interested in the topic.°

° Although I expected class to have a place in what I would eventually write about villagers' experience of nature, I initially did not expect it to play the central role it does in this book. It was only in the face of the continual emphasis villagers put on class that it shifted to the center of my thinking about life in Childerley. Strathern (1981), which I read during my first stay in the village, also pointed me in this direction.

Phil Masters, a finance professional in his midthirties, was one of the people who took me aside early on. I was having a drink with Phil and Gretchen Masters one evening at their home. Phil had proudly offered me a Budweiser, which I had somewhat awkwardly turned down for something more local, saying it was like an American offering an English visitor fish and chips. The joke fell flat, but a relaxed mood soon took hold as we sipped our drinks and got acquainted. My beer remark led to a discussion of the different customs and habits of Americans and the British, and then differences in rural life. At this point, Phil broke in.

"I suppose you've been told by other people already about how divided the village is." I said something neutral, and he continued, "There are two groups, and never the twain meet. The people who live in the other end of the village all go to one place, and the rest another. They all go to the Fox, while the people who live in the big houses at this end of the village go to the Horse and Hound."

Phil paused and reflected for a moment.

"There are three groups, really. There are the people in the council houses at one end, the very rich in the huge houses at the other, and people like us someplace in the middle."

Reverend William Cazalet, Childerley's rector, was another who in my first months pointed out the importance of class divisions. A solidly built man in his late forties, his face and hands are deeply lined from a life spent walking, gardening, crawling under cars, and working on a never-ending stream of building projects—anything but drinking the obligatory tea from fine china that is the more stereotypical village rector's custom and trade.

"Childerley still is to a certain extent slightly feudal," he explained. "There's still an *us* and *them* about the village—we the farm workers or the council house people, and them the sort of rich bobs up the other end."

He went on to give a vivid example of Childerley's "slightly feudal" character.

"But it was still more feudal than that when I arrived. They had their own set pews in the church. Major Spiers sat in one. The Trewhellas had their own. The Chaffeys had their own. The rectory had their own pew. The front section, that front block, were reserved pews for *the* people, and the plebs went from there backwards. And that's the hangover from the old days. . . ."

He tossed back a sweep of hair that had slipped across his forehead.

"In the first year that I was here," he continued, "a young lad who had arrived in the village—he was only about thirteen—[came and] sat in a pew. And the person whose 'pew' in inverted commas, it was, when it actually wasn't, came along and turfed him out. Told him to go to the back of the church. It could have turned him off the church. Fortunately, it didn't. That was when I got to grips with the thing, and started saying it's not on. . . . Quite a few people were sort of twitchy about it."

Most residents avoided using "that awful word *class*," as one man put it, in our discussions of village society. Divisions were often expressed geographically, as Phil Masters did, even though the different classes live side by side in many parts of the village. Like Reverend Cazalet, many villagers used the term *feudal* to point out class to me. Others, like Abel Harrowell (and the rector), used the familiar opposition "us and them."

"I could point it out in every village. . . . No. It's there. There's a lot more of 'them' than what there are of 'us.' Forty years ago there was a lot more 'us' than 'them'"

On the other hand, Andy Sparrow, a forty-two year old schoolteacher and a Labour voter, had no problems using the word *class* with me.

"You've got here in this little village the well-to-do who've bought their status and their land and their position, and you've got the middle commuter sort of class, and you've got those who live in the council houses. And there's quite a divide, quite a strong feeling. . . . If you look at the village and if you ask the Smith's, say, opposite, what they think of the others—they're the oldest sort of working class family with roots in this village—there would be a feeling of 'them and us.' They get their employment when they out and clean for other people, and that sort of thing. They get their employment in the pub. They see themselves as working for the others, and the others see them as working for them. And there's a bit of that class feeling left."

A number of residents suggested that class divisions were in fact stronger in country villages like Childerley than in the cities. Audrey Spencer explained why poorer people find class differences stronger in the countryside.

"You notice the difference in a village like this between the rich and the poor. . . . Some people say there's no such thing like class anymore. But they don't know. They're just from down in the towns. But up here there is. Down there the people are all the same, and you don't notice it. Here you're living right next to them. . . . You move out here, and you see the money they spend on their children, for education and things, when you can't even afford a pair of shoes for your kids to go to school in!"

Andy Sparrow made a similar observation: "In cities, you're one of a crowd. There are so many people there's an anonymity about it all. And what really counts is the amount of money you make, in terms of where you live, and how successful you appear, and that earns you your status. Your status is not so important.

"Here in the countryside it's far more stratified, because the people who make the money come out to live in the countryside when they make their big pile. They buy their big house, and they impose their status on the place. And others don't move around so much. You've still got the squire, in some villages like Barringham. And you've still got a more stratified degree of the class structure."

Moreover, Andy noted, the ethnic homogeneity of the countryside makes class more prominent.

"Although there is a class [as well as] a cultural and an ethnic element to all cities, in the countryside the class is far stronger. You don't have the ethnic element."

But most, like thirty-eight year old Lily Hobbs, Childerley's postmistress and wife of a management consultant, saw the problem of class as more general. I asked her if she felt there was a good sense of community in the village.

"No, not really," she replied, "But I don't think you get that anywhere. It's the English again. Also there's wide gaps. You've got the people at this end of the village, those at that end, and the people in the middle. . . . It's the English, I'm afraid." In her answer, I think, she was trying to connect a poor community spirit with the stand-offishness and "wide gaps" of class.

Thus, there is widespread agreement among the residents that class remains central. But older villagers say that there has been a significant change in the social structure of Childerley and villages like it. Although Childerley is still "slightly feudal," it is not nearly as feudal, they told me, as it was before World War II. Ascription seems to have given way to more achievement; the countryside has become more like the city.

At eighty-three, Sir Harold is one of the Childerley's oldest residents. A bearer of a hereditary title, he is also one of the village's best-known residents. He was once the squire of Cockham, a nearby village, but he sold his manor there in 1953 and moved to a much more modest house in Childerley, where he has lived ever since. Sitting beneath an eight-foot high, gold-framed Chippendale mirror that once hung in his father's manor, he described the changes as they have appeared to him. His perspective from the top of Childerley's social scale is an interesting one, worth hearing at length.

"The whole society is different now. You see, after the war we had what amounts to a bloodless revolution. Society became much more condensed, shall we say. There was no longer as much distance between people—it kind of filled the gaps. And the whole nature of money changed. Before the war we had seven gardeners [at our house in Cockham]. It cost me as much then to pay those seven gardeners for a week what it costs me to hire a man for a day to work around here now. [When I was a boy], my father had a smallish country house in Kent, twenty-five bedrooms, that sort of thing. Yes, we had a lot of servants then. I of course had my own manservant who was always with me wherever I traveled. I always kept a manservant then. I hardly knew how to pack my own bag! And my father had one, and my mother had several maids. We had a car, of course, several cars, three in all. There was one for my father, one for my mother, and then just an old sort of thing for the servants to use. My father's butler was going to buy a car, I remember, but he didn't want to upset my father. So he bought a motor-bike with a side car instead."

I broke in.

"Now why would that have upset your father?"

"You see, if he had bought a car he would have been rising above his station. So many traditions have changed. In all these villages there used to be what we call a squire. Do you know what I mean when I say 'squire'?"

"Yes, yes."

"He was sort of the headman of the village. Most of the village worked for him and he owned all the land. That's the way things were when I was a boy. . . . All the villages were like that then, the families from the manor houses sitting in the front. Everyone sat in their same pew. . . . There used to be a hierarchy, didn't there, and I rather liked that. You knew where everyone was going to sit in church, which pews. Now, when I go, I like to see the same people sitting in the same pews. That way I know who is there that day and who isn't. It's comfortable."

We talked about some of the other changes that concern him, such as the use in the church of the Alternative Service Book in place of the 1662 Book of Common Prayer and the increase in traffic in the village.

"What do you think the biggest change has been?" I asked.

"Well, as I was telling you, there aren't any poor people anymore. Society is much tighter now, much less difference. Now everyone has plumbing. When we came, a lot of these places still had earth closets. In fact, we put the first water closet in at our house in Cockham in the thirties. But now there aren't any poor people. . . . You don't say, 'Oh, poor old Mrs. So-and-so,' because Mrs. So-and-so isn't so poor. In fact, she might have more money than you. It's this bloodless revolution I was telling you about."

"When was the big change?"

"It was the war that did it. In the First World War, the men in the trenches were separate from the officers. But the Second World War was different—they were right there in the trenches together. Everyone was equal. So when they came back at the end of the war, the men had different aspirations. They didn't want to work as servants anymore. . . . Just look in this village. There are all these people coming in with new money that have far more than we do. . . . There used to be what I call the higher echelons, that is to say, the gentry—people with a good family but no money." He paused and chuckled. "Which I would consider us in. Now we don't really have that in the village any more. The big houses have got people who have just come into money and probably have more than me."

Sir Harold's "bloodless revolution," which "condensed" society until there were no longer any poor people, is a considerable exaggeration. Class differences have been far from eliminated. True, Childerley no longer has a squire. It is also true that even those at the bottom end of the scale now generally make more and have better housing than they did. But there is still a world of social distance between, say, Roy Prior, a factory worker, and Colonel Spreadbury, the head of a capital investment fund and owner of the village's largest house and a third of its farmland.

Yet it is not hard to understand why Sir Harold does not emphasize these realities. The absolute mobility of people into higher class categories has changed the shape of the world he once knew. As more people have "come into money," Britain's—and Childerley's—social structure has become more top-heavy. There are many more wealthy people around today to buy Childerley's old Big Houses, or to convert a barn into a new one. More people are socially close to Sir Harold, and in this sense there has been some "condensation." But there are still a lot of people socially far away from him.

Part of what Sir Harold sees as a more condensed society is the decline of such class prerogatives as the reserved pew and his father's butler's sense of his "station." Although in neighboring Barringham people still defer to the squire, the old Victorian civilities have largely disappeared in Childerley, as they have elsewhere.

Charles Goddard-Brown is another resident who laments the passing of the courtesies he once received. Mr. Goddard-Brown has a family connection to the aristocracy, although he has no title himself. One day in the paneled study of his seventeenth-century home, he complained about the increased use of Christian names, instead of family names and titles, in daily conversation.

"It's wrong that this 'matey-ness' should take over completely. I don't like the use of Christian names all the time and trying to be a sort of matey person to everybody. I think one's only matey after you've established a relationship, which is based on mutual respect. You take into consideration why you had mutual respect in the old days when you had the class system and the feudal system."

But evidently very few people today do take this into consideration. Virtually everyone in the village calls Mr. Goddard-Brown "Charles" to his face, or—worse yet—"G. B.," a nickname he picked up years ago. I rarely heard anyone call him "Mr. Goddard-Brown." I ceased doing so all the time myself, after a while. (Nor did he seem to mind.)

The outward proprieties of feudal arrangements may have indeed declined. And for all his grousing about it, even Charles has accommodated himself to the changes. But the class system that pertained in "my day," as Charles sometimes describes his formative years before World War II, still has a hold on the village. To the extent that Charles and others in a similar position in the village act on it, that system is still in place. In his words, "I do not altogether go along with a complete feudal system, but I do go along with a certain amount of it."

This is how he described that system to me:

"Alright, we must talk social, talk social because that's the only way I can put it over. I would say that judged from the prewar social set-up you'd have the upper class, confined entirely to the dukes, lords, the peerage. Then you'd have the upper-middle class. . . . [These were] not businessmen. People with a certain sort of—at least two or three generations; at least two generations—of reasonable wealth." He paused for a sip of his tea. "If they were suddenly up, they would not be considered upper middle, I shouldn't think, whatever money they had. See, it's only just recently that that's changed. [Even in my day] there were—alright, call them yuppies. . . . They were just a little bit rich but they weren't really sort of accepted. Not in the normal run of things. Then you'd have the middle-middle class, and then you'd have the lower-middle class. And then you'd have the working class."

"Now what would be the distinction between lower middle and working?" I asked. "Would the shopkeeper have been lower middle?"

"No, Well," he explained, "I suppose you could call it, they'd be artisan a little bit. But they'd be working class—upper-working class. They wouldn't be considered the middle class. Lower middle would be bank managers, dentists. I mean, frankly, in my day you didn't socially know a dentist. . . . If you were in the services, then you were basically lower end of the upper-middle class. You would be upper-middle class, really, but you'd be the lower end financially."

"Where would the rector be? He would also be lower end of the upper-middle class?"

"Yes. . . . You see, in many cases you find that the eldest son inherited the estate. The second son either went into the church, the services, the Foreign Office, the Colonial Office. So you got all the upper-middle-class males mostly serving the country in some shape or form. The attitude, the thing was, to serve the country in some capacity, either abroad or whatever. A lot of them, mind you, also went into industry and education and that sort of thing. And then, you see, industry was never really very— it was a bit, sort of, you know—it just wasn't accepted."

Having read Martin Wiener's *English Culture and the Decline of the Industrial Spirit*, which argued that the English upper class has always disdained industry, my ears perked up.°

"Is that really so?" I asked. "I mean, this is something that I very much read about as being something that was part of . . ."

Charles broke in with his infectious, gallumping laugh.

"Oh, yes, oh yes, yes," he said. "This was going on, well, definitely through to the beginning of the war. . . . The major social change has taken place since the nineteen fifties."

What Charles was describing was the same social tension many villagers commented on, a tension between achieved status based on money and education and ascribed status derived from one's family background. Despite the passing of "Victorian values," as villagers sometimes referred to the social world described by Charles and Sir Harold, ascription does remain an important force in village life.

Mrs. Greta Moore feels herself a case in point. Her father was a low-level government official, and her late husband sold agricultural machinery. She herself has never worked and has no university degree. She has lived forty years in the parish, and says she has been a regular at

° This distain, says Wiener (1981), is the root cause of Britain's economic malaise. I'm told the book was widely read by officials in Margaret Thatcher's government.

church, the Women's Institute, and local events all that time. Still, Greta finds that she is not quite accepted by the village's upper crust. She talked, with some discomfort, about class with me during an interview at her home. She described social life in the village as "A bit snooty. It's absolutely true. The high-up sort of people think they're very grand, don't take any notice of the lower ones. And that to my mind is horrible, the social-class distinction. I like making friends with all classes. I don't care. But some think they're so grand they turn their noses up. You don't have that in America at all, [do you]?"

"Well, we do," I responded, "but it's based on some different things. . . . What would you say the distinctions are based on here? Is it principally a money thing, do you think?"

"No, background," she replied. "Money might have something to do with it but . . . they think themselves so grand, some of these people, that they can't ask us lower people to their houses. They just keep themselves to themselves. It doesn't worry me, but that's how it is."

Charles Goddard-Brown put the matter crisply. He was telling me about a man of humble origins who, through a combination of good luck and shrewd judgment, has amassed a considerable fortune since he moved to the village.

"But you see, he's not socially accepted, and I doubt whether his children will be. It depends where he goes; it depends what happens. He might be accepted at a different social level if he goes somewhere else, with reluctance. And if he maintains that status somewhere else, then his children will be accepted. But he won't be accepted here, amongst a certain class. . . . The secret of it all, I think you can say, is that it takes two generations to become firmly established in another class. That hasn't changed."

And if Charles says it hasn't, then it hasn't, at least to the extent that he and others act on this belief.

It is not only the "high up sort of people" like Charles and Sir Harold who make this distinction. Working-class villagers often separate those with old money who deserve respect from those with new money who usually do not. Money is not the only source of class, even to those who are at money's command. Sarah Weller and Harriet Cooper explained why they usually don't honor their newly moneyed employers.

"They still expect you to have respect for them just because they've got money," Sarah said.

"But I'll tell you what," Harriet observed. "The true gentry are not like that. It's the people that become rich through businesses without having that life of always having had money. How can I put it? I've worked for both sorts. [One lady,] because it was her father's riches, she could be the madam. And she at times was the madam. You know, you were just a skivvy to work for her. That's the sort of people that make it bad."

Harriet applies the two-generation rule here, as this "madam" had come into money only in her father's generation, not her grandfather's or great-grandfather's. Walter Morgan, a forty-three-year old plasterer who lives in Axworth, agrees.

"It's those up and coming types that are the worst. Those that have got it, you know, for generations, don't have to worry about showing it."

Working class villagers also see the importance of family background in achieving mobility in their own lives. Katie Weller is the twenty-two-year old daughter of Sarah and her husband Fred. Sarah is a domestic and Fred is a farm worker. Katie keenly feels the ascriptive restrictions of her background. We were talking in her mother's kitchen one afternoon about her decision to move to Winford, the nearby town.

"In the town I can make a fresh start," said Katie. "You are what you make of yourself. I can better myself and get what I want. But here, no matter what I would still be the same."

"Still be a farm worker's daughter," Sarah interjected.

Katie continued. "That's why if I did move back into the country, I'd live in some other village, where I wouldn't be known beforehand."

But class in Childerley is not entirely ascriptive either. In taking the decision to try to leave ascription behind, Katie is arguing that social standing should be based on achievement, at least in part. Others in the village have gained fortunes, degrees, and other credentials that under-score the vital importance of achievement as a source of motivation for village residents. Traditional ascriptive criteria still guide assessments of class position, although not exclusively nor perhaps as much as in Charles Goddard-Brown's day. But either through ascription or achievement crite-ria, Childerleyans feel class emphatically remains an important social marker in the village, in line with the findings of the Oxford and Essex surveys.

IV

MOREOVER, THE VILLAGERS have little trouble assigning each other to social classes. By talking to the residents about their perceptions of each other's standing, I was able to determine the community's assessment of the class of 88 percent of adult Childerleyans. Much of the information I have I drew from several residents with whom I discussed the village in considerable detail during the course of my stays in Childerley. One individual even went through the parish register of electors line by line with me, telling me what he knew of each villager, which took several afternoons to complete. In some cases, if I was unable to get a direct assessment of someone, and yet knew enough about the person, I made an assessment myself, using the criteria offered by the villagers.°

It's important to take a moment to discuss those criteria, for they say a lot about what the villagers mean when they talk about class. Max Weber, a theorist sociologists often turn to for help in these matters, suggested that we could lump the sources of power within a community (for power is what these criteria seek to evaluate) into three. Correspondingly, Weber saw three types of social groups. Those deriving from economics and market position he termed *classes*, those from social honor he termed *status groups*, and those from political affiliation he termed *parties*.[19] Generations of sociologists have found these distinctions extremely helpful.

Childerleyans do not use this academic terminology, of course.°° Usually, they lump Weber's first two categories together, and sometimes all three. Mary Weller, another daughter of Sarah and Fred, sees only two social groups in the village. This is how she described them:

"That's all there is, really. There's people like us, and then there's the sort of rich people and snobby people."

Here she combines the market power of being "rich" and the honorific power of being "snobby" into criteria for the same social group.

People in a community usually do not have the information at hand to make the distinctions sociologists like to make, and so they don't. The most direct measures of class in Weber's sense—income, net worth, the market value of a person's particular skills and credentials—are rarely widely known, at least in specifics. Weber, of course, recognized that economic position in the market is normally closely associated with social honor and, often, political affiliation as well. (And vice versa.) Childerleyans like Mary Weller also recognize this association. They use this insight to understand—and in fact, at least in part, to create—the hierarchy of

° There is a long tradition in community studies of determining social class in this way, what Warner et al. (1960) called "evaluated participation."

°° For an exception, see the earlier quotation from Andy Sparrow in which he separates *status* from *class*.

social groups in which they live. And the term (having not read Weber) villagers commonly recognize as referring to the whole hierarchy of social standing (although many prefer not to use it) is that awful word, *class*.

Thus, to evaluate someone's social class, Childerleyans combine as best they can what they know of all the forms of social power at that person's command. There is nothing surprising in the criteria they use to make these determinations. Among the indicators Childerleyans consider (when known) are income, occupation, family background, the home a person lives in, the car a person drives, life-style (dress, favored activities, choice of pub), education, the amount of property a person owns, and who talks with whom.[20]

Because I am principally concerned here with social relations in the community (instead of, say, a nationally-based quantitative analysis of social mobility), community assessment of "class" is, I believe, the most significant way for me to describe Childerley's social structure. Moreover, I found surprisingly little disagreement about how a person was in general perceived, no matter the injustice some residents felt in a particular community assessment. Greta Moore's story, heard earlier, is a case in point.

There is a problem with such an approach, though. Childerleyans have several different ways of dividing the village into classes, and it's hard to choose one as the best for characterizing the community view. There are three common models: a two-class model, a three-class model, and a many-class model.

The two-class model is the dominant model used by those at the bottom of the social hierarchy. In this rather Marxian framework (although few villagers would recognize it as such), there are basically only rich people and poor people, bourgeoisie and proletariat, those who own and those who owe. The earlier quotations from Abel Harrowell and Mary Weller are examples of this. Those who see themselves as landing somewhere in the middle of the social field almost always stress the presence of a third group—the "middle bit," the "middle commuter sort of class," the "people like us someplace in the middle"—between the two extremes. The earlier comments of Phil Masters and Andy Sparrow are examples. Those of highest status, like Charles Goddard-Brown, usually employ the system with the most gradations, and place more emphasis on noneconomic factors as well.

No system of categorizing class is the sole knowledge of one village group. Most villagers are at least somewhat aware of other systems than the one they usually use. The two-class model is the most widely used.

All villagers use it at least as a shorthand, a kind of folk *ideal type* for capturing the basics of a more complex system. "Haves and have-nots," "us and them," "the people at this end of the village" and "the people at that end of the village," "people like us" and "council house people," "upper classes" and "working class"—these are all dichotomies wealthier villagers commonly use. "Us and them," "rich and poor," "upper class and working class," "moneyed people and ordinary people"—these are all dichotomies the poorer villagers commonly use. Villagers often mix the matching of the terms, referring, say, to "us" and the "rich people," as Mary Weller did.

Elements of the many-class system are also widely known and used. For example, the "ordinary people" and the people "someplace in the middle" abide by or at least recognize the distinction between a real upper class of old, usually landed money and an upper-middle class of new, sometimes landed money. A similar distinction is behind the derogatory term "yuppie," which was much in vogue during the fieldwork. This was usually applied more toward the middle of the middle class to cover those with new money but without significant land holdings. (It is worth noting that the more feudally inclined villagers, like Charles Goddard-Brown, sometimes extended yuppie to include upper-middle individuals. In one case I heard Charles Winkworth, one of the largest local landowners and the second richest village resident, described this way.) The least overlap seemed to be between the ordinary people and the terminologies for the middle range of the class structure. On only a few occasions did I hear working-class villagers use "middle class" and related phrases, and never did I hear them subdivide it into upper-middle, middle-middle, and lower-middle classes. Like everyone else, they relished the term "yuppie," but usually in two-class terminology as an alternate oppositional term to "us lot" or "ordinary people."

From these models, I have chosen to emphasize the two-class system, as it is the most widely used and therefore the most central in defining group boundaries. By the two-class system, Childerley is 42 percent "have-nots" and "ordinary people" and 58 percent "haves" and "moneyed people." (See table 1, where I have also presented the figures for the three-class and many-class systems.)

But other surveys have not been carried out this way, making comparisons difficult. In order to provide points of comparison, I also determined social class using the occupational-skill scale of Britain's Registrar General, the occupational-prestige scale of the Oxford Group, and the occupational-power scale devised by Erik Olin Wright.[21]

Table 1. Class Composition of Childerley
Community Assessment

TWO-CLASS MODEL	MULTICLASS MODEL	THREE-CLASS MODEL
Moneyed people 58%	Real upper class 2%	Upper crust 14%
	Upper middle class 12%	
	Middle middle class 44%	Middle class 48%
	Lower middle class 4%	
Ordinary people 42%	Upper working class 17%	Working class 38%
	Lower working class 21%	

88% sample, 1988

Table 2. Comparative Class Composition of Childerley
Registrar General Categories

		NATIONAL TOTALS		CHILDERLEY TOTALS[c]
Class		RG, 1981[a]	Essex[b]	
1	Professional, etc, occupations	4%	4%	23%
2	Intermediate occupations	22%	25%	23%
3N	Skilled occupations, nonmanual	22%	22%	5%
3M	Skilled occupations, manual	26%	27%	16%
4	Partly skilled occupations	19%	16%	17%
5	Unskilled occupations	7%	5%	16%
6	Armed forces	. . .	1%	2%

a. Registrar General figures, 1981
b. Essex Group figures, 1984
c. 52% sample, 1988

I list my results in tables 2, 3, and 4.° These tables point out a noteworthy aspect of Childerley. The highest and lowest social classes are considerably over-represented in the village, in comparison to national figures. The Oxford scale's three-class division shows this vividly.[22] Nationally, the "service," "intermediate," and "working" classes total 27, 36, and

° My coverage of the villagers is lower for these three tables than for the community assessment table—51 to 52 percent, as opposed to 88 percent. I often knew villagers' community assessment, but not enough to determine their place

Table 3. Comparative Class Composition of Childerley
Oxford (Hope-Goldthorpe) Categories

CLASS	NATIONAL TOTALS[a]	CHILDERLEY TOTALS[b]
Service class	27%	35%
I Higher grade professionals, administrators, and officials; managers in large establishments; large proprietors	9%	22%
II Lower-grade professionals, administrators, and officials; higher grade technicians; managers in small business and industrial establishments; supervisors of nonmanual employees	18%	13%
Intermediate class	36%	22%
III Routine nonmanual employees in administration and commerce, and personal service workers	20%	8%
IVa&b Small proprietors, artisans, etc., with and without employees	8%	9%
IVc Farmers and smallholders; self-employed fisherman	1%	5%
V Lower-grade technicians, supervisors of manual workers	8%	0%
Working class	37%	43%
VI Skilled manual workers	13%	14%
VIIa Semi-skilled and unskilled manual workers, not in agriculture	23%	21%
VIIb Agricultural workers	1%	8%

a. Essex Group figures, 1984
b. 52% sample, 1988

37 percent respectively. In Childerley the totals are 35, 22, and 43 percent respectively.[*]

The presence of many wealthy and esteemed people is, of course, unsurprising in an exurban village like Childerley. The high number of working class villagers, on the other hand, is made possible by the large

on the occupational skill, prestige, and power scales. Also, community assessment covers the never employed, which the other scales do not. For all four tables, I considered all villagers age 16 and over not in fulltime education.

   [*] The Essex Group only included men aged 16 to 64 and women aged 16 to 59, whereas I included all villagers 16 and over. If village men over 64 and village

Table 4. Comparative Class Composition of Childerley
Wright Categories

1. Bourgeoisie	2. Small employers	3. Petit bourgeoisie	
2% 7%	4% 5%	11% 6%	
4. Expert managers	5. Expert supervisors	6. Expert non-managers	
6% 4%	2% 3%	4% 5%	
7. Semi-credentialed managers	8. Semi-credentialed supervisors	9. Semi-credentialed workers	A
8% 5%	4% 2%	14% 3%	
10. Uncredentialed managers	11. Uncredentialed supervisors	12. Proletarians	
3% 2%	3% 1%	43% 53%	

B

A-axis: skill-credential assets in means of production
B-axis: organizational assets in means of production

The left-hand percentage under each class is the Essex Group figure for 1984; the right-hand percentage is the Childerley figure, based on a 51% sample of the village population in 1988.

amount of public assistance housing, plus the many tied houses associated with jobs on local estates.* What the thinning in the middle seems to represent is a gap in accessible housing for those who are unable to afford the expensive local housing market yet who do not qualify for council housing or work in the sort of trades associated with tied housing—what in the multiclass community-assessed scale is called lower-middle class, which comprises only 4 percent of the village.

There is another point of comparison worth explaining. Look at the Oxford figures (table 3) for Childerley. Note that for upper and middle levels, there is quite a bit of difference from the community assessment in table 1. The Oxford categories show a larger upper than middle stratum, the reverse of the community-assessed three-class model.

Wealthier villagers, I suspect, would regard the Oxford service class as covering a lot of social terrain. In the village, the "upper crust" of upper-middle and true upper classes usually does not include the doctors,

women over 59 are removed, the Childerley figures are slightly less polarized, but essentially the same: 33% for the service class, 26% for the intermediate class, and 41% for the working class.

* Indeed, this may be typical of what Harper (1987) calls "uniform villages." See chapter 2 for details on village types.

solicitors, working farmers, architects, managers, restaurant owners, chemical engineers, and school teachers of the service class. Unless they have considerable inherited financial or cultural capital (which some of them do in fact have), villagers with these service-class occupations are regarded as mere middle middle by the upper crust.

To make it into the upper middle (and thus into the upper crust) you need to be an owner of a large business, a high ranking military officer, just plain rich, or a person with valued cultural attributes, like Charles Goddard-Brown. (Charles, recall, has a close family connection to titled aristocracy.) These are the people who own most of the village's farmland and hold most of the prominent positions in the community, such as chair of the Parish Council, the Conservative Club, and the Women's Institute. They also tend to be older than the middle middles.

At the top of the upper crust are the "real upper class." Most prominent are the aristocracy and their closest relations, no matter what their income level. Also included are very large untitled landowners if their money is old and their life-style and bearing appropriate. Childerley has four of the former and two of the latter. These few individuals are the ones that have "got it proper," as villagers sometimes say. Yet even when combined with the upper middles, numbers are still low. Childerley's upper crust is consequently much smaller than the Oxford service class.

V

CHILDERLEYANS ARE NOT ALONE in their consciousness of the importance of class. The Essex Group found that 92 percent of their 1984 national sample could assign themselves to a social class. This figure shows only a slight decline from the 93 percent of a 1970 study of Londoners and the 95 percent of a 1948 national poll of England.[23] No questions were asked about how the respondents conceived of others in their communities. But, as class is a relative matter, we may assume that they would have been equally able to assign class identities to other people.

The Essex Group did include another relevant question, which yielded a striking response. They asked: "Apart from class, is there any other major group you identify with?" Only nineteen percent had *anything* to add.[24] A quarter of these mentioned a business or professional group, a fifth a religious group, and an eighth an ethnic or racial group. In fact, of the 4 percent of their sample that consisted of people of color, only half mentioned race or ethnicity. Survey research has its limits, but John Western's ethnographic study of the middle class of one of Britain's largest communities of people of color, Barbadian Londoners, is consistent with this surprising finding. These successful citizens desired most to be seen as simply that: successful citizens.[25] Gender is the most universal source of social identity, but it was evidently not consciously held with such strength or in such a way as to be tapped by the phrase "major group," and only 6 percent mentioned it, almost all women.

Despite postwar (and even earlier) immigration and strong regional differences, Britain remained remarkably homogeneous for a nation of 57 million during the period of my fieldwork (1987–1991). Only one person in twenty-five claimed a racial and ethnic heritage other than white.[26] Only one person in five claimed a religious affiliation other than the Anglican Communion.[27] What was left as a source of conscious collective identity beneath the level of the nation? Evidently, class was still the primary one, and Childerley remained a "slightly feudal" village. But, as we shall hear, this was not something most Childerleyans were happy about.

F O U R

The Front Door and the Back Door

We like to think we're the same as other people, except
for the fact that we live in a castle.

Consort to Lady Saye and Sele, 1990

I

ONE MORNING A few weeks after I had moved to Childerley, I
was home alone when I heard a knock. I went to the front door
and opened it. The stoop was empty. I had a quick look around,
still saw no one, and closed the door. Confused, I tried to settle back
down into my chair. There had definitely been a knock, I told myself in
some perplexity, although it hadn't had quite the normal sound. Then
there was another knock. I leapt up and headed for the front door again,
when the back door opened. In stepped Ted Spencer with a "how is the
Michael today?" and the battery charger I had asked to borrow.

I was a little embarrassed by the incident. When I reflected on it
later, I realized that I had unconsciously adopted a practice characteristic
of most moneyed residents of Childerley—that of using the front door
when visiting other people's homes and for bringing people into one's
own home as well. So ingrained was this practice that my ears could not
resolve where the sounds of Ted's knocks were coming from. Ted, like
most ordinary villagers, characteristically uses the back door when visiting
friends and relatives, even though this usually requires making a longer
trip around to the rear. I doubt Ted would ever use the back door at, say,
the rector's house. But he was paying me a compliment by choosing to
use the back door of my house (although he did wait until he'd knocked
twice before opening it himself).

By itself the difference between most moneyed and ordinary villagers
in the use of front and back doors is of no great consequence, save occasional moments of awkwardness. But this is not the only difference in
patterns of living. "Theirs is a different world to ours," as Audrey Spencer   51

put it to me once.° Each of these worlds has a distinctive feel and flow, I think she was saying, a shared style of living and sense of self I will call *back door* for the working people and *front door* for the wealthier villagers.

By back door I mean a style that is more informal, group-oriented, local, interactive, and experiential. By front door I mean a style that is opposite in all these dimensions: more formal, individualistic, far-flung, private, and distanced. Each acts as what Raymond Williams tellingly described as an "informing spirit" that pervades the experience of life in the two groups.[1] Pierre Bourdieu calls it a *habitus*, an inner "system of dispositions."[2] These habituated differences express themselves in the daily habits, manners, outlooks, taste, and other social sensibilities of the two groups.

A visit to the Spencers or to their neighbors, the Cooks, is a good introduction to what I mean by back-door style.°° Neighbors, friends, and kin are constantly in and out of the Spencers', popping round for a chat, a coffee, the loan of a tool. Hardly a day goes by without at least a couple of these exchanges. People rarely phone ahead. If you were an accepted member of their circle and you came around for a visit, you would by-pass the front door and the doorbell. Instead, you would walk around behind the garage, over the heap of bicycle parts, toys, flower pots, and tools to the back door, which is usually open, except in the worst weather. The front door is much easier to get to, but it is used mainly by strangers, officials, representatives of the Village Fete Committee collecting contributions for the annual bottle table, and the like.°°° As an accepted member of the group, you would enter through the back, perhaps without even a knock or a hello. The back door leads into the kitchen, where Audrey might be fixing a cup of coffee or working on supper. If it's empty, the sitting room is where people are likely to be, watching the telly, talking, smoking. You would walk in, say an informal hello, and sit down. Likely, you would not stay long—fifteen minutes or half an hour—and you would leave with no more ceremony than when you came.

In the Spencer's house, people are rarely alone. The center of activity

---

° Benjamin Disraeli put it more starkly, calling England "Two nations, between whom there is no intercourse and no sympathy; who are as ignorant of each other's habits, thought, and feelings, as if they were dwellers in different zones, or inhabitants of different planets." Cited in Hacker (1992), ix.

°° This sketch of the "Spencers," and the following ones for the "Cooks" and the "Brambleys," are all as of July 1988.

°°° The Village Fete is an annual festival, often with an agricultural theme, held in most villages in England.

is the sitting room with the big color television, which is nearly always on (although it is often ignored). In the evening or on the weekends, the sitting room is likely to be crammed with Ted and Audrey and their five children—Patsy, Mary, Sylvia, Janet, and Tom. If friends are over, there may well be four or five people on the three-person couch, others sprawled out on the carpeted sitting room floor. This is where the family usually eats, and there is much running back and forth to the kitchen. Even at night, the close group life continues as the four girls share one bedroom, Tom and a neighbor boy over for the night share another, and Audrey and Ted the house's third; meanwhile, Mary's current boyfriend sleeps on the living room couch.

There is always activity in the Spencer house, people jumbling and tumbling together.° Visitors and family members come and go constantly, keeping the social situation in perpetual change. Commonly a dozen people enter the house at some point during the day, and often more. The children often squabble—not in a mean-spirited way, but so as to add to the activeness and sound level of the house. Several conversations may go on at one time, occasionally shouted down by someone who wants to hear a good bit on the T.V.

The Cooks are an older couple and their home is calmer. But there is still the constant flow of people in and out the back door. Their children are all grown, yet there is never a day without a visit from at least one of their three daughters, two sons, and grandchildren. Usually there are two or three visits, and sometimes more. The Spencers and their children are also often over. Most mornings, Audrey stops by for a cup of tea or coffee before heading out for her job cleaning at one of Childerley's big houses. The Spencers' kids wander in and out with an eye for Mrs. Cook's pastries or to see if Mr. Cook is doing anything interesting and maybe wouldn't mind having help with his current project, or to borrow the proverbial egg, cup of sugar, and cup of milk. As Mrs. Cook explained to me once, "We still have a little bit of community here."

Erving Goffman suggested that social life is conducted in "regions" in which different behaviors are appropriate, distinguishing particularly between the "frontstage" and "backstage."[3] The frontstage is where careful, formal "performances" are conducted, often by a "dramaturgical team" of group members who work together, seemingly without communication between themselves, to create the proper impression for non-

---

° The photographer Nick Waplington captures this feeling perfectly in *Living Room* (Waplington, 1991).

group members. Very often these performances have been rehearsed, with speeches and roles planned in advance. Frontstage behaviors are characteristic of the boundary zone of a group. The backstage, on the other hand, is an informal region only open to true members. Here, deep and secure within the group's boundary, the frontstage guard is let down. This is where people tell off-color jokes, put their feet on the table, belch, and yell at each other.

One characteristic of the back door-style of working-class Childerley-ans like the Cooks and Spencers is that the backstage region is very large. People spend more of their time there, and it has more people in it.° There is much entering and exiting, a constant flow of social exchanges that, even when desired, makes planned performances more difficult to arrange and pull off. Consequently, life follows an informal, fluid pattern largely without the curtains, spotlights, and separation of actors and audi-ence typical of the frontstage (although by no means without drama).

The moneyed people in the village, however, seem to have a different temperament, a different sense of the proper rhythms of social life. A visit to the home of Ellen and Henry Brambley and their fifteen year-old daughter Alice is a good introduction to their characteristic front-door style. I advise calling ahead first, even if you know them well, as they would consider it more polite. Besides, there's a good chance that they will be out. When you arrive, head for the front door with the big brass knocker. In fact, you won't be able to see the back garden where the back door is as the positions of the house, garage, and a high brick wall com-pletely seal it off. (There is a garden door in the wall, but it is always closed and locked.) When you reach the front door, definitely knock. If someone answers, you will likely exchange greetings and maybe even have a short conversation over the threshold before being asked, "Won't you come in?" The front door leads to the enclosed porch where guests and family leave their shoes. Then another door, and into the front hallway, decorated with antiques and old lithographs in carved frames. One door leads to the dining room with its beautifully polished table and straight-backed chairs. The other leads to the sitting room, to which you will be personally guided.

During your visit, you will probably find that your access to the rest

---

° Although he did not develop the point, with his unparalleled eye Goffman (1959, 133) saw this too: "working class men tend to be members of large teams and tend to spend much of their day backstage."

of the house is carefully controlled. The Brambleys are very concerned about privacy, inside their home and out. In a pattern familiar to homes of the wealthy throughout the West, they maintain a clear boundary between guest areas and family areas. Unlike working-class families, the Brambleys keep a separate loo for visitors, something they can afford and have the space for. The upstairs, where the bedrooms and family bath are, are strictly off-limits—unless you are being given a house tour, guided by a family member, and then only if the house has just been cleaned. (I never saw an unmade bed in a moneyed house during my stay in the village, although I saw bedrooms in the homes of ordinary people even when they were strewn with clothes.)

The Brambleys have many fewer exchanges with other households. None of their kin live in the immediate area, and they barely know their neighbors, even after living five years in the village. They've never even been inside the house of the neighbor on one side. They have plenty of friends, of course, but no close ones in the village. Consequently, it's unlikely that anyone else will visit during the course of your stay, except possibly a village friend of Alice's. If someone did, very possibly they would be asked to come back later.

The Brambleys know people all across the south of England, and their dearest friends live in Yorkshire now. Perhaps twice a month they will drive to southern Hampshire, to Kent, to Guildford, or to Dorset to see some of these friends or to explore the countryside. They are particularly fond of Oxford and the New Forest. Several times a year they go into London for a show, for shopping, for a meal, or just to take in what Ellen calls the "cultural excitement" of the city. Ellen just took Alice to France for several days of travel through the cathedral towns of the north. They may live in the country, but they have cosmopolitan tastes and a love of far-flung travel and of news of the world, which they take pride in following closely.

In contrast, the orientation of the Cooks is more local. Two of their children live in the village, two more in villages less than ten miles away; the furthest lives twenty-five miles away. Their best friends live in Bartley, a parish adjacent to Childerley. They see them every week at least, and usually more often than that. Compared to the Brambleys, the Cooks rarely travel far. They do go to Cornwall every year, where one of their sons keeps a caravan in a holiday park. Once a month they like to drive twenty miles to visit Albert's sister who still lives on a large country estate where both Margaret and Albert worked many years ago. They took a trip to the seaside not long ago as well. But Margaret hasn't been to London in years and just took her first trip to France, a surprise planned by her children who paid for the five-day coach tour. She had never been out of the country before, and Albert still hasn't. Neither of them has ever been on a plane.

One common form of exchange villagers like the Brambleys do engage in is to have someone over for a meal, or to go to someone else's home in return. Often these are very elaborate meals, particularly Sunday lunch, with course after course of immaculately prepared dishes appearing like magic from a sealed kitchen into which the dirty dishes later disappear. But among ordinary villagers, this formal sort of meal exchange is rare. Audrey Spencer, for example, says she has never been to a dinner party.[4]

Even when people do visit or are invited into the Brambleys' sitting room or the kitchen, the guests, even close friends, will be excluded from most backstage activities. Of course, this goes on in the back-door homes of the Spencers and Cooks as well, but considerably less frequently. For one thing, with so many people constantly flowing in and out, it's a significant organizational problem to control social situations so carefully. Moreover, the smaller size of working-class homes limits the degree to which the greater number of people in them can be regulated, restricting the possibility of maintaining rigid boundaries between family areas and guest areas. In comparison, the backstage area is considerably narrower in the lives of Ellen, Henry, and Alice Brambley. They spend less time there, and the only people in it are members of their nuclear family and, sometimes, a few very close friends. Their sense of when backstage behaviors are appropriate covers fewer occasions in their lives than it does for a family like the Spencers.

The lack of a free flow of household exchanges, the narrower backstage area, and the concern for privacy are part of a more individualistic sense of self. For example, in the Brambley house, family members are often alone. Alice is often up in her room, reading, studying, practicing her flute, or engaging in some other solitary pursuit. Henry and Ellen both work full-time. (He's a civil engineer and she's a schoolteacher.) When at home, they too spend much of their time alone. Henry will be at work in his shop, built onto the garage, while Ellen is out in the garden "puttering about," as she says. She loves to take long walks alone through the woods and fields near their house. Thus, when you were led to their sitting room, it was probably empty before your arrival.

If you wanted to have an extended private conversation with one of the Brambleys, you would not find it hard to arrange. But the greater group-orientation of the Spencers means there would likely be some awk-wardness and joking as the kitchen or one of the bedrooms was cleared out. And there would probably be many interruptions by the curious. To be sure, the Spencers have a big family in a small house, and more effort is required to maintain the social space of a long private talk. But, in part because of this, they are not as used to long private conversations in their own home, and would show more discomfort about arranging for one than the Brambleys.

The greater group-orientation of working-class villagers is also re-flected in their closer standards of interpersonal distancing. There is the regular load of four or five people that the Spencer's couch must bear. When an expedition is mounted for a day on the coast or just to the town for shopping, people may jam together into a single car, sometimes three in front, four in back. Of course, the Spencers have only one car, as well as a small house for a large family. But they feel no particular discomfort with the frequent situations of thigh-touching closeness in their lives. Ted, Audrey, the older children (including the twelve-year old), and many of their friends smoke, and the sitting room is usually pretty hazy. The smoke is not seen as intrusion on personal space, as moneyed villagers often find it to be—even those who smoke themselves. Rather, it is the product of a group activity, which probably adds to the definition of the group space. To be in cigarette smoke is to be in a group setting.

The informality of back-door style is also expressed in the way ordi-nary people in the village present their bodies to those to whom they are talking. Moneyed villagers tend to present themselves facing straight on with the shoulder-lines of both parties in a conversation running parallel, or nearly so. This makes the body itself almost an extension of the face in face-to-face conversation, something else to be scrutinized in the inter-pretation of speech and intention and something else to be carefully con-trolled so as to convey the desired impression. Working-class villagers, in contrast, more commonly position themselves at an oblique angle to each other, still maintaining some direct eye and face contact, but relaxing the experience of a conversational encounter by limiting the size of the "face" which must be controlled. Rather than opposing lines, they tend more toward circles and oblique angles, so that their bodies are not directly opposed. There is unstated wisdom in these differences. The oppositional postures wealthier villagers seem to favor are appropriate to the one-on-one conversations that fill much of their lives. The generally more oblique postures of working-class villagers are suitable to the larger gatherings in which they more often find themselves. In fact, for them a directly oppositional stance might be interpreted by their associates as unwelcoming, as it excludes others. It could even seem threatening.

Some writers who have observed differences in body posture across class lines have attributed the less oppositional stance common among working people to deferential and defeatist attitudes.[5] This may well be true in many conversations between individuals with a substantial difference in power, particularly in frontstage situations. Its persistence among the working class in settings with no power differentials, where all are of roughly the same class and status, suggests that a different informing spirit is also at work. In contrast, moneyed villagers still tend to maintain oppositional postures even among people of their own class and background.

The same dominance of oblique angles between people in social situations extends into the way sitting rooms are arranged and used in working-class households in the village. In most of the tied cottages and council buildings, the fireplace is set squarely in the middle of the principal wall, usually the wall opposite the doorway. This four-square arrangement of walls tends to lead to similarly rectilinear placement of chairs and sofas along the walls, with the fireplace as the focal point. The result is a formal, oppositional setting inappropriate to the back-door style. But in the modern working-class village home, the formal placement of the furniture and fireplace is diffused by the presence of what is, in effect, a second hearth: the television. This second hearth usually sits off to one side of the fireplace in a corner of the room, almost unavoidably at odds with the sight lines of most of the seats. With reference to the fireplace, people sit in opposition to each other, as the room's form dictates. But with respect to the television, the attention lines run at an oblique angle to seating positions. This crossing of sight lines caused by the two hearths allows informality to win out over the sitting-room-as-frontstage design of the architect. Many moneyed villagers have televisions in their sitting rooms too, but they almost always switch it off for visitors.

A visit to each of the two pubs also makes clear the differences between the styles in degree of group orientation, formality, and interpersonal distancing. In the public bar of the Fox, people tend not to stand or sit oppositionally. Most of the men, particularly on a big night, will huddle around the bar in a great mass. In this huddle with its constant surging motion, it is faces that one directs attention to, rising and almost floating above a dark, lower zone of bodies, barely distinguishable from each other. Formal scrutiny of what would be called the "body-face" is not possible. In the midst of this mass, one feels almost palpably part of a single group entity, if one is accepting of the situation.* (If you are not, if you feel that you do not "belong" or if you are applying different standards of interpersonal distancing, there is hardly any situation which will make you feel more an individual, and one whose personal space is much encroached upon.) Those sitting at the tables along the walls tend to leave the bar side of the table open so that the group sitting there is not sealed off from the others. Chairs and benches whose position at the tables would force one to sit with back to the bar and the center of the room are usually the last to fill, promoting the greater group orientation of back-door style.

In contrast, in the Horse and Hound people sit directly opposite each other in small separate groups, backs facing backs at other tables. The group around the bar is much smaller, and there is less effort on the part of those sitting at the tables to be part of the goings on there. I asked Mary Spencer if she had ever been to the Horse and Hound, and she said, "Yeah. Once. Don't like it. It's too, sort of, quiet. I'd rather go to the Fox because there's more conservation going on down there." For those who want a quieter, more solitary time, the Fox does have the lounge bar with its restaurant-style seating and separate entrance (although few use it). In the H and H, front-door style pervades the whole place, and everyone enters by the same door, as in the house of a moneyed person.

Intertwined with the informality and greater group orientation of the back door is a norm of group behavior Patricia Fleming has described as "negative egalitarianism."[6] As a description, this is not a perfect term since it seems to carry an air of criticism of this norm. But Fleming is right in identifying the practice. The front-door world is one of hierarchical formal organizations like the Parochial Church Council with leaders in officially recognized positions who make decisions for (and presumably on behalf of) all. But the working class largely rejects this hierarchical style, with the glory it showers on the individuals in those official positions. Except within the family, the norm is for group decision making. No one is to appear in too much of a leadership position. For example, one man who came to work in one of the Big Houses tried to set himself up as a social leader in the working-class community. He was initially accepted and well-liked, as he had a gregarious, friendly disposition. For most of a year, he could be found at the center of many a good time. But bit by bit, he fell from favor as he infringed on the norm all too often. "He tries

---

* Mikhail Bakhtin (1984), 255, put it well: "The individual feels that he is an indissoluble part of the collectivity, a member of the people's mass body. In this whole the individual body ceases to a certain extent to be itself."

to take over everything," I was told by several people. "We should railroad him, I say," another man told me. "We can do that in this village."

Arthur Cater, an old village man, told me a story that reflects this back-door social norm in regard to material possessions:

"I shall never forget the chap. There were six of us in the dairy in them days. One of our mates, he bought one of these little motor bikes. Of course he thought he was, you know, very clever because he had a motor bike and we didn't. He goes to Harchester one night, you see, and on the way back, his light fell to earth, and he got caught up with the police [for not having a light]. And he had to go to court. But Lord Lefroy was on the bench that day, so when the case came out he asked some different questions and that. He said, 'I understand you work for my neighbor, Lord Tidmouth.' 'Yes, m'lord.' He said, 'I understand you work in the dairy. Why,' he said, 'you'd be getting a fairly good wage then.' 'Yes, me lord.' 'Well,' he said, 'in that case, instead of the ordinary five shillings, we charge you seven-six.' I can see that chap [as if] he stood there now when he came back from court. And what he said weren't nobody's business. Instead of five shillings, seven and six!"

Through constant stories and jokes of this sort, strong pressures are put on those who violate the norm.

I infringed on this norm myself on one occasion. A farmer in a neighboring village runs a paint-warfare game in his woods in which two sides armed with paint-shooting guns try to capture each other's flag. For a £10 fee, each player gets a small supply of orange paint balls to fire at the opposition. Once players are splattered with paint anywhere on their bodies, they are out of the game. Generally, two teams will play several games over the course of three or four hours.

One Saturday afternoon, I went with the lads (and one woman) from the Fox to play another team. I quickly found that in order to hit anyone you had to put yourself in grave danger of getting shot yourself. And I was also puzzled that no one seemed to be going after the flag. So instead of concentrating on shooting people, I went right through the woods and made a dash for the other team's flag, grabbed it, and got clean away despite many shots in my direction from the defendants. (The guns are very inaccurate.) Two games later, I did it again. After the last game, when we had all returned our equipment, I went over to our group, which was standing around reliving the day's glories. Feeling good about winning the two games for our side, I rather expected to hear some praise for my exploits. Instead, I was distinctly cold-shouldered. Finally, someone turned to me and said, "You Yanks are all the same. Just like in World

War II, we did all the fighting while you got the glory." No one laughed.
I was devastated.

This was not merely a boundary-making, anti-American statement.
My American-ness was often a source of pride for the groups I mixed
with, the pride of being able to include someone different. Rather, the
fact that my difference was turned against me after the games demonstrated the need these villagers felt to uncrown the standing I thought I
had achieved.

Back-door "group-egalitarianism," as I would prefer to call it, can also
be seen in the common practice of mutual buying of rounds in the Fox.°
Although people will often buy rounds for their friends in the Horse and
Hound (as happens regularly in pubs and bars the world over), the practice
is seldom conducted with the same intensity there. Yet nearly every night
in the Fox there is a group of friends, mainly men, drinking together using
the rounds system. In this form of drinking, usually among a group of
three to ten people, each participant buys drinks in turn for the whole
group. This means everyone spends the same amount of money. But it
also means that you must keep on drinking until it is your turn to buy a
round for everyone else, and even then it is hard to leave the drinking
round, because there is likely to be someone who still hasn't had the
opportunity of returning your favor. Under the group-egalitarian ethical
code of rounds buying, just as it is improper to drink free on other people's
money, so too it is improper to leave someone unwillingly in your debt.
Also, in this way everyone has an equal opportunity to flash about a crisp
ten or twenty pound note.

Now it is a matter of simple math to see that in a group of, say, seven
to ten people, consuming a lot of alcohol is quite unavoidable. In fact, if
you are a little slow at drinking down your pint of English bitter, twenty
ounces of high-alcohol beer, you will find, as I did, that one and sometimes
two additional pints have been pulled for you even before you have finished your current one or asked for another. Strong pressure in the form
of cajoling and teasing is placed on all the participants to drink each round
completely, and not to switch to half pints or to give a pint away.°° To
do so would be to make a statement of rejecting the group. Consequently,

° This could be contrasted with the "individual-egalitarianism" of the front
door. The difference is that group-egalitarianism is an equality of outcome, while
individual-egalitarianism is an equality of opportunity, regardless of outcome.
   °° As I am not accustomed to this level of consumption, I was happy to
discover that one successful strategy was to carry my pint with me when I went
to the men's room and to decant a good bit of it. I suspect others often did the

seven or eight pints followed by several shots of whiskey is a common amount for each round's participant to drink in an evening, the alcoholic equivalent of about fifteen cans of strong American beer.

The consumption of such vast quantities is, of course, a serious social problem. The health of a number of village men has been undermined by this practice, and it is a major financial drain for a workman supporting a family on £5,000–6,000 a year. I estimate some villagers spend over £500 a year in the Fox, and one man victimized by alcoholism and rounds buying was in debt to every regular in the pub. Still, the willingness to submit to the deep, dark leveling of being drunk, very drunk, together is to make a commitment of unashamed solidarity that deliberately flouts the values of front-door society. The fellowship of drink, a central feature of most human societies, is an important means by which many village men enact the egalitarianism and the social boundaries of the back door.

II

WHY DO THESE DIFFERENCES between the front-door and back-door styles dominate social life in Childerley? At bottom, I suspect, are the different material circumstances of the working class and the moneyed people in the village and the effect that these have on life experiences. Similar contrasts in habits and home life across class have been noted in many other settings and cultures, leaving material differences as the only constant factor.[7] Karl Marx overstated the case when he wrote that "it is not the consciousness of men that determines their being, but, on the contrary, their social being that determines their consciousness." But he was right in saying that "material life *conditions* the social, political and intellectual life process in general" creating "definite forms of social consciousness."[8] Emile Durkheim, although he did not give the same importance to the role of the economy in shaping the organization of society, also stressed the effect of social organization on social consciousness.[9] How could it be otherwise, for what we do surely affects what we think and feel?°

Thus, those whose working lives stress competition and career mobility are likely to see themselves more individualistically. Those who follow

---

same. And I also suspect that my little dissimulation was not always unrecognized by other drinkers. They politely (and mercifully) overlooked it, though.

  ° Here I am sneaking a quick look at the conceptual "map" of social life charted by "reflection theory," described in chapter 8. I will be discussing this map in considerable detail there and in the last chapter.

spiralist careers, where moving up means moving out to a new job far away, will tend to have fewer local friends and kin and more far-flung social ties. Those whose daily work requires constant persuasion, social manipulation, and calculation of social and economic gain are likely to feel less comfortable with the activity and fluidity of back-door style. Those in a position of political dominance will find that the public eye glares more constantly upon them, and so they will want to hold the world at a distance and lead a more formal and controlled life. In contrast, those with little access to the main institutions of social power are likely to feel alienated from formality and to resent hierarchical authority. And those who have small cars (if they are fortunate enough to have one at all) and small houses will be used to living a close, interactive, group life.

Yet is is important not to overdraw the contrast between the front door and the back door. While conceptual contrasts are essential to human thought, the dangers of overstating and reifying such contrasts are well-known. The imputed characteristics of groups hardly ever pertain to all individuals in them, and may only pertain within the social context of that group. In different circumstances, we all become different people and think and act accordingly. There are times when wealthier villagers do use cultural back doors, and ordinary villagers front doors. For example, most moneyed men in the village (probably when they were younger) have likely participated in rounds buying at least a few times, and gotten communally drunk. The front door and the back door are not tattooed in the mind. Rather, they are taken-for-granted patterns of living, social conditionings appropriate to and derived from the context of class life in an English exurban village.

We have to be careful about the front door and back door not only at an individual level, but at a group level as well. I have in mind a particular group of moneyed Childerleyans quite accommodated to both doors. These are the residents of "the Community," the six families of London professionals who live in the converted manor house at the edge of the village. Although all the families in the Community have at least one adult in high-salaried, credentialed, front-door employment, many of their habits of living are quite back door.

Helen and Brad Burton-Collins's home is an example. They put a lot of thought into redesigning their unit of the former manor house to their liking, in part because Brad is an architect. The result is a home that retains some of the front-door grandeur of the original space but is informal at the same time. For example, they left the former music room virtually untouched. (It has spectacular eight-foot high windows overlooking the parkland outside and a twelve-foot high ceiling with, as I recall, plaster moldings.) Here they keep their library, a grand piano, and some fine antique furniture. This is a space well suited to the quiet reading, practice of musical instruments, and other solitary activities the Burton-Collinses's enjoy.

But they took what was the billiards room and, after putting in a wall to make space for a hallway and stairway, turned it into a large kitchen-cum-dining-room-cum-family-room. This is the central social room of the house. A couple of big sofas and cushy chairs line the walls of one corner. The kitchen part wraps around the opposite corner—counters, stove, and fridge. A sturdy wood table big enough for ten sits in the middle. In another corner is a door out to the garden, and it is amply fitted out with coat hooks, shelves, and wellies.

There is a fluid activeness to the spirit of life in this room, and a constant stream of people comes through it during the day. Neighbor children from the other five units come bouncing through to see what Helen and Brad's two girls are up to. Adults drift in for a coffee while Helen and Brad cook, or stop in to let them know about an escaped sheep, downed tree, leaky shed roof, or other Community crisis. (These come up almost daily.) People often don't call ahead—they just come over and let themselves in, either through the hallway door or the garden door. (Both of these doors are on the same side of the building, and neither is clearly a front or back door.)

Brad and Helen often have house guests too, through their participation in an organization called W.W.O.O.F.—Weekends Working on Organic Farms—in which people come up from the city to help out for the weekend in exchange for food and country air. About every second weekend Helen and Brad have a couple "Wwoofers" about, adding to the fullness and flow of the scene. When the Wwoofers (or other guests) are around, Helen and Brad maintain a fairly soft boundary between family areas and public areas in the house. The bedrooms and the only toilet are upstairs. They did not trouble to put in a guest toilet when they redesigned the unit, so all guests must use the same one as the family. Helen and Brad also encourage people to look around the upstairs, no matter what state it's in, to see the remodeling they've done or to have a look at the progress on their latest building project up there. Three-quarters-finished improvement schemes can be encountered just about anywhere in the house.

But having described the many back-door habits of these economically front-door people, I must now stress the fact that Helen and Brad (and other couples at the Community) are well aware that their home doesn't fit into conventional patterns. In adopting this uncharacteristic mode of living, they are well aware that it differs from their own upbringings and that of their coworkers and friends. Back-door style for people of their class is a statement of conscious difference, a difference they take pride in. It is a statement they would only find meaningful in an economic and cultural context where the contrast between front door and back door dominates.

III

ANOTHER WAY DIFFERENCES in material circumstances occasionally express themselves in Childerley, and in villages like it, is in social conflict. An incident that took place in the nearby village of St. Mary Bourne illustrates the tensions that exist.° From appearances, it's a very "villagey village" with its ancient, close-packed houses, fine church, watercress beds, and attractive situation on the banks of the Bourne, a tributary to the Test.

On the night of May 14, 1988, the village's rural quiet was shattered by the breaking of glass and the crunching of metal. That Saturday evening a band went on a rampage and vandalized about thirty cars with bricks and bats. Tires were slashed, windscreens smashed, bodywork dented. Many of the cars bore names like Mercedes and BMW. Earlier that month, the "Wessex Freedom Force," a previously unknown group, had delivered a warning that it would bomb wealthy incomers out of the countryside. The tabloid The Sun leapt to the newsworthy interpretation that a "class war" had erupted in the countryside.[10] According to BBC radio, the "yokels" had had enough of the "yuppies" in their village.[11] But no one claimed responsibility and, like the Captain Swing rebellion of the 1830s, the perpetrators melted away namelessly into the community.

It is not certain that the violent acts of that night really were specifically directed at the newer, wealthier residents of St. Mary Bourne. A number of the cars smashed were not smart and upmarket, and a couple were owned by people who had lived all their lives in the village. It may well have been, as some argued, the handiwork of a swirling crowd of drunken young men, each taunting the others on to audacious transgressions against the norms of society in general—not wealthy newcomers in

° As this incident received national media coverage, I have felt it unnecessary to use a pseudonym for the village.

particular.° The truth may never be known. But what was certain were
the terms used to describe the groups involved, a shared vocabulary of
group boundaries: yokels and yuppies; us and them; ordinary people and
moneyed people. To be sure, there was disagreement over whether the
incident truly demonstrated antipathy between the two groups denoted
in this vocabulary, but not over the existence of the groups, or the vocabulary.

Among working-class Childerleyans with whom I spoke about it, there
was no doubt that the vandalism in St. Mary Bourne was indeed class
warfare. A couple spoke admiringly of it. "I wouldn't be surprised to see
it happen here," one man told me. The "divide," the "strong feeling"
recognized by Andy Sparrow and some of the other villagers quoted in
chapter 3 has its roots in a material conflict experienced in communities
on both sides of the North Atlantic throughout the international property
boom of the 1980s—the gentrification of local housing.

Often seen as an urban issue, the wave of gentrification also lapped
into rural and exurban areas across England, as rural living became increasingly desirable.[12] The basic issue is that the arrival of the wealthy
drives up the price of housing beyond the reach of poorer families who,
in many cases, have lived longer in the locality. Location within the commuting watershed of London and environs intensified the process in
Childerley. Southern England prospered during the 1980s, in contrast to
most northern regions, largely because of the wealth of London's financial
districts during the economic expansion of the period. Consequently,
many people could afford to pay more for a country place. At the same
time, development remained under the tight control of the British planning system. Demand went up enormously, and supply expanded only
somewhat. Between 1981 and 1987, housing prices rose 300 percent in
Hampshire as a whole, and even more in the Hampshire countryside.°°
In Childerley, a three bedroom Victorian cottage would have fetched
about £50,000 in 1980 (already well beyond the reach of many of the
poorer residents), and probably would have gone for £250,000 in 1988.°°°

° This was the interpretation given to me by some wealthy residents of St.
Mary Bourne with whom I spoke personally.

°° This was the third highest rate of any county in the country, exceeded
only by Surrey and Berkshire. In contrast, a northern county like Durham showed
an increase of 130 percent, lower than the rate of inflation over the period. In
the country as a whole, prices rose 210 percent. (Aslet, 1988).

°°° The British housing market has softened considerably since 1988, as it
has in other countries, and prices in the village have dropped some.

Although in the aggregate rural housing supply went up a bit during this period (planners did allow some development), for the rural working class it contracted considerably. Many of the houses that wealthier people bought were old country cottages and farm houses, often in poor repair. In the 1950s, most of these had been held by large estates and let to rural tenants, either as rental property or as tied cottages. Other working-class residents lived in council estates. Local people worked on local farms and estates almost exclusively. Childerley's farms, for example, employed about seventy people. One village big house employed seven full-time gardeners and a domestic staff of around a dozen.

Mechanization of agriculture, rising wage expectations, and the collapse of the estates after the war dried up most employment in the village. At the same time, it dried up the need for employers to provide housing for the working class. Former tied cottages gradually went up for sale, and wealthier people who commuted to the towns snapped them up, often combining two or more attached cottages into one. Working-class villagers could commute to the towns to work, and many did (and do)—but only if they had an affordable place to live. With tied cottages disappearing along with rural jobs, the council estates became their refuge. Yet in the 1980s, the Thatcher government's decision to sell off council properties to their tenants (who could, after five years, sell them on the open market) began to erode even this last harbor.

These trends have old roots and it helps to place them in a longer perspective. Initially, the loss of rural employment, the prospect of higher wages in the cities and towns, and a desire to escape the image of rubes and bumpkins contributed to the century-long decline in rural population experienced in most Western industrial nations after about 1850. The very wealthy, for whom none of these factors were ever issues, never left, in keeping with the English rural aristocratic tradition. And there was always a slow back-to-the-country trickle of middle-class people, for whom these factors were no longer issues. They bought a few village homes, sometimes as a second home, sometimes as a place to commute from if train connections were good. Yet through to the 1950s, rural population continued to decline.

Beginning in the 1960s, and a little later in Childerley and other villages a bit distant from London, the trickle became a steady stream, and then a torrent. Greater wealth, rural electrification, wider car ownership, better roads, and a deconcentration of employment helped make rural living possible and desirable for many former city residents. Rural decline turned around and became growth.

These economic and infrastructure changes, as I discussed earlier, were only facilitating factors in the new rural migration.° What the additional cultural factors are is one way to describe what this book is about. But for the moment, the important point is only that the wealthier residents tend, on the whole, to have lived less time in the village than the working class. Four of the current moneyed families arrived before World War II, nine between 1945 and 1960, and five more between 1960 and 1970. Twenty-six current families came in the 1970s, and fifty-six in the 1980s. Even taking into account earlier families that have moved on, the movements of the 1980s represent a major watershed in Childerley's history. Consequently, over half of the moneyed families have been in the village less than ten years, four out of five for less than twenty years.°°

In comparison, twenty-two—one quarter—of the working-class households have roots in the village that extend before World War II. Thirteen more extend to before 1960. Eight more came in the sixties. The seventies saw a jump in working-class arrivals similar to that of the middle class as fifteen more of the current households moved to the village. In the eighties, the rate almost doubled again as twenty-seven more found a place, either in the council estates or in tied cottages associated with remaining farm and big house jobs. But even with this recent growth, one out of two working-class families have been in the village over twenty years, which is less than is often assumed among the villagers, but still considerably more than for moneyed families.

The greater localism of the back door is due in large measure to mobility restrictions that accompany the economic situation of ordinary Childerleyans. Education and class ascription limits their access to high paying jobs, so few can buy a home. In a country where less than ten percent of the housing stock is privately rented, this obliges most to seek council housing for an affordable place to live.[13] (By comparison, privately rented housing is about forty percent of the United States market.) Unfortunately, council housing is in short supply. The local authorities who manage a district's council housing regularly run waiting lists with thousands of applicants, only a small percentage of whom can be accommodated in any one year. The authorities use a point system to select people from the list. As the system gives priority to people who have been on the list the longest and have lived the longest in the district, those seeking

---

° See chapter 2.
°° I derived these figures from the annual parish electoral registers back to 1920, supplemented with field information from the villagers, where available.

a place outside their home district are at a considerable disadvantage.°
Farm workers and others in tied cottages can afford a wider search, because housing comes with the job, and actually no current farm worker
in Childerley was born in the village (although one man was born in an
adjacent parish). But these jobs are scarce everywhere, due to mechanization, and so do not serve as an option for many.

In addition to housing problems, there are restrictions in the job
market that help confine working-class villagers to the local area. In uncre-
dentialed and semicredentialed employment such as most working-class
villagers hold, network contacts within the locality are key to finding a
good job. As Abel Harrowell explained to me, it's a matter of "Being
lucky. You know a friend that knows a friend, and there you are. That's
it. Like my lad. He's still at school. He's got a work experience coming
up [as part of his school requirements]. I'm very friendly with a local
agricultural engineering firm down the road here, and I've worked with
a mechanical foreman down there. I say, 'my lad's got mechanical apti-
tude. Any chance of a good work experience?' 'Send him along.' That's
being in the know. And a little bit of luck. You were in there first, really."

Being lucky. But you are not likely to be "in there first" unless you
live close enough to be "in the know" and to have a good chance of having
friends at the firm. In addition, having a locally known family name can
be a credential worth more than any degree. But it does depend on
whether or not the family is respected in the area. As Abel explained,
"locally a name either holds or it doesn't hold."

Because their housing and employment options are so much better
in the local area, working-class villagers have good reason to feel materially
threatened by the encroachment of wealthier people on the area's housing. One obvious solution is to build more low-cost housing. The Thatcher
government balked at doing this through expanding its council house
construction program (a limited number of new council houses were built
in this period to replace old stock), and instead continued to sell them
off. (No working-class villager, I should point out, objected to privatization
of council housing itself—just the lack of much new building.) And many
moneyed residents, with the support of the planning establishment, ob-

---

° Two national programs, the Tenants Exchange Scheme and the National
Mobility Scheme, seek to facilitate interdistrict moves. But they have not proved
adequate and rates of interdistrict moves for council house tenants is less than 40
percent of the national average. Those in privately rented housing, by contrast,
move to a new district at five times the rate of those in council housing (Champion
and Townsend [1990], table 7.6).

jected to any opening up of private development. Consequently, the pool of low-cost housing in Childerley continued to shrink.

As many working-class villagers live at the margin of poverty, these threats are very real to them. While no longer poor by global standards, as many in English villages were before the war, many villagers live on tiny budgets in an economy in which money is virtually the only means of exchange and in which expenditures for such things as a car and good clothes are increasingly essential for holding down a job. In such an economy, an annual salary of £5,000 to £6,000 for a full-time job in a local factory or on a local farm does not go very far.

Many villager families do not even have the capital to open a savings or a current account (a checking account, to Americans). When bills need to be paid, these families will set them all out on the kitchen table and tuck so much from their pay packet or cashed pension check into each envelope. Then someone will take them all down to the post office and get money orders made out for each bill. The old-age pensioners live on particularly restricted budgets, and a number forego a telephone. One village couple lived until 1984 in a house with no hot water, one cold-water tap, and only an outdoor toilet. One single mother in the village supports her four young children on the wages she makes from part-time housekeeping and on irregular contributions from her estranged husband.

The conflicts between the classes are not only a matter of their different material circumstances, but also of the contrasting cultural styles that stem from them. Working-class villagers often expressed to me outrage over their perception that the moneyed people were trying to remake the village. Audrey Spencer and her eldest daughter Patsy were among those who expressed their views on the remodeling of houses to give them more of a front-door look. Patsy brought the topic up.

"They bring in their own things and they flash ideas about what they're going to do to this house and that house. And us lot, we keep everything more or less the same."

"We liked it for years and gone without for years," explained Audrey. "And they just change it all, change the houses, modernize everything, to make it comfortable for them. But they're killing the actual village life."

Some moneyed residents felt that a new village pond would give Childerley more of a "village character." But several working-class residents described the plan to me as a waste and a scheme to raise property values. Then there was the plan to clean up the village graveyard. John Walker is a retired mechanic who came to the village in 1960, and his wife is descended from an old village family. Here's his reaction.

"The commuters have ruined the village. They want everything tidy so it has no soul. *They* have no soul. Do you know how you can tell when the commuters have arrived and taken over a village? If you see the gravestones all lined up beside the church and the yard all a lawn, you'll know they're here. [They want] to make it more tidy—so they can drive around on their tractor mowers. I was in the Fox not so long ago and this commuter was in there telling them about how the graveyard should be tidied up and the stones moved. And some of the locals he was talking to had relatives buried in there! It's their suburban mind. Everything has to be the same, all tidy and conforming."

Front door, I would call it. Although no moneyed villager I spoke to actually wanted to remove the gravestones, John is right in saying that several objected to the graveyard's over-grown and tumble-down character. Take Gordon Ives, a moneyed villager active in local affairs. He complained to me about the unwillingness of the "council house people" to get involved in "improving" the village and to "clear away the rubbish, make the graveyard look reasonable and presentable."

It is significant that, in this clash of front-door and back-door values, the graveyard was tidied up. The moneyed people, quite simply, occupy the positions of power in the village, and things usually turn out their way. The moneyed people often do attempt to include working-class villagers in the planning of various activities, such as the annual village fete, the harvest festival, the construction of the new pond, and the maintenance of the graveyard, green, and other common land. Imbued with a community spirit of inclusion, many of the leading residents active in village affairs lament that the working class refuse to get involved in planning or often even to show up at local events. The door is open, as Gordon Ives explained:

"If anyone wanted to organize something, they would be very welcome. They just don't."

One of the principal reasons, ordinary villagers told me, is that the wrong things go on at these events. They don't seem like their events, just moneyed people's idea of it.

"I've been to one or two of the events," John Bone explained, "but I always seem to be a bit of a loner. They always seem sort of stilted. . . . [The annual village fete used to be] a village occasion, and everyone knew each other. You used to have tug-of-wars against another village, and things like that."

Many ordinary villagers also harbor resentment about having to pay for events, and perhaps also for being expected to make an appearance to validate them. Katie and Sarah Weller, for example, were critical about the harvest festival.

"They have the harvest festival," said Sarah. "You can't afford to go, the ordinary people. Whereas before, it was a free thing for the workers, just to thank them for the harvest. But now you have to buy a ticket to go. Dress up. You can't afford it! The ordinary people don't go. The people that have done all the work, the actual village people, can't afford to go."

"And when they do," Katie added, "they feel out of place because everybody's above them. It becomes something for people with money."

"And they think that's country life!" said Sarah. "But they've lost the atmosphere."

Cy and Amy Lawrence don't buy this explanation. They say that "the village" has tried to design these events with the working class in mind by having such things as a flower show or by not charging, but efforts to involve the working class inevitably fail.

"It's just an excuse, really," Amy protested. "We've tried all these things, and they just don't get involved. No one supports them. It's the us and them, isn't it, and I'm afraid you can't change it."

All the enthusiasm of the community leaders cannot change the fact that they are the ones making the decisions and setting the agenda. Therefore, ordinary villagers are suspicious that they would be allowed token control, but no more. The door is open, but not in a way that they would want to use it.

"I said that when I was going to retire, I was going to stand for the parish council," John Bone explained, laughingly. "But I haven't bothered. That was only sheer spite."

And they sense condescension and distance in the attitudes of many wealthy villagers.

"They're not friendly to ordinary women," Harriet Cooper, who lives in one of Childerley's council estates, said of the Women's Institute. "It's all rich ladies who have nothing better to do than be catty with each other. It's sad, really."

Sarah felt that the moneyed people at the Young Wives Group, another village women's organization, were friendly in a way, but still looked down on her.

"They say, 'Oh, join the Young Wives' and whatever. You goes early, and there you are washing up and doing all their dirty work, while they do all the organizing. . . . If I do work, it's for me, not to help them out while they get all the praise. Because they do look upon you as poor. . . .

You know, you're useful to do their dirty work and that's it. I don't know. They're very friendly, more or less, but they, they are rich! And you'll never be as good as them, and they always let you know it."

Equally important is the fact that the moneyed people are still the employers of a good many of the ordinary people in the village, either on the farms or the big houses, or in cleaning, maintaining, and remodeling the cottages. Much of the village working class is economically dependent on the wealthy, and they know it. And those that aren't today perhaps recognize they could be in the future, should they change jobs. They are in a disadvantaged position to rock the village boat. Their subordinate place in this power arrangement leads to a mixture of deference and defiance familiar to power differentials the social world over.

One of their principal ways of expressing their defiance is not to show up at the events organized by the moneyed people or not to participate in the organizations they are often asked to join. In this way, they can resist the structures that constrain them, but without compromising the necessity that these same structures sustain them, however poorly. James Scott's description of commonplace, everyday peasant protest in a Malaysian village, which expresses itself "in ridicule, in truculence, in irony, in petty acts of noncompliance, in foot dragging, in dissimulation," fits much of working class defiance in Childerley.[14] Refusal to participate is one of the working class's means of resistance to the moral economy of village life imposed by the moneyed people. I often heard little stories and statements of defiance as well, all privately expressed. Fred Weller's story about Charles Winkworth, is an example.

"I used to do odd jobs for Mr. Winkworth, a bit of welding here and there, sort of thing. But he never paid me. And when he did, it was all ten-pence pieces and change like that. He never seemed to have any money, and always had to rush around the house looking for a bit of change, sort of thing. I think it was a bit of an act, if you get what I mean, to make himself seem poor. So finally one day he calls me over for a big welding job, and I say to him, 'Well, what about my money for the last six jobs?' He said, 'Oh, right. I'll pay you for all of it when I pay you for this.' So I say, 'No you don't. I want all of what you owe me before I do a thing more—and I don't want no pennies either!' And you best believe that he found the money right quick!"

Quiet protest is also directed at the "yuppies," not just the very wealthy like Charles Winkworth. I had guests up from London for the weekend, and Harriet Cooper invited us all over for tea in her back garden. Sarah Weller, who lives just down the road, dropped by as well with her youngest daughter. We sat around together enjoying Harriet's mince tarts and a good chat. There's a ditch along the side of the road just opposite the Coopers and, on the way over, I had noticed that someone had filled it in with bricks and bits of broken concrete. I asked about it and Ed Cooper, Harriet's husband, said that the new bloke across the street was filling it in. He intended to cover it over with topsoil and make the verge level again, Ed explained.

Then Sarah said, with a smile, "What they don't know is that when it rains bad in the winter, the road floods. That ditch was originally put in to keep the water out of the garden. They're sure going to be surprised next winter!"

Everyone laughed heartily at the thought, and it was quite plain that Sarah at least did not intend to tell this new, moneyed family (living in what was only a few years ago a farm workers' tied cottage) about the possibility of a flood. Private shades of St. Mary Bourne.

I also heard many stories of deference, the other side of the moral economy of power in the countryside, particularly toward the large landowners, the "real gentlemen," as opposed to middle-class people.[15] Arthur Cater spoke in this way about Major Spiers, who owned the principal manor house in the village, now divided into flats, until his death a few years ago.

"Major Spiers. There was another gentleman. He was a real gentleman. He'd help anyone out that needed help that was genuine. A lot of people missed him in Childerley when he died. Yes, because he used to do a lot of good in the village, especially for the church."

Peter Bridle had much the same to say about Colonel Spreadbury, who is the biggest landowner in the village, and for whom he drives a tractor. I asked him once what it was like working for him.

"He's a gentleman. I won't hear a bad word said about him. He's a real decent, nice bloke. A real gentleman he is. It's the [farm] manager I don't like."

David Cooper, Harriet and Ed's son, works side-by-side with his farmer, a smaller landowner who doesn't use a farm manager. This is how he described their relationship.

"My boss is a real good bloke. He can have a laugh, a drink with the lads. At work I call him Mr. Morris, but outside I call him Peter. You got to have a little respect. And he treats me with respect too. He's absolutely serious during work, but he can go to the pub and say, hey, it's not my round so bugger off—you know, joke and have a good time."

Here David describes what Howard Newby has called a "dialectic of deference" across the status differences, with "respect" flowing upward and downward.[16] Although it is dubious that this balance is often attained in practice, it remains an important ideal for both sides. For the working class, it justifies their subordinate economic position by presenting evidence that they are just as good as anyone else. For the moneyed, it allows them to conceive of themselves as essentially kind-hearted and egalitarian, even though they are in a position of power. Tony Steers, a farmer from Axworth, recognizes that the care he takes toward his workers' needs and the respect he shows them is actually "a bit paternalistic, I suppose. [But] I love working with the working class. They're much more direct, like children."

The dialectic within the village and farm is really one of deference flowing upward and respectful paternalism flowing downward.

There is also a dialectic surrounding envy. In a culture that stresses material evidence of success, working-class villagers cannot help but ponder the wealth that lives next door and across the road from them.

"Nothing is any trouble to them," Sarah Weller once bitterly observed to me. "Because when they want something done, they just go out and buy it. And it's done."

Consequently, Sarah doesn't feel comfortable talking with moneyed villagers or mixing with them at the village fete, harvest festival, Women's Institute, and other community occasions and organizations.

"I don't want to talk to them because all they talk about is their holidays and where they've been. And I can't ever do any of those things, because I don't have the money."

Her daughter Katie, who was there, added, "You don't have anything to say about where you've been, so pretty soon they're doing all the talking. They might ask what you did last night. And you say, 'watched television'—and the night before, and the night before that, sort of thing."

"I guess I don't talk to them," said Sarah, "because I don't want to know about all they've been doing. It might just make me envious."

Envy flows upward and very often, unfortunately, derision flows downward. Gordon Ives, for all his active involvement in village affairs and church charity, is not very understanding about the situation of the working-class villagers.

"It's all take and no give with them. This is the trouble. They all want something for nothing. Do they know where money comes from? Do they realize that people work for it?"

The ideals surrounding this dialectic are negative ones. And while this dialectic also helps each group to understand their position, it does not help to bring them together.

IV

THE FACT THAT so many barriers exist to bringing the classes together in a democratic, egalitarian, and open way is a major source of moral uncertainty for Childerley's residents. For as important as class is in conditioning the habits, tastes, life chances, honor, social power, and patterns of friendships in the village, it is something most villagers told me that they very much disapprove of in British society. Over and over again village residents expressed this to me, so often, in fact, that I have to argue for its vital importance in understanding their social awareness.

Take the conversation over supper I had at the home of Steven and Joanna Oakley, both professionals in technical fields. Another moneyed village couple were over as well, and conversation turned to differences in accents both between and within the United States and the United Kingdom. I mentioned that, while there are many subtle differences in accents in the United States, most Americans are only consciously aware of gross ones, like northern versus southern accents. In fact, I said, I personally couldn't do any better in Britain, and I wondered if it were really true that the British can make the fine distinctions Shaw described in *Pygmalion*. The others all chimed in with anecdotes and imitations. Then there was a pause, and embarrassment seemed to swell into the conversational gap.

Joanna perhaps spoke for the others when she said, softly, "You really *can* tell exactly where someone comes from by their accent. It's awful, really. It's the class system again, isn't it."

Harriet Cooper usually uses the terms "ordinary people" and "moneyed people," as do most working-class villagers. But she knows the word *class* and what it means, and hates it. The topic came up in a way that revealed a little bit about the downward mobility she has experienced in her life and her feelings about the justness of class. I was describing to her the arrangement at "the Community" (which few Childerleyans know about).

"That sounds like a good idea," she offered. "It's probably the only way ordinary people can buy a house today."

"Well, they're not exactly ordinary people," I replied. "They mostly have professional jobs, architects, that sort of thing. They're neither rich nor poor."

"What we call in this stupid country the middle class. That's what we were considered to be when I was growing up because my dad was a naval officer."

I heard these phrases and similar ones more times than I could count. "This stupid class system," "this awful word class," "it's always this damn class thing, isn't it." Most village residents would agree with what Greta Kingman had said: "And that to my mind is horrible, the social class distinction."

Were these statements conjured up for the benefit of my American ears because, coming from a reputedly classless society, I might not approve of the continuing importance of class in Britain? I think not. Villagers took pride in many differences they perceive between Britain and America: British tradition and monarchy versus the raw, plastic, uncultured newness of United States society. Churchill's old joke about the two nations divided by a common language. Why then did they not take pride in this one? I think it was because they did not wish to be seen by *any* outsider as supporting class distinctions.

Possibly villagers suspected me of being a left-liberal university type (which is true), and tailored their remarks accordingly. There may be something to this—although I generally tried to contribute, when asked, only those aspects of my political views that I thought fit those of the company I was in. In other words, I tried to be polite without being untruthful. And I imagine the villagers usually tried to be the same with me. The fact that so many villagers thought disapproval of class would be something both they and I would agree on I take to be very significant.

Moreover, the sense that class is unjust is apparently not limited to Childerley. Seventy percent of the respondents to the Essex survey thought that the distribution of income in Britain was unfair. Significantly, few thought government or collective action could do much about it, and they favored instead personal efforts to consolidate their private welfare. The Essex researchers described this resigned attitude as "informed fatalism"—the sense that, idealism to the contrary, class in Britain is indeed unbreakable and unshakeable. The Essex Group suggested that this sense of the unpleasant realities of life is the dominant way British people conceive why, despite decades of efforts to get rid of the leaden cages of class, their society apparently remains locked in them.[17]

Yet at the same time that most Britons reject the morality and justice of class, it remains a central source of social motivation, at least in Childerley. The desire to better oneself, as Katie Weller hopes to do, or to maintain one's social position through careerism, materialism, leisure patterns, the formation of hierarchical social groups within communities, and other forms of what Thorstein Veblen once called the "invidious comparisons" of class—all these remain central life goals of Childerleyans.°[18]

That these comparisons should be so important at the same time that their outcome, class, should be regarded as unjust presents a dilemma to Childerleyans. Frank Steers, a village farmer, expressed the dilemma well during an interview at his house.

"I can't help wonder at the end of man's mad rush and strife of industrialization and materialism. I mean, what is at the end of it all? A man needs shelter, food, and clothing. The desire for everything else at forty-five I find emptier than it was at thirty-five. It's lovely to have big cars and fast cars and comfortable cars, but actually I'm no better person for having achieved that. So maybe if I think that the things that are important is to have a herd of decent cattle, and lead 'em with a stick with a nice dog and work a few sheep, why don't I get on with it now—and forget all this fancy cars and what have you I've got out there, and striving to get as much dosh [money] [as I can]? So why don't I just drop out now and go and do it?"

He could only laugh at his predicament, and he did.

The dilemma that one is "no better person" for having achieved the aims of class motivations is, of course, at least as old as the teaching that the meek shall inherit the earth. But in an age with so little meekness in the acquisition of material and status satisfactions, the message hits especially hard, particularly in the context of the ideal of the open society.

The leading role that class plays not only as a source of social motivation but also in shaping the habits, tastes, sense of self, feelings of membership—in short, the *social identity* of Childerleyans—intensifies the dilemma of class. The contradiction is stark. Here is a village in a society in which the main source of conscious social identity is considered by most to be repugnant and unjust. The result is that attitudes toward class are more than just fatalistic. Caught on the horns of a society that seems simultaneously to advocate and denigrate class and class motivations, Childerleyans may be said to regard class as *morally ambiguous*. Childerleyans have much in common with the "moral geography of the Dutch mind, adrift between . . . the gratification of appetite and its denial, between the conditional consecration of wealth and perdition in its surfeit"

° The fact that class remains a central source of social motivation, if not *the* central source, may go a long way toward explaining why there isn't the organized movement against it that so many have looked for—despite widespread belief that class is unjust.

that Simon Schama has described among seventeenth century Calvinists in that land—the "embarrassment of riches," Schama calls it.[19] But this is only half the story, for there is also for villagers like Harriet Cooper the embarrassment of poverty and the moral ambiguity of bad fortune in an alleged economy of choice and merit.

Rachel Wood also feels the moral ambiguity of class. She sought in Childerley a place free of the material competitiveness she experienced in her former suburban neighborhood. She was therefore distressed to find that the motivations and divisions of class in the village can be read right from the village's architecture.

"As you go through the village, you can see which are the council houses. You suddenly think, oh that's the workers, that's the farm workers. And that's the council [estate]. And there is that distinction, which I don't think there should be. . . . I don't know . . . I feel it should all blend a bit. Otherwise you lose the atmosphere of it being an actual village. It becomes segregated, somehow."

Rachel herself lives in one of the oldest and prettiest cottages in the village, a half-timbered place which really does have "roses round the door." Both she and her husband were born of working-class parents and are understandably proud of their solidly middle-class home, Land Rover, second car, washing machine, and freezer. The conflict between her own material success and her egalitarian views of how life should be is not lost on Rachel. Nor is the irony of how she is herself, in coming to the village, promoting the very tensions she laments there.

"When I came here, I saw a program on the television. And they were talking about villages and people moving into a village, and how sad it was that people couldn't afford to stay there. And I really did feel then that I had done the same thing. Which I wouldn't have wanted, if somebody had pointed it out. I wouldn't have wanted that."

Mary Hebberd, who lives in Childerley's larger council estate, has similar doubts about the class motivations of many ordinary people. She is rather ambivalent about the sort of working people who are "always stirring things up."

"There's a real us-and-them feeling in this village, down in the council houses. Some people there think that just because they are, you know, one type, that they are worse or better than the others. It's a shame, really, that people will see it that way. Everyone comes from the same place and winds up in the same place, so why it should make any difference in between I just don't understand. But it's always been that way, and always will be, I suppose."

The kind of moral ambiguity about class that I am describing is not inconsistent with the conservatism of Childerleyans like Mary—and most Childerleyans are conservative, indeed often very conservative. This conservatism embraces egalitarianism as much as liberal and socialist thought does, for in our times the concept has become almost synonymous with justice. But important differences emerge in how equality is defined. Unlike many on the left, conservative villagers like Frank, Rachel, and Mary see the market as an egalitarian force. As Frank put it, "You must be responsible for yourself. . . . Let [industries] feel the edge of the market. Let them be competitive. Let them get rid of all that dead labor. That's how I see the country going, whether you agree with it or not."

We are all equal members, at least ideally, of the same free community of competent, self-responsible actors, Frank is saying. But the moral tissue of this view does not quite hold together for most conservative villagers. A spirit of communality, of human solidarity, is central to the constitution of any human group. Such a solidarity presumes at least the equality of being a member of the group (in this case, the free-market community), and generally more than that. How much further equality should extend is always the subject of debate—the question of how to accommodate difference within the equality of group membership.

Here conservative villagers confront from the other side the market and its promotion of the private individual, forever consuming and seeking capital to do so. Here they confront the different positions in the market everyone has, differences which, perhaps inevitably, lead to the economic and cultural contrasts of the front door and the back door. All Britons are members of the same market community. But the "freedom" of this market draws the villagers away from the equality it provides by simultaneously promoting their differences, differences of income, capital, and class. This freedom allows Rachel to gain the capital to buy a house and join the village, but only at the moral expense of demonstrating her privileged financial state. This freedom allows Frank to buy a fast and comfortable car, an emblem of difference his egalitarian ethos forces him to regard as "empty." As Mary observed, "Everyone comes from the same place and winds up in the same place." Thus, these villagers find the market to be an extraordinarily contradictory basis for community, for it at once pulls apart the feeling of communion it puts together.

The philosophy of these villagers might be called *economic conservatism*. The moral contradiction of the market economy, however, doesn't confront a traditional Tory like Charles Goddard-Brown in the same way. His form of conservatism, what might be called *status conservatism*, leads him to be as suspicious of the market as any leftist. Charles is a leading member of the local Conservative Club, yet he found Margaret Thatcher's meritocratic market quite alien to his thinking. "The Thatcher government," he told me in 1988, "isn't a conservative government, you know." And from his point of view, he was right. The truth is, although it has far from done away with inequality, the greater postwar stress on the achievements of consumption and credentials—emphases Thatcher advanced, however unevenly—reduces the importance of the ascribed equalities and differences Charles still adheres to.

And that's a serious moral threat to Charles's sense of what equality—call it fairness—is. For there was a certain equality to the Victorian notion of community, even though there was a hierarchy of class difference. It was the equality of membership in a village, a town, a nation, working together on the common project of empire, each in his or her appointed role as father or mother, lord or laborer. Although there was social difference, all were bound together by the values Charles still talks about to anyone who will listen—respect, service, and mutual obligation. With this very different conception of the moral basis of community, Charles is not worried about the contradictions of sameness and difference in the market.

But even status conservatives like Charles experience ambiguity in class values. He still believes in the necessity for class hierarchy, but now he feels defensive about it.

"Let me be frank. All the modern changes in society that began in the 1950s feel very alien to me. . . . Sometimes I wonder about the afterlife and wonder about what they have in store for us in heaven. It could be hell, you know. I see it as something like air traffic control. Imagine all these different planes going along in different flight paths, each in its own strata, one at twenty thousand feet, another at twenty-two, and so on. What worries me about heaven is that they might try to mix things up and get everyone flying at one level, and then there would be nothing but chaos and constant crashes. Do you see what I mean? Everything works out all right as long as everyone sticks to their proper level in the air, as it were."

Charles may sound confident about the old ways. But there is profound doubt here. Postwar changes have so undermined the basis on which he learned to justify hierarchy that in his analogy Charles worries that even God himself rejects class difference.

Although younger listeners often smile when they hear it, this is what Charles and villagers with similar outlooks mean when they talk about the "politeness" of the past. Albert Bickley, a former civil engineer and one-time tenant farmer who retired to a small bungalow in the village ten years ago, explained it this way:

"Back in those days, it wasn't a bad thing to go into gentlemen's service. It taught people politeness, and that's gone today. No one was mistreated. On the contrary, it was a great thing to be in what we used to call the 'big house.' My uncles, my aunts, my cousins—they all did it. I can remember once going to visit my aunt at the Big House where she worked. There was the head butler, about eight maids, gardeners—the lot. Today people don't even know how to hold a glass. They just grab it from the top, see, like this, with their fingers all over the rim. Now our mother taught us never to do that. You would never do that in service either. The maids all knew how to do things right. And they wonder why people get such stomach disorders today."

But now these villagers are deprived of this rationale for social difference and its associated civilities as the best basis for organizing a community and an empire. Wealth and hierarchy then fall prey once again to the old Christian and socialist critiques that they are simply self-serving. Such villagers must either reject the mental habits of a lifetime or retreat to the phrases of proud incomprehension I so often heard from them: "in *my* day," "you probably won't agree with me, being younger," and "I'm terribly old-fashioned, I know."

Through this defensive nostalgia, villagers like Sir Harold attempt to fend off the ambiguity of class that necessarily confronts even them. After the interview discussed in the previous chapter, his wife, Lady Saxton, came in with a tray of piping hot imported tea and store-bought biscuits. There was no maid anymore, but they began to reminisce about when there was.

"He probably has been giving you an old-fashioned view," she began. "Still, I can tell you that the countryside is much different now. The whole atmosphere has changed. . . . Do you remember? We had fifteen bedrooms and six sitting rooms and three in every department in the house at Cockham."

Sir Harold nodded in assent. "Yes, three in each."

"No, that was in Cambridge," Lady Saxton continued. "In Cockham it was just two in each department in the house. Now what we pay for one day's gardening work for one man paid eight men for a week. The big change was World War Two. That leveled everybody. It didn't matter who you were, everyone was on rations. I remember I had only two gallons of petrol a month to run my car. That equalized everyone, brought them all down to the same level."

"Yes. I was telling him that."

"And do you remember?" Lady Saxton went on. "Whenever I came into the shop, the woman would stop what she was doing, leave the other customers, and serve me right away. It was always M'Lady this and M'Lady that. And all the chaps would take their caps off when I walked by. Now you are lucky if they shout 'Ello.'"

There is, of course, another route. That of simple denial. That's the approach of John Bulley. He's fifty-five, divorced, and in early retirement from his career as a shipping company executive. We were sitting in the solarium of his thatched, seventeenth-century farm house. I had asked, "One of the things that some people have said to me is that there are some strong divisions within the village. I don't know if you've encountered these. Not everyone agrees."

He replied at length.

"I haven't encountered them because I don't look for them. I don't have the slightest doubt, though, that they do exist. But then I would say that they have existed since time immemorial. I personally don't find it a barrier in any way at all. But people can invent. They sometimes, I think, excuse their own short-comings by saying, well, of course, people are stand-offish or they belong to that class or that class and they won't have anything to do with me. It might be that if they looked at themselves they would discover that they weren't the sort of people anybody would like to have [as friends]. I guess I accept that there are divisions. [But] I don't accept that they are necessarily the fault of any particular class or religion or any other thing that causes barriers. I sometimes think that the people who find themselves most affected are perhaps themselves the cause of the barrier."

His terrier came bounding into the solarium and knocked over my drink. When we had resettled into our seats, he continued:

"I think I would say of this village—now it may not be true of them all, I don't know—that class in its old-fashioned term is very low down on the list of distinctions. . . . I know it's terribly easy to say that every time you find that you don't become a bosom friend of someone to say, 'Well, it must be that they think they're above me or I'm beneath them,' or something. I discard that absolutely. I think it's a sign, first of all, perhaps of a slight inferiority complex. But also, there is so little time. . . . You can only have a circle of friends of about ten at a maximum. And it's only natural that you will choose a circle of friends from people who fit most accurately into your own life style. . . ."

He paused.

"I tend to know best people in the village who have had the same experiences in life, which gets you back, if you like, to the same background and back to this awful word *class*. But it has nothing to do with that. I mean, unless you're thrust together in a war or in some ghastly situation like a storm at sea or something or a shipwreck with a person of a completely different background and class, it is unlikely that you're going to spend [the effort] or find the opening to start talking to them about things, because you haven't got the time."

Other people's inferiority complexes, a lack of common topics to talk about, and the limited time one has for others—this is *not* how John explains class. This is how he explains it away. That he needed to do so is, I think, further evidence that class has become a morally unstable foundation for social value and social identity, at least for Childerleyans.

Each Childerleyan has his or her own way of saying it. I would describe the common problem they face as simply this: The need for a source of identity and motivation that each regards as not based on social interest. This is something class no longer offers them. Frank Steers says he now sees money and cars as "empty" sources of self. John Bulley tells himself that any class basis to his lifestyle is purely unintentional, at least on his part. Rachel Wood says she wouldn't have wanted her perfect cottage "if someone had pointed it out"—pointed out, that is, that somewhere along the line a poor person must have lost out for her to get it. Harriet Cooper can only see social interest, the social interest of others, in the fact that she is no longer identified with the middle class. The critique of interest thus undermines for Rachel, Frank, and John the identity they might otherwise readily claim, and undermines for Harriet the identity she is now asked to be content with.

Thus the notion of class has become unstable and lacking in legitimacy, yet it remains a central source of conscious social identity and motivation, as well as habits and life chances. How do Childerleyans resolve this dilemma, this crack in the moral foundation of British life? They do it by collective action, but of a very different sort than would lead to the major changes in the relations of economic production many, rightly or wrongly, have hoped for. They do it, as we shall hear, by choosing to live in another England. Not the England of class life, but the England of country life, closer to nature.

FIVE

Country People and City People

I should have then this only fear:
Lest men, when they my pleasures see,
Should hither throng to live like me,
And so make a city here.

Abraham Cowley, 1647

I

RACHEL WOOD'S THATCHED cottage nestles into a curve in Childerley's main road, a curve that's probably existed since some Saxon cow, centuries ago, wandered over for a better bit of grass. (Or so a village wag has it.) She keeps quite a menagerie of dogs, chickens, pheasants, and rabbits in her back garden. One morning, amid the chirps, barks, and squawks, she described to me how she and her husband chose to move to the country, and in the end to Childerley. It had to be this area, because of his job.

"We saw Bishop's Common was far too built up. Bartley we liked. But again it was very much that people who owned the properties didn't live there. We looked at Redmarsh, but that was too built up for us."

She got up to quiet one of the dogs.

"And suddenly I went in to the estate agent, and I just said I want something in the countryside. Well, this cottage was there. I saw the picture, and I said, 'That's my cottage.' That was it. It just happened. And the fact that it's in Childerley, I knew nothing about Childerley at all. But when I came, I was delighted it was still a village . . ."

Why did they decide to leave their comfortable suburban home for a place far older, and far smaller? Not because of class aspirations, Rachel said.

"I didn't think of myself as being one of those rich people that could afford to live in Childerley. It hadn't occurred to me. I don't think we are rich anyway. We're absolutely broke! But I just wanted to go back to belonging somewhere."

She had put it more forcefully earlier in the conversation:

"When we came here, we were desperate for a village. We wanted to be part of a village. And I wanted to recapture that feeling of belonging that I had."

A feeling, she said, she has not had since she was a child.

The desperation that Rachel felt was the desperation of identity in doubt. Childerleyans experience a fundamental anxiety about the moral validity of class, the primary source of conscious social identity provided by their larger society. While all the village residents recognize themselves as members of social classes, in general they do not feel good about it. Most moneyed villagers do not enjoy thinking about themselves merely as "one of those rich people," as Rachel put it, and the ordinary villagers do not enjoy thinking of themselves as merely the poor.

What they do feel good about is being someone who lives in the country and, more than that, being a "country person," a "village person," a "country girl," a "villager," or a "countryman born and bred." Discarding those of class, these are the shoes with which Childerleyans usually prefer to walk.

What became a major focus of my study was how Childerleyans claim and grant membership into a highly valued social group: "country people." Those outside this group they call "city people." From this distinction, villagers derive that feeling of belonging Rachel spoke about, a feeling of acceptance into an identity that they regard as morally good. When I asked Childerleyans why they lived in the village, this was the conceptual map virtually all of them used to locate themselves for me.

In order to think of themselves as country people, Childerleyans need ways of defining what country is and what makes country people distinctive. Since the 1940s, considerable scholarship has been devoted to demonstrating that, in the face of modernity, these distinctions no longer exist (and maybe never did). At most, scholars have concluded, the differences are unimportant.[1] Childerleyans, however, have little doubt that they exist, and that they are important. They see two principle contrasts. First, they feel there is far more community in the country, at least in the true country. Second, they regard a life in the countryside as a life closer to nature.

The villagers may be wrong. Yet in the much celebrated words of William I. Thomas, "If men define situations as real, they are real in their consequences."[2] If so, then the differences between the country and the city must be real, for Childerleyans firmly believe in them—and these beliefs have real consequences. From these beliefs villagers gain a source of identity they regard as highly legitimate, something they no longer get from class. As we shall hear, they also gain a more legitimate way to talk about and experience the motivations that stem from class and from class divisions. These are real matters that really matter to the villagers.

II

IT WAS ONCE COMMON WISDOM in the social sciences that social life varied markedly along the rural-urban axis. This view, which came to be known among sociologists and geographers as the "rural-urban continuum," is an old one. Simply stated, it holds that community—and, in many versions, nature too—is more typical of rural than urban places. In strong statements, cities are even held to be the antithesis of both nature and community. Versions of this idea can be found in the poetry of Virgil and Horace, and it reappeared as an important theme in the thought of early modern times.

Modern thinkers proposed a number of dichotomies of social life which seemed to lie, at least in part, along the rural-urban axis. For Georg Wilhelm Friedrich Hegel, it was "family-society" versus "civil-society." For Max Weber, "traditional" versus "legal-rational" authority. For Emile Durkheim, the "mechanical solidarity" of similar people versus the "organic solidarity" of dissimilar people who are nonetheless dependent on each other.[3] Karl Marx saw a plodding "idiocy" and "stagnatory and vegetative" character to rural life, as opposed to the potentially revolutionary context of urban living.[4] Georg Simmel portrayed cities as distant from nature and as having a distinctive "mental life" which combined calculation, quantification, and an "objective spirit" with a "blasé attitude" toward others—a kind of numbness that results from the constant passage of humanity.[5]

Ferdinand Tönnies was the most influential writer on rural and urban differences and deserves a more detailed look.[6] He distinguished between *gemeinschaft* and *gesellschaft,* commonly translated as "community" and "society." By gemeinschaft, Tönnies referred to social relations underpinned by sentiment, tradition, and permanence. Tönnies had in mind friendship, neighborliness, and kinship, as well as ethnic and religious ties, all closely tied to land and place. In contrast, gesellschaft relations were those driven by calculation, interest, and impersonality. Here Tönnies was thinking about the worlds of business, law, regulation, and science. Means-orientation versus ends-orientation—that's another way Tönnies explained the difference. It is significant that Tönnies explicitly avoided placing gemeinschaft and gesellschaft along the rural-urban axis.[7] Although he recognized that gemeinschaft is best known as typical of rural areas and gesellschaft of urban ones, Tönnies pointed out that "the essence of both gemeinschaft and gesellschaft is found interwoven in all kinds of associations."[8]

Tönnies was particularly influential on a famous group of sociologists and social anthropologists associated with the University of Chicago, known as the "Chicago School." Living in one of the fastest growing metropolises the world had ever seen, Chicago School scholars sought a language for describing the changes rushing through their city between the world wars. So they took the ideas of Tönnies and others and placed them explicitly on a rural-urban axis.[9] In the famous words of Chicago School scholar Louis Wirth, a city may be defined sociologically as a "relatively large, dense, and permanent settlement of heterogeneous individuals." Here people led an "urban way of life" characterized by "segmentalization of human relations which are largely anonymous, superficial, and transitory."[10] In another well-known work, Robert Redfield charted the rural pole of Wirth's urban way of life. He theorized that life in the "small, isolated, nonliterate, and homogeneous" society of rural folk promoted feelings of gemeinschaft. In such a setting, behavior is "traditional, spontaneous, uncritical, and personal" and characterized by a "strong sense of group solidarity."[11]

Following World War II, however, a number of writers began to criticize the idea of a rural-urban continuum. A host of researchers went out into urban and suburban neighborhoods to see if life there really was as Wirth had described it. And instead of transitory and anonymous superficiality, they all found social order and many bases of community. They found families, neighbors, and coworkers. They found people associating with others of the same ethnic group, class, and stage in the life cycle.[12] Researchers studied rural areas too, and several called into question Redfield's characterization of rural folk as isolated, unchanging, homogeneous, and uninterested in calculated gain.[13] A study of several villages north of London, for example, found little of the ideal community of rural places. Social relations there seemed little distinguished from those of cities.[14]

All of the contrasts scholars placed along the rural-urban axis had been attempts to characterize the transformations wrought by modernity. The new studies led to two basic criticisms of these characterizations. First, whatever modernity was, it did not prevent the presence of gemeinschaft in cities, and it may even have provided new means for the expression of community. Second, it appeared that modernity's transformations were no longer limited to urban areas as advances in transportation and communication began to unite the whole world into one economic and social complex. Empirically, the idea of the continuum no longer seemed to hold up, or was at most, in the words of Richard Dewey, "relatively unimportant."[15] Ray Pahl put it more strongly: "Any attempt to tie particular patterns of social relationships to specific geographical milieux is a singularly fruitless exercise."[16]

In fairness to Wirth, Redfield, and others who helped establish the rural-urban continuum as a one-time fact of social science, it is not clear that they would have disagreed with these findings or felt them incompatible with their own work. Like Tönnies, Wirth and Redfield had sought to establish "ideal types," that is, theoretical constructions that point to the importance of certain social forces, but that—at best—only approximate reality. Wirth made clear that what he called the "urban way of life" was not actually limited to cities, although he did feel it had originated in, and was common in, such places. Similarly, Redfield would not have been surprised to see in other settings elements of the rural folk ideal.° But other researchers felt that, in the face of the real situation, these ideal types were misleading and romanticized.

The criticism that community could not be tied to locality led to criticism of the concept of community itself. Think of that ultimate oxymoron from the daily news, the "business community." Villages, cities, asylums, prisons—sociologists have at one time or another called all of these "communities." Thus George Hillery complained that "community has become an omnibus word . . . which embraces a motley assortment of concepts and qualitatively different phenomena."[17] Margaret Stacey took this line of reasoning to a radical conclusion. In an influential article, she held that because of "the obstinate, but still mystical, remnants of the romantic model . . . as a concept community is not useful for sociological analysis."[18]

This remains the dominant view within sociology today. For example, the entry on "community" in the 1988 *Penguin Dictionary of Sociology* reads "the term community is one of the most elusive and vague in sociology and is by now largely without specific meaning."[19] Major synthesizing

---

° In my reading, Redfield meant only to oppose a "folk way of life" to an "urban" one, not country life to city life. Such a folk life largely originated in, and was common in, country areas. But we should therefore expect to find aspects of folk life wherever we find folk—in the country or in the city.

works in the field barely mention community or relegate it to the past with a wave of the hand.[20] Even in rural sociology, a discipline long associated with research on community and the rural-urban continuum, a leading scholar has recently written of the "exhausted ghost" and "outmoded and no longer relevant" concept of community.[21] Wendy Griswold puts it even more bluntly. "Communities," she says, "are imaginary."[22] Not only can community no longer be tied to the rural-urban axis, scholarly consensus holds, it may not even be a useful description of social reality.

III

CHILDERLEYANS DO NOT AGREE. They have no doubt that life in the real country is unlike that of the city.

John Bone is one of many villagers who spoke about the distinctiveness of the countryside's closeness to nature. He described his feelings to me one morning over a cup of tea, both of us leaning back in our chairs with our feet on his kitchen table.

"Country life to me is—well, if you look out over there, there's quite a nice view. Now, I can go out over there every day, and every day you see something just slightly different. Now there's blooms just starting to get on the trees, getting ready to burst. And all over there, I know all those woods and fields by name like the back of my hand. Cause I've lived in the area for so long. I know what life's going on in there. . . . I mean, you see the country life."

Andy Sparrow, the schoolteacher, traveled extensively in rural Africa. When he returned, he found he "couldn't stand city life" and moved to Childerley soon afterwards. I once asked Andy what the word "country" meant to him.

"If you said that to me sometimes, I'd think of Africa," he said, "because the country there was such a formative thing in my development. I loved the wild ways. I loved the mountains. I loved the wilderness and the freedom and the sense of being just a small part of vastness, of emptiness. I loved being close to the natural world. So that would come to my mind. Or Childerley might come to mind. Woods, fields, the plowed fields, the sheep, the cows, the walks I go on, the dells, the badger holes, the fox holes, the rabbits, the lot of woodpeckers you see, the deer."

Frank Steers sees his farming as far more than a business or some sort of agricultural factory floor. He loves being out in countryside, absorbed by its distinctive enjoyments, wandering his own fields. I asked him what he likes best about being a farmer.

"The bit I really enjoy is walking around in the evening taking the sheepdogs, going around looking at the sheep, standing in amongst the beef, and looking at good cattle. And that's something. Different things excite different people. And a flock of sheep on the move or looking at really lovely beef cattle, it excites me like others are excited by a decent impressionist painting or a smart car or a beautiful woman—I'm also excited by those things!" He laughed and continued, "It's a sensuous thing almost. The beauty in the countryside is something too, just walking around in the autumn in the mist. Once your eyes have been opened to beauty, you can see it everywhere, can't you. Then certain forms of it take your eye, whether it's a certain style of painting, or just the beauty of what you see round about you—the trees, the sky, the ever-changing sky, cattle and sheep. That's all very, very satisfying. It's part of the privilege, really, and enjoyment of living in the country."

Most of the villagers I came to know made similar statements at one time or another, although not always so vividly as John, Andy, or Frank. They talked of how important the woods, fields, and animals of Childerley are to them. They exhalted in a joyous, sensuous feeling they described as coming from their immersion in nature's beauty. They spoke of a sense of privilege, the privilege of living so close to nature. As one retired farmer put it, "We're very lucky, really, to have spent so many years amid such beauty."

In addition to this closeness to nature, Childerleyans were also virtually unanimous in ascribing a distinctive lifestyle and pattern of social relations to true country life.

"Peaceful," is the way Mary Prior described it. "It's a whole new 'ballgame.' You know, there's a quietness about genuine country people that sort of just plod along. The no-hassle of life. . . . People have got time, time for living, time to talk, which I think is smashing. I mean, even in our little country shop, they've got time to serve somebody rather than expect them to rush around and get it all themselves and get 'em out as quick as possible."

Nigel Brown, an eighteen-year-old son of a local farmer, echoed this theme:

"It means a quieter life-style to start with. I don't know. You could call it an escape from the rat-race. . . . Kind of a much slower way of life."

Rachel Wood said it too: "In the towns, people are in a rush. That's the difference! In the towns, you get in your car [for everything]. I had a neighbor, lived there thirteen years. But I never spoke to her because she'd come out of her door, get in her car, go off, come back, and go indoors. . . . Here, the pace is that much slower."

Moreover, Rachel suggested, in the country you can escape from the material competitiveness of town life.

"When I [first moved to my former suburb], I was talking to somebody, and I said we were thinking about buying a freezer. 'Oh haven't you got one? We've got two.' That was how it was. If somebody's got a new car . . . it's a status symbol thing. You're suddenly putting yourself on. You must have a new car. You must have a washing machine. And we couldn't really care less what anybody had. Bicycle, car. It didn't matter. We find that that's how the towns live, and we wanted to get away from that."

There is a helpfulness in country life, most villagers agreed, a unity that ties residents together across class lines.

"We've got friends from all walks of life," John Bone explained, "and we all help one another. If you want something done, you go down and see so and so and he'll do it for you. No question of any monetary exchange. You do it. And if he wants something done, he'll come and ask you, and you do it just the same. This is how the true country life, to me, is going on."

The helpfulness and togetherness ideally part of country life is actively sought after by a number of moneyed villagers through participation in local volunteer work. A small but active core of residents devote a lot of their free time to volunteer projects. Keeping the village green trim and neat. Publishing a monthly village magazine. Building bus shelters.

One Saturday morning a group of us were scraping the massive iron frame that suspends the church's eight bells, in preparation for painting. High up in the drafty bell tower, between scrapes, a discussion arose on what volunteer work showed about village community spirit. As often happened, the villagers raised a topic they thought would interest me, but it was also a topic that interested them. These periodic discussions in kitchens, on walks, at supper, under cars, or over tea or beer gave them a chance to hear each other's views and crystallize their own, creating their culture as I was discovering it.

Stephen Oakley, who holds a doctorate in microbiology and commutes some thirty miles each way every day to work in his lab, I think summed up the view of this group of moneyed villagers when he said, "You wouldn't get this in suburbia." For the chip-covered crew of scrapers that raw morning in the bell tower, living in a village was an opportunity to be part of a real community where you knew your neighbors and people helped each other.

"Living in a small community's very nice," Stephen told me later, "because you can't not know people. If you're in suburbia, you can live next door to somebody and not speak to them. . . . You can do that here, but it's unusual here. Because you're in a small community, you take notice of people and you get to know people. And it becomes much more of an overall community."

Many Childerleyans also talked about the countryside as a better place for family. The phrases "better for the children" and "good for the family" are conversational cowslips in the village. Like that famous English country flower, they are touchstones of what is right and good about country living. Parents often cite the cleanliness and safety of country life, as well as the sense of the countryside as a place of traditional family and religious values. Mary explained it well:

"We're very lucky in this village. We've got a Christian-based school, so they get Christian values before they kick off [into adult life]. So from the word go they're taught to respect themselves and other people. I feel so sorry for some of the city children because they haven't got that. Parents having to work. Or sometimes they don't have to, they just—they do, and the children become latch-key kids."

And not only social values. Frank Steers described the advantages of bringing up children close to nature.

"It's been really great bringing the kids up in a natural environment. They're sort of natural kids, and I think that's better. I wouldn't want to have brought them up inside [a city]. And they're real happy kids. They love it."

These advantages are hard to find in the modern world, say many Childerleyans. That's part of why Lilly Hobbs relishes living in Childerley.

"Life is like it was in the past here. You feel like you should lock it up every night. Coming home at night when we first moved here we used to think we should be closing a gate behind us at the bottom of the hill."

Quietness, a slower pace, smallness of scale, knowing everyone, help-ing others, tradition, refuge from the rat race, advantages for family and children, freedom from material competitiveness, religious morality— these are ideals that Tönnies would immediately have recognized as *gemeinschaft*. That's the right term, I think, for the villagers describe the ideal of community in the widest sense, as something more than the ties among people in a local settlement. As did Tönnies, they connect community with tradition, family, and antimaterialism.

Many villagers also connect it with another form of gemeinschaft, the "imagined community" (to use Benedict Anderson's revealing phrase) of nation.° For these villagers, Childerley is (or, as we will see shortly, is supposed to be), more than just a country village: It is an *English* country village. A deep tradition in Western thought says that the true spirit of a nation is to be found in the country. There is no better example of this tradition than *country*'s double meaning as both rural region and nation.[23] And no nation better exemplifies this double meaning than England.[24] Stanley Baldwin put it this way in his 1926 book *On England:* "England is the country, and the country is England."[25]

George Frizzell, a retired businessman living in one of Childerley's nicer thatched cottages, agrees. He's lived his whole life in country villages, the last few years in Childerley.

I once asked him, "Would you consider yourself more British or 'country'?"

He furrowed his brow for a moment, and then answered, "I can't see what you mean by British or 'country.' I've never considered British versus country. To me, that isn't a question."°°

Nation can have an echo—sometimes audible, sometimes not—in another form of gemeinschaft: race and ethnicity. In an all-white village in a nearly all-white nation, I often found it hard to distinguish the sounds of the two forms. Sometimes I did not. George Henwood, a villager of liberal means and conservative ends, placed only the thinnest of veils over a connection he made between country life and ethnic purity.

"Our cities have been destroyed," he said. "[London's] just a cosmopolitan cesspool. . . . Of course, there are still very wonderful bits. But, shall we say, the—well, let's put it this way and not call it a cesspool, but it's been polluted. It's been polluted and it wants cleaning up, so the trout can move up a little bit."

Gordon Ives would probably agree with George's angling metaphor about the colder, purer waters upstream where trout thrive. Some villagers had arranged for a Hampshire folk group to give a concert in the village

° Anderson (1983). As Anderson wisely notes, all communities are imagined (although real nonetheless, at least in their consequences). But few require the leap of kinship that nation does.

°° Infuriating as it rightly is to some, in this conversation Henry and I were using a convention common in the village: that of treating English and British as synonymous.

hall. To give it a nice community touch, there was a dinner beforehand, with wine, candles, and tablecloths. It was a fun, loose evening for the fifty or so, mainly moneyed, villagers who attended. During the clearing up after supper, I went to sit at another table. A conversation about the tiresomeness of London was in full swing. Someone had gone there for the day and was recounting the burdens of making the trip, indeed of simply trying to exist in London, even for a day. In the ensuing discussion, others supported this point with stories and views of their own.

"The problem is," Gordon offered, "London isn't really English anymore."*

In all their varied forms for varied villagers, nature and community are the hedgerows that bound and define countryside talk. By these land-marks, Childerleyans know when they are in the country, and when they are not.

IV

AS FAR AS I COULD DETERMINE, every village resident agrees that there is such a thing as the country, distinct from the city—and every village resident agrees that this distinction is very important. Indeed, I suspect most would find academic questioning of it a ludicrous waste of time. And many—for example, Sylvia Norgate, the non-employed wife of a banker, and her friend Alice Gilbert, a retired secretary of a local historical soci-ety—find proof of this in Childerley.

"I think you were very fortunate to pick Childerley," Sylvia told me one evening over sherry.

"That's right," Alice agreed. "Childerley is a particularly friendly vil-lage. It was only a week after I moved here before I met someone. Childerley is a real village, different from most of the other villages around."

But not all the villagers agree that Childerley is itself "a real village" in the real country. I was not long in the village before I began to hear sentiments such as these:

"It isn't a friendly village."

"Childerley doesn't have an identity. This is a dormitory village."

"The big problem is that the community spirit is gone, or at least much declined. There's no longer any common purpose, no common goal.

---

* My notes on this incident are not as complete as I'd like, so I cannot report with confidence what the response of others was to Gordon's comment.

That's what is needed to hold a place together. I can't really see where it's all leading to."

"This is not really a rural area. . . . It's not so farmery here."

"It's not the same as it was. The new farming's got so far away from nature. They used to farm *with* nature in the old days. It makes you wonder how much longer it can continue. The soil's gone. No hedges. No wildlife or flowers."

"It's become sterile. The sort of nitty-gritty has gone out of it. Now everything is all preserved and washed and painted, but the, what I mean, the heart of it has gone. The buildings have been preserved but the character has been lost."

"It's changed a lot. Childerley is losing its face as a village. It's not, ah, a villagey village, if you understand what I'm saying. It's not so rustic anymore."

"Village life has gone up the creek."

This, in fact, is the majority view. Most residents feel, often painfully so, that the "rural idyll" of nature and community is not a realistic description of the current condition of Childerley. Although these villagers agreed that there is something special and compelling about Childerley that is worth protecting, they often pointed out that life here is not sealed off from the urban facts of the present. There is no "gate at the bottom of the hill." Even most of those who at times spoke of Childerley as actually fitting the country ideal later qualified their views with phrases like "as villages go." Nearly all the residents would agree with at least that much of the academic view of rural-urban differences. Yet this does not stop them from thinking that it should be otherwise, and that it once was.

And that it could be worse, far worse. Despite the village's failings, most residents, it would be fair to say, feel that nature and community are more a part of life in Childerley than in the typical English city. That's important to keep in mind for understanding the attraction they feel for Childerley and places like it. Even so, probably no resident is unaware of the exurban question: Is this still the real country?

Childerleyans find themselves asking this question when they look at both the natural and the social conditions of the contemporary village. Mary Drake, one of the oldest residents born in the village, and her nephew Bert, a mechanic, were among those who felt deeply the changes in the village's natural environment. They described to me one afternoon in Mrs. Drake's sitting room the cornucopian color, taste, abundance, and natural glory of earlier times.

"Everything's changed now," Mary said. "You don't have the flowers that you used to, or the berries."

"It's all the chemicals that they use in farming these days that's killed it all," Bert explained.

"There used to be strawberries," Mary continued, "oh such berries, right down there by the corner. Remember that, Duck? And down the lane, there were blackberries and wild gooseberries. There was such color too. Remember the blue-bell woods?"

"It's worst around here, what with their type of farming," Bert added. (But first I think I caught an inward wince from him at being called, at age forty, "Duck.") "We were out in Dorset on a back country lane, and it was all overhanged with leaves and trees, like, and flowers everywhere along the sides. Like the way the lanes here used to be."

"The verges are gone too. They keep widening the roads for cars."

"In Dorset there's more colors—greens and reds and blues. But here it's just green, just green. And what's the reason for? The grain into storage and then it rots."

Bert was describing the intensity of modern production agriculture, with it's aggressive use of herbicides and reseeding of pastures with fast-growing grass varieties, where formerly a mixture of grasses and flowering plants had prevailed. The land looks different to him now. Meanwhile, overproduction of grain has become a serious storage problem for the European Community.

Not only the look of the country has changed; its taste has too, as Mary explained.

"Nothing tastes like it used to, does it Duck? The meat, the milk, chicken. You can't get good food like we used to have. It's all different."

"It's all the chemicals they put in it today," said Bert.

Villagers often interwove themes of nature and *gemeinschaft*, passing easily from one to the other, both when they described the rural ideal and Childerley's failure to live up to it. Harry Heath, a sixty-seven-year-old retired banker who has lived in Childerley for more than two decades, was one. Most of Childerley's land is farmed by large operations headquartered outside the village. Harry connected what he saw as the anonymous economic motivations of these farming arrangements (what Tönnies would have called *gesellschaft*) with the substantial changes in landscape and wildlife Childerley has recently experienced.

"Nearly the whole of the land is really run by some syndicate, which is just controlled perhaps by one remote man twenty miles away. And he's disinterested in the village and everything else. . . . They've lost all the personal control and touch. It's like the big company, the multinational, who comes along and takes over. The bosses are remote from the workers and there's no feeling of community or family. It's an unhappy situation. And that's reflected in the loss of the little fields with lovely thick hedgerows and lots of birds and meadows with flowers in it. Now you walk along and a machine has chopped the hedges down to . . ." He indicated a height of about three feet with his hand.

"The birds and animals have got no habitat. And the fields are just like miniature prairies, they're so vast."

Working-class Childerleyans also decried the loss of the community of the past. Joan Bradley, a housekeeper, was born in the village sixty years ago. She reminisced about old times one afternoon over tea, and later wrote down these thoughts for me.

> I preferred the old village life. It was real friendly, like one big family. We always used to go out visiting. You didn't need a telephone. You just went and asked someone. If anything happened, if someone was sick or something, everyone knew it soon enough. When I was a girl, you made your own entertainment. You read, the women sewed, we played cards. We would listen to the wireless. You were more self-sufficient. Everyone knew each other. Now your neighbors don't know you. It's not the same anymore.

Ruth and Robert Hill are new to Childerley. Robert is a management consultant and Ruth is a housewife, and they live in one of the village's most picturesque old cottages. They came expecting, or at least hoping, that the village would be like the one big family Joan Bradley described. Instead, they find that they really haven't met very many people in the village, except those of a similar social class and age.

"I think it has something to do with our characters," Robert said. "I suppose some people make friends with their next door neighbors because it's their next door neighbors. I think we tend to only make friends with them if they were similar sorts of people to ourselves anyway. . . ."

"The trouble is with us moving in here," Ruth observed, "you're introduced to so many people, and you might meet them once and don't see them in six months, and you just don't remember."

"We have met quite a few, but we are different," Robert concluded. "We don't get on with them the same as we do with people in the same sort of background, I suppose it is."

Sarah Weller suggested that the children in the village school do still have a bit of the real old-fashioned, know-everyone-in-the-village sort of community. But as soon as they graduate at age eleven, it all ends. The working-class children go to the state school in Winford and the moneyed kids go off to private boarding schools across the country. She described the experience of her daughter, Katie.

"In Katie's generation, she had about six or seven other boys and girls her age [who were good friends at the village school]. Out of all that lot, only Katie and another girl went [on] to the school in Winford. The rest all went off to private schools, to Eton or wherever. They're all of a different class, you know, never went to a secondary school. No matter how many friends you've made at school, they're gone because their life's changed. They lead a different life style at boarding schools. And Katie kept in touch with quite a few of them until they were sixteen, seventeen years old. It just petered out because their lives are so different."

"I mean, it's hard," Katie added. "I had a friend that moved up to Scotland when I was about—she was about seven, wasn't she? In the end, she stopped writing because we was just so different. And we used to go play all around the village and everything."

Margaret Cook and Audrey Spencer agreed that there is little trace of the big village family left.

"The Squire and his wife . . . , they knew all their tenants," Margaret said, remembering. "It worked on the principle of being a big family, really. In the olden days, the Squire's missus used to go out and visit somebody, or take them a little basket."

"You respected the people you worked for because they looked after you," Audrey interjected.

"Whoever went into hospital," Margaret continued, "they always made sure that the family that was left behind was looked after. And so [the husband] was still able to go to work. Somebody would see the children home from school, off the bus. There were puddings made, or dinner made, and washing done. People *did* in those days. You helped each other out. . . . It made you feel you were a part of the community."

A historian could take issue with parts of this assessment of the past. Between 1880 and 1950, English agriculture was in the grip of a deep economic depression. Rampant poverty, poor diets, dilapidated housing, widespread child labor, and lack of job security characterized most rural areas during this period and testify to the harshness of life in the village "family" of lord and laborer. Rather than displaying the affectionate ties of an ideal community, many villages were best characterized as being bound together by what Raymond Williams called a "mutuality of the oppressed."[26]

Historians would confirm, however, some of the other impressions villagers have. For example, modern agriculture has indeed caused dramatic changes in the British landscape. After World War II, Britain sought to establish as much self-sufficiency in food as possible, and now grows 80 percent of its requirements, up from the 40 percent of prewar years. Because of government incentives to maximize production, thousands of hedgerows—perhaps the most characteristic feature of the landscape of southern England—were ripped out. Many copses were also cut down, and pastures and field borders plowed to make way for bigger fields and bigger machinery. A survey of Childerley's hedgerows taken by the county council revealed that 15 percent of the parish's hedges have been removed since 1947. Considering how little woodland there is in even a relatively well-wooded parish like Childerley (and, for that matter, how little there is in Britain as a whole), that amounts to a significant loss of wildlife habitat. Moreover, most of the hedges that remain have been cut way back, further reducing their value as a refuge for Childerley's wilder residents. And, as many villagers argue, there is substantial evidence that the introduction of pesticides and other agricultural chemicals has had an additional impact on the wild plants and animals that remain.[27]

But for our current purposes, the historical accuracy of the villagers' views is not of central importance. We should ask a different question: Why do the villagers praise the ideal of country life as what has led them to live in Childerley, yet at the same time so sharply criticize the contemporary village on precisely the same grounds?

Ideals are, of course, very rarely lived up to. As the sociology of deviance has recognized since Durkheim, failings are essential to the motivating power of an ideal. Deviance clearly defines, for all to see, what is right and just. As Kai Erikson has written, "deviant forms of behavior, by marking the outer edges of group life, give the inner structure its special character and thus supply the framework within which the people of the group develop an orderly sense of their own cultural identity." No one in Childerley has gone to jail for violating the ideal of country life. But trespasses against its directives for living do highlight its principles, providing "a point of contrast which gives the norm some scope and dimension," as Erikson put it.[28]

The contradiction between ideal and real gives the notion of rural-urban differences its edge, the cutting surface that makes it a powerful cultural tool for Childerleyans. As Raymond Williams noted, the ideal of rural life has always gone hand in hand with a sense that such a life is in decline, a Golden Age which is always slipping away. In sounding this "rural complaint," as Williams termed it, Childerleyans make the case for the appropriateness of community and nature in the countryside—heightening the importance of maintaining this boundary by stressing its permeability.[29]

V

DESPITE ITS FAILINGS—and in large measure because of them—the residents thus define the appropriate social situation of Childerley as that of a gemeinschaft in nature. This definition has real consequences: It provides a flexible boundary across which Childerleyans allocate identity. Paralleling the distinction between city life and country life, residents often spoke of marked differences between "country people" and "city people."

The residents use many terms to distinguish these two groups, including a number of familiar pejoratives. The residents refer to themselves as true villagers, country cousins, country bumpkins, locals, country girls, countrymen bred and born, Hampshire hogs, salt of the earth, real countrywomen, village people—as well as what I have adopted as the broadest term, *country people*. Others they describe as city dwellers, bloody townies, Londoners, yuppies, city slickers, city-ites, outsiders, foreigners, day-trippers, town people, as well as *city people*. Together these terms comprise a vocabulary of rural identity.

In using these terms, Childerleyans claim and grant membership into a bounded social group—real country people versus city people. The phrase city people, in the views of most Childerleyans, fits many current residents of the village. And it is these city people and city influences to which residents mainly attribute Childerley's failings as a natural gemeinschaft.

John Bone, as true a Hampshire hog as there is in Childerley, explained the difference he felt between country people such as himself and the city people both within and outside the village.

"They want town refinements in the country. All the things they've got in the town, they want in the country. And it doesn't quite work that way. You see, I'm a countryman bred and born. Lot of people that come down, they have absolutely no idea of country life at all. You can't blame them for it. But people don't understand the way country people work, really. I suppose, it's probably the same [with me]. When I went up to London, people used to laugh at my accent and treat me as a country cousin, because I have a country accent."

Frank Steers feels much the same pride in his family for not being comfortable with city life.

"[My children] don't understand the city. Every time we go up to London, they look at it and they just can't imagine ever living there and neither can I. So we're sort of country bumpkins, and we feel at home here and we feel like fish out of water when we go into the city and feel the city vibes. I personally feel quite frightened by [the city]."

I regularly asked Childerleyans what it would take to get them to live in a town. This question usually brought firm looks and the typical response of "I could never live in a city." Andy Sparrow spoke for many of the villagers when he told me, "I feel pretty out of place [in cities]. I don't see much of city life, and I feel a bit alien when I go there. I mean, I go to London for all the shows and that sort of thing. But the squalor, and the people, and I find that mind-blowing. I just find consumer society mind-blowing."

Yet the city people keep coming into the village, bringing city ways and city thinking with them, the villagers told me.

"I hate these bloody townies," complained Frank Steers, "who come in and here we are trying to farm and they come in and they manicure the place up and then they become quite defensive about how they want it for themselves. And if there's a bit of mud on the road—I'll tell you what happened the other day. One of my neighbors, his cattle were in the field. He turned a bull in with them to get them in calf. So the bull services one of the cows, and this was visible from somebody's house. Immediately there was a big scene created because this 'disgusting thing' was seen from their house."

The problem, according to Frank, is that country people are simply different from city people.

"Sometimes friends of ours from the city, they come here, and they feel insecure in our fields. And walking around the farm at night without any lights, they think that's very dangerous. The fact that there's the physical signs of animals terrifies them. But [when I go to the city] the thing I'm frightened of is being mugged and losing my money and getting lost and not knowing where I'm going. Getting run over because I don't understand the traffic system. Things like that. I just don't know the rules, and they don't know my rules when they come up here."

The word *rules* is significant, for as is plain from the words of these village residents, just moving to a place like Childerley does not lead to being accepted as a real country person. Considerable barriers to membership exist. Not surprisingly, one that the villagers frequently mentioned was the test of time—how long a person has lived in the village. Aware of this test, Stephen and Joanna Oakley, who have lived for nine years in one of the most sought-after cottages in the village, were cautious about claiming the right to be considered country people. As Joanna explained, "We would like to think we're country people. Put it that way."

"We don't make any great claims in that direction" Stephen interjected, laughing.

"I should think we're getting there," Joanna concluded. "Perhaps fifteen years and we'll have qualified!"

But in an exurban village like Childerley, acceptance is not based simply on local roots and residence time. The feeling of being "Whalsa," which Anthony Cohen reports for the Shetland Island of Whalsay, is not strongly evident in Childerley today.[30] Rather than dividing up the village into who is "Childerley" and who is not, the main distinction is between who in the village is a "real country person" and who is not. Lifelong or very long term residence is now so uncommon among adults in Childerley (only twenty-eight were born in the village) that few could claim identity using that measure. Consequently, Childerleyans take other considerations into account, both when they think about their own identity and that of other residents.

These considerations became clearer to me (perhaps because I'm a sociologist) when I began to think of them as four general measures. The first I'll call *localism*. By this I mean to refer to the residents' sense that a real country person ought to have lived in the village for a substantial portion of her or his life. Ideally, he or she would have been born in the village and have pre–World War II family roots in it. I think probably all villagers would agree that those who qualify here are unambiguously country people.

A second I'll call *ruralism*. By this I mean two things the villagers usually connect: The length of time a person has lived in rural areas (including those other than Childerley and nearby villages) and holding a rural job like farmer, farm manager, farmworker, or estate worker at one of the Big Houses. A close family connection to someone like this will give a person a measure of ruralism as well.

Take Abel Harrowell. Like Joanna and Stephen Oakley, he has only lived in Childerley for nine years. But as a farmworker and lifelong rural resident, he is widely accepted as one of the real country people—a true villager—despite his short residence time in Childerley itself. With perhaps just a touch of doubt, he explained why.

"I was born in a village. Alright, I've moved about a bit, and I've moved to another village. Yes. And I've ended up in a village. I mean, obviously, villages are my way of life. I'm a country lover and a villager. I am a true villager, there is no doubt about that. Even though my life has been split between two villages, it still means as far as I am concerned that I'm a true villager."

A third general measure I'll call *countryism*. Here I refer to the knowledge a person displays about, and their participation in, activities considered indicative of country life. Knowledge about farming would be an example—for instance, the ability to distinguish fields of wheat and barley before their distinctive seed heads form. Other realms of countryism include pet raising and pet care, botany, riding, hunting, walking, a knowledge of local history, appropriate country dress, and authentic remodeling. Another is the distinctive food that real country people eat. As Rachel Wood said, "My aunt always told me that I can't be a country girl until I learn to eat jugged rabbit."

That's rabbit cooked in its own blood. There is also something characteristic about the way things are done in the country, say most villagers, not just what is done. Older residents in particular feel that doing things yourself and never wasting anything are characteristic of the country. John Bone feels this strongly. Tending his garden is only one of the many things he does himself, and he is very proud of not wasting any of its produce—not even brussel sprout greens and tops.

"I think it's a sign of the times. A friend of mine, he was a doctor, and we were going fishing and shooting together. He and his wife came up the other day. His wife said, 'Get rid of those brussel sprouts. They're untidy.' She didn't realize. But you know, those greens and what are very tasty. And that's an old country custom. You ask about ninety percent of the people in Childerley and I don't suppose any of them have ever tasted brussel sprout tops!"

The last "measure" I'll call *communalism*. Most Childerleyans feel that a real country person will have a ready desire to do the things that express a tie to the community. Villagers take note of a person's commitment to the church and the parish council; to the darts team, the Women's Institute, the Young Wives Club, the cricket team, the Over Sixties Club, the Care Group; to the village shop (which is struggling) and the pubs; to the annual village fete and the Village Hall Committee; to tending the village's small areas of common land, like the green; and to the kind of informal exchanges between households thought appropriate to neighbors and friends.

Using these measures, village residents appraise with a critical eye the country claims of others. And of themselves. Ingrid Lovegrove, for example. She's a thirty-year-old former secretary, now full-time mother. Her husband is a management consultant. Although she has been in Childerley for only a year, Ingrid has lived in villages since she was fifteen. She may not be local, but she does see herself as rural. She also takes pride in her knowledge of country ways, and was critical of rich, city-raised people who buy expensive rural clothing and try to act country—the "green wellie brigade," to cite a popular term of contempt in Britain.

"Some people put on a Barbour coat and green wellies," said Ingrid, "and call themselves country people. But they don't know flowers the way I do. They might not know anything about the country." She paused, and then observed, "But even I don't know the first thing about milking a cow."

VI

VILLAGERS OFTEN INTERWEAVE their country and class identities. By thinking and talking country, Childerleyans think and talk class—and often avoid the moral ambiguity of the latter.

One place this alternative language for class can be heard is in the different ways that moneyed and ordinary villagers employ the measures of country. The working class, for example, places greater stress on localism and have stricter standards of ruralism. Stephen and Joanna Oakley hoped that fifteen years' residency would be enough to qualify them as country, but Mary Drake spoke only partly tongue-in-cheek when she described another resident this way. "He was born in Winford [the nearby market town]. He wasn't born here like I was. He's been here just fifty years, so he's really a town boy."

This higher standard is no surprise, for most of the few who would qualify under it are working-class residents. At least for themselves, richer residents use a shorter ruler here—and place more stress on other yardsticks.

Under countryism, working-class and moneyed villagers disagree even about what should be measured. Ordinary villagers show little enthusiasm for the formalism behind moneyed efforts to tidy up the village by straightening the gravestones, trimming the green, and other so-called improvements, making the village look more like a postcard. They also routinely criticized authentic remodeling, participation in the hunt, and keeping horses and noncommercial sheep. These they saw as displays of wealth, not countryism.

The same may be said for communalism. Working-class residents rarely participate in the village's many organizations, the leaders of which are listed each month on the "Who's Who" page of the monthly village magazine (which is published by the church and edited by moneyed residents). Ordinary villagers, as I often heard, see this kind of formal communalism of civic duty as the moneyed people trying to take over the village. Charles Goddard-Brown may complain about how it's always the same few who volunteer for the various village organizations.

"In the rural areas, when you come into a community you have a responsibility towards that community. You don't come in, take out what you can, and give nothing back."

But in doing so, he only expresses the moneyed view of the fulfillment of public responsibilities as a measure of communalism. In contrast, the working-class villagers emphasize the informal exchanges of the backdoor between neighbors, friends, and kin: childcare exchange, assistance in car repair, nights out drinking with the lads, cups of tea, and cups of borrowed sugar.

These differences are not only the result of the contrasting styles of the front door and back door. They also result from differences in power. Those without money are in less of a position to buy a horse and remodel a country house, and so will have to rely on other measures of rural identity. The hierarchy of formal organizations necessarily limits access to this standard of communalism. Those less well placed on the social ladder will seek the opportunities for communalism that a drink with the lads and a cup of tea with the girls provide.

When there are such clear links to social power, people are not likely to mistake them. Working-class villagers, at least, are well aware of how they differ from the moneyed villagers in their standards of countryness. These conscious differences become a way to talk about class, not merely to think it. Audrey Spencer made this clear in describing the communalism of the moneyed villagers and how they now dominate all the local formal organizations, in contrast to the informality of working-class communalism.

"Yeah," observed Audrey, "that's all things that the rich people do now. They come to the village and they do this and that, like bell-ringing, collecting for charities. They all do that. The village people, we, well, we're just funny to them."

The vocabulary of rural identity also carries class messages. Note the expression "village people" that Audrey used. This phrase (and "villagers," its close relative) can refer to all Childerley's residents. Yet here Audrey uses "village people" to refer only to working-class country people, as is very commonly done. Many other expressions for rural identity similarly have the bulk of their weight on the lower slopes of the class pyramid—"locals," "real locals," "Hampshire hogs," "country bumpkins," the "salt of the earth," and "country cousins."

Childerleyans rich and poor seemed to give these terms pretty much the same weighting. When they came to the village, Ruth and Robert Hill hoped to "mingle with the real locals." Who are the real locals?

"The ones we've met are in pubs," Robert explained. "That's the main place you can meet people. I suppose the other place you can meet people is in church. But we tend to meet the nonrich locals—I'm trying to think of the right word—"

Ruth encouraged him to be frank.

"You're being polite," she said.

"Class," Robert continued, "I suppose it comes down to that. The normal sort of working-class people in the village you meet in the pubs. You talk to them, but—"

"You never get invited back to their houses," Ruth broke in. "You don't ever get that friendly, do you? Whereas people like us that have moved in are the people that we mix with and go to dinner with, and do things like that. Certainly not 'villagers' as such."

In their usage of the phrases "real locals," "nonrich locals," and "villagers as such," moneyed residents like the Hills accept the greater legitimacy of the working class's stricter standards of localism and ruralism. They also show how these phrases can be a more polite, that is to say, more acceptable and perhaps less morally ambiguous, way to discuss class identities and differences.

Some of the terms of rural identity have their weight on the higher slopes of class. "Country people" is one of these; "countryman" and "country girl" are two others. Like the down-slope terms, "countryman" and "country people" are not purely restrictive. Working-class villagers use these terms to refer to themselves at times, as some of the earlier quotations from John Bone show, especially when others introduce them into the conversation.

The class overtones of the terms can limit their usefulness to villagers in their struggle with class morality. Jim Winter, an artist who lives in "the Community," rejects "country people" outright as a source of identity. To him the phrase conjures up images of *The Countryman, The Country Times, Country Life,* and other up-market publications. He gave me a tour of the grounds at the Community one day, and we chatted along the way about why he chose to live in the countryside. I asked him if he considered himself a country person.

"Well," he replied, "I hope I'm not considered one, living in a former manor house. To me, the phrase 'country person' refers to gentry and farmers. I don't want to be identified with either, really." He paused. After reflection, he chose these terms for his identity, "It's just in my bones to be in the country."

Similarly, Audrey Spencer tried to distance the phrase "real villager" from its lower-class weight. She didn't think it interchangeable with the local working class, as the Hills apparently thought it was. Audrey made a special point of distinguishing villagers like herself from recently arrived working-class residents who might work in a factory in Harchester or as a builder.

"They go to Harchester, or building somewhere. So they're still different. They're still town people that have come here. Even though they're ordinary people, they're still different because they've been town people."

If country identities were merely class identities, they would have little to offer Childerleyans, as they have quite enough of the latter already.

VII

WITH A COUNTRY IDENTITY comes a sense of legitimacy—of rights and motivations appropriate to country people. Such a sense is an important resource to have in life. As country people, Childerleyans have access not only to another language for thinking and talking about class, but also class motivations and class conflict.

For example, a country residence has long served as a source of cultural capital for the wealthy in England. In the terms Fred Hirsch has suggested, the countryside is a "positional good." By that Hirsch means a good which is limited in supply, and which consequently gives social esteem and power to those who have title to it. Often there is no inherent limit on a good's supply, and it is necessary to maintain what Hirsch calls its "social scarcity" by various means.[31]

If Hirsch is right, limiting the access of others to the countryside is essential to maintaining the value of this capital. Limiting development is, of course, one way to do that. Thus it is no surprise that many wealthy Childerleyans express outrage at the pace of construction in the country-side. Ruth and Robert Hill were among those that did.

"Did you read about that new housing estate in Warnham," said Ruth, "on the other side of Winford? There was some rare type of sand martin living in a [sand] bank there, and they ran the estate right over it. And what they have been doing to badger setts—I think it's just awful. That's a problem with building housing. And it is because they are going on and on and on with it! I think it's got to stop. O.K., you've got to get rid of some of it, your fields of wildflowers [and what have you]. Not everything can be preserved, and some wild animals will suffer. But I think they are going too far."

"I'm not sure we need all these houses anyway," Robert added.

Their arguments could be read as protecting their own position. But because of their identification with the culture of the countryside, Ruth and Robert do not have to think about their views in this way. They can think about them as defences of the countryside—the rightful home of sand martins and badgers—not themselves. Of course, protecting animal habitat is indeed very important, and on grounds other than Ruth and Robert's social standing. This makes the value of country as a positional good extremely secure for the Hills.

Villagers often reject the country claims of each other, as we have heard. This too limits access to the good of the countryside. Comments like the following from Charles Goddard-Brown, at least, have that effect. A moneyed resident of Childerley for over thirty years, he often criticizes the motives of the newer, wealthier residents.

"My great thing about the people who have come here, a lot of them since 1975, the majority of them have come in because they've moved up to a socially accepted position. So they've got a place in the country."

Katie Weller said much the same about the wealthy newcomers.

"They come here and they say, 'Oh it's a pretty village, nice country-side,' and that's it for them. . . . It's like a place that they think about going out to as if its just like a holiday place. They treat it as, you know, nice things to look at, and things like that. And so they've bettered them-selves coming out into the countryside. But us lot here, we've been here all our lives. . . . It's a home to us."

By bringing out into the open the issue of the positional benefits of country living for new moneyed residents, and by questioning their countryism and communalism, accepted Childerleyans—rich and poor—

selectively devalue the cultural capital claimed by residents they do not accept as real country people. Whether or not they fully intend it, that is the result.

Based on this selective cultural devaluation, working-class Childerleyans too can use their identity as a source of positional advantage. They marshall this advantage in their often bitter conflict with the wealthy over village housing. Joe Eyre is a farmworker only two years in the village but very much country because of his employment and rural background. He is one of many ordinary Childerleyans who argue for the working class's greater rights to village housing because they are the true country people and because they are the ones who really understand country ways.

"It's a funny thing now that country people can't afford to live in the country, where we belong. It's all because of the yuppies coming in. They're driving us out, the working people. It takes the life out of everything. The yuppies come in, and then they complain that there's no life in the village. I got into an argument about this in the pub the other night. But they're the reason why there isn't any life left in the village. They've taken it out by coming in! And they're probably just going to leave anyhow, after ruining it all."

Working-class villagers across exurban England have had some political success in making these claims. Under the slogan of "village homes for village people," there is now a growing movement in many counties to pressure the British planning establishment to open up some land to build low cost rural housing.[32] Among the schemes are shared equity arrangements. Families purchase a home at 50 percent of market value and own a 50 percent interest in it; the rest is paid for and owned by a private housing association set up for this purpose. Should the home be later sold, any profit is split between the association and the homeowner, giving both equity for a further purchase elsewhere.

In fact, many moneyed Childerleyans support these schemes. Childerley's rector, Reverend Cazalet, is one. He even tried to get one going in the village.

"So that people who want to live in a village can live in a village," he explained. "Because one of the problems here is the price is forcing villagers into the town. Just sheer price of property. And it's people that are townies and city-ites who've made cash [that can afford to buy], and they become villagers. And the villagers who want to be villagers are banged into town."

Reverend Cazalet did not get very far in his efforts, though, and resistance on the part of some of the moneyed residents was the main reason. But even villagers like the Hills are aware that resistance to such a scheme is vulnerable to a class critique. The tensions that moneyed villagers feel—as well as their acceptance of working-class villagers' claims to be more country than moneyed newcomers like themselves—is well illustrated by an argument that Robert and Ruth Hill had. I had presented them with a hypothetical situation.

"Let's say we double the size of the council estate. . . . We'll put in more housing, and local people will be able to stay here. They won't be forced to go out into the town."

Ruth didn't buy it.

"What did those local people used to do?" she said. "They didn't all stay in the village. Not everybody used to stay in their own village, did they? A certain percentage used to go out. They always left. So why should we now turn around and say, right, they all ought to be allowed to have a house to stay in the village? It's stupid, because it would just get bigger and bigger and bigger. It would be a town."

But Robert could see the other side.

"I think local people *must* be being driven out," he said. "I mean, fifty years ago or whatever, this house [of ours] would have been lived in by someone who was earning pennies. It was a small, cheap, falling down, very-few-facilities house, really. The only reason it's worth what it is is because people like ourselves want our nice old quaint house in a nice village. And so therefore, we are driving local people out, aren't we?"

Ruth was startled by this.

"No. Why?"

"Because," Robert replied, "there are less houses in the village for the real locals."

"Yes," Ruth responded. "But that's not our fault, is it? You're starting to get into politics now. No. It's to do with the farms [and their declining work-force], isn't it? I mean, the original workers in the village used to live in farm cottages, tied cottages, and, alright, council houses. If a farmer wants to sell off his cottage, [the workers] would never have been able to afford it, would they? Which is what they've done. So you've got to look at the reasons."

"I'm not saying there's a solution."

"No. But you've got to look at the reasons. It's all very complicated. *We* haven't driven anybody away. It's just the way the country's gone, isn't it?"

"Well, we're part of it," said Robert.

Ruth then took on the village-homes-for-village-people movement directly.

"I don't understand this argument that the 'villages must be for the villagers.' I mean, I don't understand how the villages can hold everybody. They never did, anyway. Even a hundred years ago, people used to go. So why have they decided now that it's all our fault, and that they must build 'x' amount of houses so that everybody can have a chance to stay? Not everybody has a chance to buy!"

Robert didn't budge.

"No. But as I say, this house would probably be a rented house. It would probably be owned, and certainly was owned, by a large estate."

Ruth, frustrated, finally called off the discussion.

"Yes, but it's the government's policies and so on. It's just so complicated. I can't explain it. The whole country's like it, isn't it? It just wouldn't work."

As the interview went on, we discussed the reasons why they had chosen to move to Childerley from their former London suburb—at considerable cost. They live in a quite expensive house, for its size. Robert gets up at 5:15 every morning to get to his job in a firm on London's fringe and doesn't get home most evenings until 7:30 or 8:00. He hardly sees the countryside during the week except for five minutes at the kitchen window with his coffee (something he says he always makes time for). But he must keep this job to pay the mortgage on their comely old cottage. They maintain two good cars in top working order, one for him to get to work and one for her to get to the shops. To live this country life within a conventional, patriarchal family structure costs them every bit of Robert's considerable salary, and so they often feel themselves almost poor, despite their substantial family income.

On top of that, Ruth and Robert have found that there really isn't the community in Childerley that they imagined. They still find the natural aspects of the countryside very attractive, but they lament many of the changes that have taken place.

Throughout our conversation, I was playing the devil's advocate, and they took the opportunity to reflect on what really drew them to Childerley.

"It's something personal," Ruth burst out finally, "something individual. I don't want to be like everybody else in my little box. People are different. I don't like being made to look the same as thousands of others.

I think we're individuals. I think it's getting away from the masses. It's something different."

She recognized that such a statement of distinctive individualism, especially when combined with her earlier views about limiting building in the countryside, might be taken as evidence of the kind of social motivations Hirsch's term "positional good" captures.

"I'm not saying," she therefore added, "that it's something that you can say 'I've got,' and you haven't got it. Not in that way. It's something apart. Perhaps it's just a personal thing. It's like having your little bit of England. Now that sounds really silly—I can't explain myself." Here she paused again, reflecting on her motives. Then she said, very quietly, "Probably it's a very selfish thing."

A sensitive moment followed, and then Robert kindly gave her some covering for her frank personal exposure.

"Well, we all are, when you come down to it."

Ruth and Robert are thoughtful, forthright, open people. Their views helped me understand the ideological tensions with which many moneyed villagers must live. On the one hand, they share the pervasive notion among Childerleyans that class motivations do not stand on wholly sound moral ground. And yet they still orient their lives toward these motivations, for they are also simultaneously applauded in contemporary Britain.

The issue of rural gentrification is therefore particularly tough for them because a principal attraction of a rural identity is that they can experience material motivations not as class, but as country. As Ruth expressed it in describing why she came to Childerley and what she was getting away from in the suburbs, "It's just these little people in their little boxes, and they're all the same. And they're all trying to make out that they've got more than the next one. And it's just so ridiculous. And you've got a better car. Not for me. I'd rather live in a shed in the woods."

Yet Ruth and Robert most certainly do not live in a shed in the woods. They live in a beautiful little thatched cottage, the kind extolled in countless magazine articles, television programs, novels, and children's books, and costing at least £200,000. But because of her adherence to the culture of country, Ruth usually does not have to think about it in this materialistic way. She lives there not because she is, in her view, a conspicuous consumer but because she wants to be a country person. Her search for a country identity provides her with an alternative system for understanding her motives, resolving for her, at least to some degree, the moral problems of class. The resolution is not perfect. Others sometimes suggest that there is a class element to her country ambitions, and Ruth herself sometimes even recognizes this. Although the moral foundation beneath her country home is more secure than what her suburban home offered, Ruth finds that there are some cracks in it too.

VIII

THE DESIRE TO BE CONSIDERED a country person is not merely a grab for power.[33] The moral ambiguity Childerleyans find in class creates a potential crisis for them. In seeing themselves as country people, and in making the case that others ought to see them that way too, Childerleyans try to resolve this dilemma of self and society. On the one hand, they find a more secure basis for the sense of identity which arguably all humans need. On the other, Childerleyans gain access to a more positive way to think about the class motivations which, although they feel unsure about, they do not wholly reject. The moneyed villagers thereby gain a more relaxed sense of who they are, a sense they do not have to feel embarrassed about. The ordinary villagers thereby gain a feeling of pride and confidence in who they are, a feeling often denied those relegated to the bottom of society's broad-based pyramid.

And so, the countryside provides Childerleyans with social power and social identity, valuable resources for their positional, emotional, and ideological concerns. These implications of being a country person, power and identity, are linked. The power of being a real country person cannot be disassociated from the acceptability of an individual's claim to rural identity. At least among the other villagers, a person needs to do more than merely live in Childerley to gain the cultural and political capital of the countryside. Much rides on the strength of each villager's claim.

In fact, the vast majority of Childerley's residents to whom I talked could make very good claims to be real country. In my early months in the village, I listened to many accounts of the lack of "true villagers" and "real country people" in Childerley by those who considered themselves among the remaining few. Accepting this at first, I was somewhat surprised to realize that almost everyone was saying it. I redoubled my efforts at finding "townies," "week-end people," and "yuppies," going to those "city people" others in the village had pointed out. But these people almost invariably made claims that, to me at any rate, seemed as good as the claims of many of those who had sent me their way.

Take Ruth and Robert Hill, for example. Several residents had cited them as clear examples of the city people who have invaded the village.

And true enough, Ruth really does not have a rural background. But Robert grew up in an Oxfordshire village working on his father's farm; his brother is still farming. The Brambleys are another example. Henry comes from a town, but Ellen was raised in a village of fewer than fifteen hundred people. Gretchen Masters's father is a Wiltshire farmer, and her husband Phil was raised in a village, although his parents had professional jobs. Christine and Ted May, the one a full-time mother of two and the other a highly paid investment manager, were both village-raised, and Ted's brother and father continue to farm a large holding in Kent. And so it went. But few Childerleyans know more than a small fraction of the other residents in the village, so it is easy to assume the worst.

Why have some people with equal financial resources chosen to live in Childerley and not others? The substantial claims to be country people that even alleged city-ites within the village can muster suggests that it is those who have the greatest cultural access to this social resource who tend most to seek it out. They are also those who are most likely to have encountered the value system surrounding country life and to know it well enough to maneuver in it. For the most part, it is they who are coming into Childerley, or choosing to remain there. And it is they who are fighting to preserve the social boundary of countryness around it, for reasons of position, emotion, and ideology. As Ronald Blythe put it, "It is often said that the conservationists of this village are the middle classes, but they are, in most instances, the grandchildren."[34]

And the grandparents. This was brought home to me in a conversation I had with Albert and Margaret Cook, both of whom used to work on prewar estates in considerable poverty under a lord of the manor. I heard stories about such poverty from a number of the "old-time country people," and I was struck by the frank pride with which the stories had been told to me. Margaret and Albert expressed these feelings well.

"The village has died," Margaret began, "really, the village as such. What I mean the old-fashioned kind of village where your children and kin lived down the lane. It's sad really, but that's the way it is."

I wanted to know if those times really were better for people like themselves who had to endure such thin means.

Albert replied.

"Half a crown a week and half a day [off] in seven weeks when I started. You couldn't go to church—you worked straight through. . . . We walked everywhere. Hundreds of miles, I should think. When I first worked at Axworth on the estate, I used to walk twenty-five miles and back to [my parents' village] twice a week. I walked twenty-five miles to

Axworth Monday morning, and back home Wednesday night. Then Thursday morning twenty-five miles, and back home Friday night. No one took any notice. It's just what you did. If you wanted to go someplace, you just did it."

I nodded in wonderment, hearing about this very different time.

"But I'd go right back again," Albert continued. "The young ones say you're old fashioned and you don't know. But we do know because we were there and they weren't. It *was* better."

Albert and Margaret had met on the estate. Margaret went on to describe how one friend of theirs, a kitchen maid, used to feed her family on the leftovers from the lord's table, sometimes just the drippings from the meat.

"Sometimes that was all they got. She worked in the kitchen and would get the pan from under the bird, after the lord's family and guests had finished eating the meat, which they usually couldn't eat the half of. Then she would carry this home for dinner. Mind you, it was good food, all dripped over potatoes."

"Did you ever think how it was," I asked, "that the staff were getting drippings and the lord and his lady were getting the meat, so much they couldn't eat the half of it?"

"No," Albert answered. "You never gave it a thought. That was just how it was."

Margaret agreed.

"It was the class system, really. They were rich and you were poor, and that was it. But I love going back there [to visit the estate] even now. There's such a peace about it. We should take you down sometime."

Albert and Margaret now have a home in a comfortable council estate. But they are still poor by contemporary standards. Living all their lives in rural poverty, it could be expected that they would regard their rural background as brutal and degrading. Yet they do not. In making these statements of affinity for what they admit was an exploitative past, statements they know few people who have not had their experiences would agree with, they make a deep claim to be what they say they are: country people.

NATURE AND SELF

SIX

Finding Nature

Yet nature is made better by no mean,
But nature makes that mean: so, over that art
Which you say adds to nature, is an art
That nature makes. . . . This is an art
Which doth mend nature—change it rather, but
The art itself, is nature.

William Shakespeare, *The Winter's Tale*

I

THE VILLAGERS ALL enjoyed the music that evening in the village
hall. Both singers were in good voice, and their melodeon and
guitar playing was uplifting (if at times a bit inaccurate). Most of
the songs were catchy enough that the crowd could join in on the choruses.
But it was "The Farmer's Boy" that really got the windows rattling.

> For to plough and sow,
> To reap and to mow,
> And to be a farmer's boy,
> To be a farmer's boy.

Childerleyans take pride in their sense of themselves as country people. They use this sense of their difference as a source of identity, motivation, and social power—a source they find secure and legitimate. But why
does country life offer the residents of Childerley such a secure resource
for their social needs? Why do they find it a more legitimate basis than
their social class? Why do they grant rural identity this moral status?

The answer lies in the power of an idea, the idea of nature. When
Childerley's residents talk about why they value the country, closeness to
nature is one of their principal themes, as we have already heard from
them. The Roman poet Horace wrote, "If life in harmony with Nature is
a primal law, and we look for the land where we'll build our house, is
anything better than the blissful country?"[1] Childerleyans too find a deep
moral security in the affiliation of country life with nature.

119

It's worthwhile to pause briefly and consider what role we can grant ideas in guiding people's lives. Ideas can, of course, never be entirely uprooted from the desires and needs framed by material conditions. Their power comes from more than their inherent logic alone. Perhaps the oldest critique of idealism is that material circumstances give us our ideas, that what we believe is usually in some degree self-serving. But as Bennet Berger has observed, ideas are rarely *only* self-serving. People feel a deep unease when self-serving beliefs do not seem to hang together or when they seem contradictory, such as those concerning class in Britain today. In fact, we feel particular unease when ideas do not fit with or justify material circumstances. In Berger's words, beliefs represent "the attempts of human beings to cope with the relationship between the ideas they bring to a social context and the practical pressures of day-to-day living in it."[2] An idea that both hangs together and can be brought to bear on the material, practical context of people's social lives will have particularly compelling moral value.

For Childerleyans, such an idea is nature. Although the villagers are by no means sure that the village of Childerley is a place of nature, they have no doubt that such places exist. Moreover, they do not doubt that there are country ways of living and people who follow those ways. A close association with nature, they find, is the surest way to identify what those ways and who those people are. The moral foundation of country life, I shall argue, rests upon this rock.

Still, for all its power, nature is not an easy idea. Thinking it out can easily lead one into a tangle of contradictions. How do Childerleyans conceive of nature and how do they avoid its contradictions to their satisfaction?

II

BEFORE WE HEAD OUT into this new terrain, I'd like to take a glance at the conceptual map previous scholarship has sketched of this area. I say sketched because the line that marks out where nature starts and everything else stops is an exceedingly hard one to draw. The cartographer's pen begins to shake as it approaches the paper, in recognition of a basic contradiction in the idea, a contradiction we might term *dualism*.[3] Yet if a people—such as, say, the residents of a small exurban village like Childerley—are to use nature as a source of moral value, the contradiction must be resolved.

The problem begins this way. There is an intuitive core to what nature is that most people who use the word probably share. This core includes plants, rocks, soil, water, air, and animals. Few have denied that birds, mountains, and rivers are the very stuff of nature. But what about people? Are we not animals too? What about what people make? If we are as much animal as the fox and the hare, with their dens and warrens, then are not cities, home to nearly half of humankind, part of nature too? What is plastic and concrete that a beaver dam is not? Why even exclude pollution from nature, for it is surely made by an animal and violates no natural laws, as evil as it may be? Or an atom bomb? And what about what people do, how they act and interact? Here intuition fails and centuries of debate begin.

Two basic meanings of nature have consequently emerged. John Stuart Mill described them as follows:

1. "All the powers existing in either the outer or the inner world and everything which takes place by those powers."

2. "Everything which . . . takes place without the agency, or without the voluntary and intentional agency, of man."[4]

We might refer to these more simply as the *holistic* conception of nature and the *separatist* conception that excludes human agency, and in some formulations even humans themselves.

It is not hard to see why moral argument has pushed nature onto these two opposing horns of meaning. If one holds that it is right to follow nature, one must of course say why. An answer long given is the holistic claim that people are part of nature. Therefore, we should adhere to its guidelines. But if that is the case, then it is unnecessary to tell us to follow nature, for we, as a species of nature, must already be abiding by its order. Nature's role as a point of contrast for moral instruction therefore collapses. As Aristotle once noted in arguing against "monism," as he called it,

If, however, all things are one . . . the being of the good and the being of the bad, of good and not good, will be the same, and the thesis under discussion will no longer be that all things are one, but that they are nothing at all.[5]

This difficulty with a holistic view led Aristotle and many others to take a position that separates humans, or at least much of what humans do, from nature. As the historical geographer Clarence Glacken wisely observed,

Essays confidently begin with assertions that man is a part of nature—how could he be otherwise?—but their argument makes
sense and gains cogency only when human cultures are set off from
the rest of natural phenomena.[6]

But the separatist horn of the dilemma is no easy resting place either.
Our problem, it has often been argued, is that we are not natural, or that
we are no longer a part of nature's embrace. This establishes a clear
contrast with a realm we ought, so the argument goes, to emulate. One
question that immediately confronts such a position is, why then is nature
relevant to what we do? We are driven by different principles. A second
question is, what aspects of this separate nature are we to follow: the
dancing courtship of the butterfly or the cruel and indiscriminate killings
of the earthquake, the hurricane, the famine, the plague, and the half-
starved predator? As Mill pithily put it, "in sober truth nearly all the things
which men are hanged or imprisoned for doing to one another, are nature's every day performances."[7] This might be termed the *reference* problem—which parts of nature do we mean to refer to when we advocate
looking to it for guidance? Thus Henry Sidgwick declared, "It is manifestly
idle to bid us follow Nature."[8]

These may seem insurmountable philosophical obstacles to the value
of nature for our instruction and improvement. But there are few if any
perfect ideas. And there is something about nature that causes us to return
to it over and again—despite its difficulties—as a firm base for our moral
foundations. Whole philosophical systems have been built around efforts
to locate the boundary of nature in a way that resolved the twin problems
of the superfluousness of holism and the irrelevance and moral relativity
of separatism. Lao Tzu offered the idea of the universal *dao,* or the Way,
within which we might separate between *wu wei,* or acting according to
dao, and *you wei,* acting against the Way. The ancient Greeks offered the
roughly comparable notion of *logos,* an order which permeates the whole
universe, within which we can distinguish between *phijsis,* or nature, and
nomos, or human convention. Each system gave both holistic relevance
and a separatist point of moral contrast.

Childerleyans too have found ways of drawing the line of nature. At
the very least, they have no doubt that such a line exists. They recognize
certain ambiguities in the idea, perhaps particularly the question of
whether Childerley and those who live there rest within the real country
of nature's own making. But they still find it a far less ambiguous line
than many of the others their community, their culture, draws.

III

ANN MARTIN HAS LIVED in English villages for most of her fifty-two years, and Childerley for the last five. She is self-employed, a consultant to small businesses. She is also an avid amateur naturalist, knowledgeable about plant names and the habits of local wildlife. Ann has a sharp eye for the details of the countryside, and she's a great walker.

Ann thinks about nature a lot. One afternoon in her sitting room she gave me a definition of nature that centered on a solution to dualism most villagers I spoke with on the subject also used.

"I was wondering," I had asked, "if I could mention a few things, and if you can just say whether you think they are part of nature or not. Like trees."

"Yes," Ann replied.

"Fields?"

"Yes."

"Open spaces, the countryside?"

"Yes."

"Villages?"

She paused and reflected.

"I'm not sure," she said. "You're out on the margins there. I don't have a straight yes or no. Villages. Habitations. [Badger] setts. Yes, I suppose so."*

"Cities?" I continued.

"Services. Concentration. I think that's on the outer margin. That's slipped over the edge, for some reason."

"So that's not part of nature?"

"That's not."

She continued, though, to puzzle some over this.

"That's difficult, isn't it?" she said at last. "It's only a great expanded village, really, isn't it?"

"Cars?" Here she was firm.

"No, cars aren't. . . . They're a forced means of transport. Nature is only doing what you can do yourself with what you have been directly equipped with. So nature is walking or running. Getting in a car is not nature."

She elaborated her definition of nature in the next response.

"Atomic bombs?" I asked.

---

* "Setts" are the communal tunnel dwellings of badgers, usually dug into sandy ground.

She pondered for a moment.

"Chemicals put together," she said thoughtfully. "Fusion of chemicals. No. They're not going to be nature because they were put together by force. They wouldn't—as far as I can judge, not having any knowledge of physics, really—they wouldn't happen on their own, would they? No. The boundary is, to me, everything that would not exist, that would not be available, if man hadn't created them."

She wasn't satisfied with this answer, however, and asked herself, "That doesn't make sense, does it? Because if you talk about the distortion of plants and such by genetic experiments—"

Here Ann seemed to puzzle over the view that plants exist by nature, even if humans then go and create better varieties, as in the many varieties of roses in her own garden. So she offered a qualification that recognized gray areas.

"However, that's how I am, in a very ineffective manner, trying to say that, if it's against the sort of preordained manner of living on the earth in which products were given to us which we should not massively distort, then it is not nature, I think. Yes. That's how I see it."

Ann believes there is a line that sets nature off, and this is where she draws it: That which is clearly untouched by humans is definitely nature—"everything . . . that would not be available, if man hadn't created them." The fields and open spaces of the countryside she considers in this realm. So too are those aspects of human lives which are not due to human artifice, like the ability to walk and run. "Nature is only doing what you can do yourself with what you have been directly equipped with." She found it equally clear that cars and atom bombs, things which "wouldn't happen on their own" without human "force," are not nature.

Yet she also recognized gray areas, such as the question of whether villages and particularly cities are part of nature. "You're out on the margins there." Humans, like badgers, need setts—by nature, they require habitation. But what kind of habitation? Villages, she seemed to feel, were less a product of the tendency of human artifice to "massively distort." There seemed to be more artifice, perhaps more unnecessary human force, in cities than in villages, so for her they "slipped over the edge." Some alteration of the "preordained" still allows for a natural life, as long we do not "massively distort" things.

In other words, Ann sees nature as a gradient. She applies this gradient to people as well.

"Would you consider in your own mind that certain people are more natural than others?" I had asked.

"Yes. People who sort of have more of an affinity with what is around them in a countryside setting. And who are more capable, I would assume, of survival, should the need arise, without what I see as being the constructed, the manufactured. And so I would say that there are some people that [are more natural], just because they're more likely to survive with what is God-given. Which is a phrase I use meaning what is available without having the need of sophisticated and complex construction of some kind."

Natural people, then, are those who have more "affinity" for the country. Moreover, they are people who can get along better without the "constructed," the "manufactured," and the "sophisticated."

The solution Ann offers here is an old one, what I will follow Leo Marx in calling *pastoralism*.[9] This is the idea that in some places people live closer to and more in accordance with the ways of nature than others. In general, the furthest away from nature are the lives of city dwellers and the "civilized"; closest to nature are rural dwellers and "primitives." Those closer to nature lead a distinctive pattern of social life that follows from their close association with nature. Pastoralism also often has a temporal dimension that suggests a greater closeness to nature among people of the past.

The attraction of pastoralism to Ann, I believe, is the way it deals with the problem of dualism. First, it provides a contrast between two sorts of human society, one more natural, one less so. With this contrast, moral conclusions can be drawn without falling into the tautologies of purely holistic conceptions of nature. Second, pastoralism sidesteps the charge of nature's irrelevance that separatist positions are susceptible to by showing nature's relevance for *some* humans. Third, it clearly points out what are the relevant differences, solving the problem of reference. These differences are the contrast in habits of living between societies of the natural rural past and the unnatural urban present. This allows moral comparisons to be drawn. There are two ways to read the contrast—a positive one which praises the pastoral and a negative one which condemns it.[10] Ann, like most villagers, almost always uses positive pastoralism.

As many readers will know, pastoralism has been widely rejected by academics. In America, critics will pejoratively call pastoralism the "rural myth"; in Britain, the "rural idyll."[11] Rural sociologists have pointed out that pastoralism romanticizes the poverty of farm workers and peasants, turning them into "merrie rustics" and obscuring the extent to which the economic and political forces of the city keep them impoverished. Looked at in this light, rural people are as fully a part of the city as any lawyer or shopkeeper—and no more "natural." Others have also criticized the way, ever since Rousseau at least, people have used positive pastoralism to construct "noble savages" and, since long before Rousseau, negative pastoralism to construct inferior "races" out of foreign peoples.[*]

Childerleyans would be made very uncomfortable by these criticisms of pastoralism, for it remains a powerful idea among them, one villagers like John Bone continue to employ. We were discussing his views on nature in much the same way Ann Martin and I had done. I asked him flat out for a definition.

"Nature is things unaffected by human beings," John replied, without hesitation. He went on to give an example.

"I always remember as a little kid we used to go over to the Isle of Wight to my father's parents' [house] for a holiday. This was in the thirties. I always remember being up around the castle there, and all the long grass they had [in the meadows]. And you used to hear all the crickets, see all the various birds, wild life, all the butterflies and moths, and insects buzzing around. I remember that distinctly as a little kid about five or six."

John paused and seemed to try to envision those meadows in his mind.

"In my latter years, when I was working, I spent a few days over [on the Isle of Wight]. So I made a point of going out to the castle. They had the grass in there, but it wasn't very long. It was the summer months, but there was no crickets. No, nothing that I remember as a kid. . . . There is a spot, I mean it's still relatively wild [by today's standards]. But there's obviously no wild flowers anywhere. So it really brought things home to me."

The contrast he was drawing was with a time before the modern intensification of agriculture. Today the meadows are cut over by machine rather than freely grazed by cattle and sheep, resulting in shorter grass for most of the season. Widespread use of chemical sprays has devastated the local insect population. Modern farming has eliminated nonproductive species like wild flowers from the meadows.

"I enjoy seeing things as I think they should be," John said, "naturally, with wild life."

[*] See Lovejoy and Boas (1935) for an early critique. They called pastoralism "primitivism," but I have not followed their lead. It strikes me that primitivism is better as a critical term than as a descriptive one.

Of course, even the meadow of his childhood was not "unaffected by human beings," and so, strictly speaking, could not be nature under John's definition. But like Ann, he does not see nature and nonnature in strict polar opposition. For him as well it is a gradient, although John applies the category of nature rather more strictly than does Ann, or indeed most villagers. I asked him the same sequence of questions I had asked of her.

"Trees. Natural?"

"Well, you've got a good case there. Look out that window. You've got a [Lombardi] poplar tree and a silver birch. Right? They were put there by man. They're not."

I was a little surprised, given what other villagers like Ann had told me. Did John really mean to say that a tree could be unnatural? I asked for a bit of clarification.

"Lombardi poplars don't come from England, right?" I said.

"Yeah. [So] they're not natural. They're not with the area. Now out there in my far corner, I had a Witch Elm and when the Dutch Elm disease came, . . . I lost it. There was an oak tree over there, which has been cut down since. So what I did, I took acorns from that and I've grown an oak tree and I planted it out there. . . . Now you see, oak is a natural tree in the countryside of England, of Hampshire. I'm replacing it where I can. But all these people put all these fancy trees in. It's just not natural."

"Well, what about a field . . . ?"

"Doesn't matter where you go, the only place where you are likely to find where it's relatively natural is in glades and woods. Now over in Bartley [a nearby village], [there's] some lovely woods and they've got some glades in there. Not big open areas, but an acre [or so]. And there is some wildlife there, natural . . ."

Here John seemed to consider how periodic grazing by livestock over the centuries keeps a glade open. Thus even these areas are only "relatively natural." He had an even harsher judgment for modern farming practices.

"How about farming?" I asked. "Is farming natural?"

"Farming is not natural. I mean, very few farmers use natural fertilizers. They haven't got the [live]stock to do it. It's all artificial. They use sprays. And that's killing the wildlife, there's no doubt about it. You see, being a shooting man, I've very conscious of the wildlife . . ."

"Is the hedgerow natural?"

"Well, yes and no. If you go back to the, oh, medieval days, there weren't many hedgerows. There was more open land, you see, and more common land. It was grazed, but the wildlife wasn't affected so much. In those days, they didn't have pesticides, so you went on naturally. It's only when they formed [the big] estates that they planted the hedgerows."

He reached down to Lady, his retriever, and stroked her ears.

"But by doing that they've preserved. Because they intensified the use of the land to a certain extent, therefore the hedgerows acted as a back up, as cover. And now of course, they're taking the hedgerows out."

Hedgerows are thus a gray area in the gradient for John. Although they are constructed, the nonconstructed—wildlife—have taken up residence there.

"How about cities? Are they natural?"

"Well, they're not natural, of course. . . . But they provide a service, or they should do, surely. We all got to buy things. . . . So cities do provide a service. But obviously they're not natural. . . ."

John paused again, and then commented, "You go into farming areas, and that's where nature ends. Everything else—suburbs, inner cities, all that—it's completely false."

Like Ann, then, John sees things which are definitely natural (wildlife, woods, wildflower meadows, and whatever is unaffected by humans) and definitely unnatural—(cities, suburbs, modern farming, and the "completely false"). In between is a middle ground of the "relatively natural" that includes glades, hedgerows, and aspects of older farming practices such as using manure for fertilizer. It is the gray areas that make or break a definition for a logician. For Childerleyans, the existence of a gradient is what gives an idea like pastoralism its moral relevance.

I had not yet asked John about villages. When I did, his language changed. He began to speak more in terms of the contrast between the country life he feels he follows and the city life of so many others—a contrast he based in nature.

"What about that middle area?" I asked. "Villages. How about villages?"

"Well, there is a certain amount of country life [there]. But then, the people in villages are not country oriented. . . . This is [the way] so many people are. They can't be bothered to prepare the food. They all go straight to the supermarkets and buy all prepared. Now to me the natural way, if we go back to our prehistoric days, the general purpose in life was to live. You had to eat, so you went to find your food. Well, I'm a shooting man, a fishing man, so I get stuff for myself. . . . That's when you are more back to nature. You're trying to be almost self-sufficient. . . . To me, the natural way is trying to use natural food, like I am."

Although the countryside and the current life styles of those who live there are no longer fully natural, John feels that his is, or at least much more so. He doesn't use only prepared food. He gets much of it himself, albeit often by using machines, like his gun. He doesn't engage in contrived activities; he remembers that the purpose of life is "to live."

"Let's put it this way," he explained. "I'm a country person, having lived in the country. . . . Now I think I'm far closer to nature than [my neighbor]. He calls himself a countryman. And they're no where near it! They're the green wellie brigade, really."

So country life and country people are things of nature. At least that is true for what John and Ann see as real country life and real country people.

IV

BUT WHAT EXACTLY do the villagers mean by "nature"? It became clear in our conversations that Childerleyans meant more than just that which is untouched and unaffected by human construction and sophistication. Villagers see a range of underlying principles in nature. To put it another way, what Ann and John gave was a description of how they contrast nature with everything else, a kind of negative definition of nature which describes what it is not. We should explore their more positive accounts, for they reveal additional ways the villagers handle the contradictions of dualism.

Once I urged Ann to say a bit more about what she means by "God-given."

"When you say 'God-given,' " I asked, "what is for you the relationship between nature and something theological?"

"I don't think that there's a God up there. I think Jesus Christ lived [though]. He was an ordinary—he was a very extraordinary human being of great intelligence, of great compassion, and of great inner strength. And he was there just at the time that the Jews were being massively persecuted, living in and being dominated by the powers. And this man goes on in hope. Because he had this great quality of goodness in him."

She picked up the plate of biscuits and extended it toward me. I took one, and she continued:

"So then you might say, are you saying there is a God? If goodness is God, then there is a God. I don't think there's anything immortal. Unfortunately, I don't think that there is this whatever is it up there who will receive us kindly, or not kindly, or whatever. But I do believe there have probably been quite a few Jesus Christs, people of immense good-ness. And those that we have got to know is because they were in the right place at the right time. And there were some who weren't, whose goodness wasn't amplified by the conditions of their time. But if it is possible to say that such great goodness is what is meant by God, then historically it is so."

This same goodness Ann sees revealed in nature—even in its appar-ent evil. England over the three years preceding this conversation (which was in March 1990) had experienced an unprecedented series of severe windstorms—virtual hurricanes. Hundreds of thousands of trees had come down in a country where less than 10 percent of the land is woods. (Even with vast areas of deserts, farms, and grasslands the figure is roughly 40 percent for the United States.) Many homes were without power for two weeks in the worst of the storms. Treasured landscapes vanished, leaving lines of shattered stumps behind. A few people were killed. Noth-ing like these storms had been recorded for three hundred years.

"Does that mean," I asked her, "there can be cruelty in nature, can be evil in nature? For instance, the storms that England has had . . . in the past couple of years. [Are those] storm[s] evil?"

She did not pause.

"No. That's not evil. It's the natural order of things, like the food chain. That is what is. That is reality. That is what is. And it presumably has a purpose. . . . It did in one fell swoop get down trees that otherwise may have drifted down over the next two or three years."

So Ann extends this good purpose to nature. Without the storm, many trees would have fallen haphazardly and perhaps killed even more people. (In a storm, I think she was implying, most people know enough to stay indoors; consequently, falling trees land on fewer people than they other-wise would, had they fallen any old time.) Through nature's goodness, she finds harmony in apparent discord.

Like pastoralism, this too is an old idea. Plato called "goodness" the "governor of the intelligible order," "that most sovereign cause of nature and the universe."[12] For Plato, this good was God, what he called the "Demiurge," the artisan-deity.

Aristotle, though, demurred from the Platonic view that goodness is nature, nature is goodness, and that ultimately everything is both natural and good. Noting that with such holistic notions it is not possible to draw moral contrasts, he advocated a more separatist conception. Something is "due to nature," said Aristotle, only if it "has in itself a source of change and staying unchanged."[13] Anything which has its source of change outside itself—Aristotle used the example of a bed constructed by humans—was not due to nature. Humans are themselves due to nature, as they have a source of change and purpose inside them. But what humans make through art is not. Note his careful distinction between "due to nature" and "nature." For Aristotle, nature was only the source of change, not the things—trees, winds, people—that had that source inside them.

Just as Ann offered a perspective Plato would have understood, other villagers said things which resembled Aristotle's views.

"I used to try and tell my children," said Rachel Wood, "the leaves on trees—every single one is different. Everything is different. We've got to keep looking. It's continually changing. The countryside is continually changing. As long as man doesn't change it too much!"

Later in that conversation she described her concern about a scheme to divert a local river in order to build a road.

"That seemed a shame that that river [which] had always run its natural course, for years—I don't know how many years it had been there—suddenly somebody was going to move for a road. And I just thought that was sad, because I do like them to stay the same. It's chosen its own route."

Here is Aristotle's emphasis on how the things due to nature have their own internal source of change. The countryside is "continually changing," Rachel observed, without any external factors. The river had "chosen its own route." Humans have their own internal source of change, but the changes they cause in other things, Rachel says, like diverting a river, are not changes due to nature.

Andy Sparrow agreed.

"Nature is all that is beyond the touch of the manufactured," he said. "Before the touch of the manufactured—before the touch of human capacity to change things and create different materials out of raw material."

There is something Aristotelian in Ann's views too. Cars and atom bombs, she said, things which "wouldn't happen on their own" without human "force," are not nature. But the human ability to walk and run *is* natural. Aristotle would have said "due to nature," but the difference is slight. Both agree humans did not contrive their own legs.

Of course, no human has ever broken a single law of nature. Plastic follows nature's laws as much as plants do. In Aristotle's words, "art. . . . imitates the works of nature."[14] Human artifice is not nature, but the same *logos,* the same logic or order, permeates both. This gives all existence a certain unity, Aristotle thought. In fact even for Aristotle the final cause behind this order was, as for Plato, the "Good."[15] Ann also connected these two views. Here, then, both she and Aristotle found a separatism within a holism.

John Bone made a comment that paralleled another aspect of Aristotle's view of nature. Aristotle thought the *logos* he saw in the world could not be accidental. "Nature," Aristotle wrote, "does nothing without some purpose."[16] There must be a *telos* to things. John made the same point.

"Let's put it this way," he said. "We've now been able to survey most planets around. We appear to have the only one which is inhabited. We don't know why. Why have we got all this flora and fauna? From the tiniest insect to the elephant, which is the biggest we've got, to man, which is probably the most intelligent. . . . You've got the insects [which] live off of the flora. The insects that feed the birds. Birds feed, let's say, the animals. And the animals to feed the man. When you start looking at it in that sort of complex, really that's the secret of life for all. So everything's there for a purpose, in a way."

Harriet Cooper agrees with John and Aristotle.

"A lot of nature has been destroyed, [for example] the hedgerows and everything pulled out and the fields made huge. But actually they're coming back to find that the hedgerows and the streams have *got* to come back. They're losing the birds that were taking all the insects that were causing a lot of disease. Nature evolved that way so that each thing could do its own job. And I think they're beginning to find that that has got to come back. The hedgerows have got to come back. . . . Nature has got to come back, as it used to be."

Each thing of nature has "its own job." Humans, although in some sense separate from nature, ignore this unifying reality at their peril.

Since Aquinas, Christianity has often relied on the notion of design—purpose, jobs—in nature to prove the existence of God.° The complexity and diversity of nature's wondrous harmony of interconnection could not have been worked out by chance, the argument goes. Frank Steers made this argument too.

"I see nature as God's creation. He made the oak tree, and it's all designed. And the Book of Genesis is to me more and more wonderful every time I read it. . . . I see it as incredibly—it's almost true! Do you know what I mean? I can read it and I can see, you know, God created

---

° Aquinas drew his ideas mainly from the Stoic school that grew up shortly after Aristotle's death and also from certain passages in Aristotle on purpose in nature. See Glacken (1967).

and He was pleased with it. In the same way that a man makes a shep-
herd's crook and carves the bit in the end, and he's chuffed [pleased] with
his results. And you get the feeling that He's brooding over it and looking
after it even now. And there will be a seedtime and harvest, until He
decides there's not going to be. In other words, man can do a lot to harm
it, but without His ultimate authority, it's going to still be there. . . . The
Almighty must have thought it all out, planned it. It's fantastically well
made. And we just chop it down, use it, push it around, and everything
like this. I think it's disrespectful, really."

A design in nature argument is another way to get around the contradictions of dualism. The mark of God's crafting is everywhere, said Frank.
Although he did not say it to me explicitly, I think Frank would also
extend this crafting to the form and existence of humans (although not to
what humans do). God's design therefore provides a unity to everything.
Yet nature is still something opposite to us, making it a point of moral
contrast. We may "chop it down, use it, push it around," but it is "disrespectful" to abuse God's own handiwork.

It's worth speculating for a moment how these correspondences between the views of ancient Greek and early Christian scholars and those of
modern Childerleyans came to be. Not from reading the original sources, I
feel fairly sure. Rachel, John, and Harriet are not widely read, and although Andy and Ann are, they both denied having ever read Plato or
Aristotle. Frank often reads the Bible, but he has not read Aquinas.

Are these, then, ideas that knock around in the cultural toolkit we
each carry and that we each fill from the same hardware store of common
knowledge? And is that hardware store stocked by intellectuals who have
read the classics and promoted these ideas?

Partly. But even so we must still ask why Childerleyans find these
particular hammers and wrenches so appropriate to their lives. I am inclined to suspect that common moral dilemmas of the individual in society,
dilemmas common across time and space, are at least as important. What
made these ideas seem relevant to the classical authors makes them seem
relevant to Childerleyans today. I am even prepared to believe that Rachel, John, Harriet, Ann, Andy, and Frank came up with their views
largely on their own in the face of these common questions about life.
There is a lot of truth in Andy's explanation for the origin of his own
conception of nature.

"I've dabbled in [philosophy], but all second hand. . . . We did do a
little bit on philosophy at the university. I wouldn't say that that had
influenced my belief. [My conception of nature is] a rationality a lot of

people come to by just looking at the facts of the human species and life and the planet."

For one thing, for all their ideological importance, these are not topics people regularly discuss. For another, the ideas of nature that Childerleyans discussed with me also contained resemblances to ideas from well outside what some have considered the Western tradition to be.

Frank Steers's explanation of nature is a case in point. The Western conception of God is famously transcendent—God as separate from nature. Yet Frank seemed to push this conception right up to the border of immanence—God in, suffused throughout, nature. God did not just walk away from nature after He finished with it, said Frank. He is "brooding over" nature and "looking after it even now." Rachel Wood went even further, finding His presence almost palpable.

"God," she said, "the only way I could explain Him to myself . . . is that He was something that I couldn't see but He was there. As though He'd brushed your face like a breeze. You felt the presence."

Or there's Charles Goddard-Brown's theory of nature. He also offered views that some historians of philosophy consider atypical of the West.[17]

"Well," he said, "I suppose what I feel about nature is that nature as I know it, or [as] I've grown to know it, is the result of millions of years of balance, with everything interrelated through trial and error. [And] which is still in the process of adaption as one new thing comes in and produces pressure there, or disease. When I say pressure, I mean it can be anything. It can be a disease. It can be anything negative, destructive."

"You mean a force for change of some sort?"

"A force for change, yes. But a force that is either destructive or constructive. So you have a destructive force that comes into [being], and then it's countered by a very slow adaption of everything until we get back to another balance. And of course, if the balance goes too quick without some other force coming against it, then it can also become destructive. I mean, the force for good can become the force of destruction. . . . You've got to have plus and minus in perfect equal in order to get the ideal situation. And this is always changing in the world. . . ."

Charles does not exclude humans from this natural process of balance and counterbalance:

"Then human beings come into it. I mean, we are part of it. We are only a part of it, literally a part of nature. . . . I believe very much in the lovely language of the 1662 Book [of Common Prayer], God saying 'dust to dust.' That's what I feel. We are part of it all."

"So is everything that people do part of nature?"

"Yes."

Before the interview began we had been talking about the increasing number of cars passing through Childerley. Charles lives right on the main road and the traffic sometimes is loud enough to rattle his windows—and his peace of mind.

"Would, for example," I therefore asked, "a car be natural?"

"A car? Well there again, what people do is either destructive or constructive. And anything which is destructive to the accepted balance I dislike. But I will accept that there has to be change. Take cars, for instance. Alright. [There] is something which is destroying the balance of nature. And pretty obviously it was beginning to destroy the balance of nature right from the word go. It's all a question of the relationship of cars relative to road space."

"As we were talking outside."

"That is the basic thing. It's a question of ratio. If it becomes too great, then it becomes a destructive force. If it's just right, it can be a positive force, as far as it allows you to go to other people and therefore spread ideas, social things, et cetera, help. And that is all good. But when it comes to a certain [point], it becomes destructive. Any forces that we use for good can become destructive because they've gone too far. The weighting has become too great.

"To me," Charles said, summing up, "the perfect thing is a deciduous type forest and the greenery and the order and all that sort of thing, which to me is lovely and perfect. . . . And so anything which upsets it [the balance], which is too extreme, which produces a nasty taste in the mouth or a nasty effect in the mind, to me is something which is alien and foreign and destructive, and I hate it. So that's what nature means to me."

These are strikingly Eastern views. Charles is no hippy, no advocate of the sixties counterculture and its dabbling in Eastern philosophy and other cultural alternatives. Indeed, he regards the sixties as the era most responsible for the decline of the "old-fashioned" values he still holds to. Yet here is *ch'i,* the Chinese idea of a vital breath or "force for change," a metaphor I introduced into our conversation but which Charles readily picked up on. This force has a positive manifestation and a negative manifestation, a *yin* and a *yang.* Together their interplay introduces a dynamism to the unity of *dao,* the great harmony or "balance" of the universe. It also provides a moral contrast between the balance Charles sees as "the perfect thing" and the disruptions of balance which he hates. Through this unity of opposites, Charles gives both holism and separatism their due.

It is conceivable that Charles has read Eastern philosophy. I never thought to ask him. But he certainly did not give an orthodox rendition of Eastern ideas. Moreover, he has no problem mixing Eastern-sounding ideas with, for example, citations from the Book of Common Prayer or Darwinian notions of adaptation "through trial and error." He, like many other villagers, showed a creative grasp of the subtlety necessary for resolving dualism. Childerleyans may pick up some of their tools at the hardware store, but, like craft workers of old, they still do a lot of hand work on their own.

V

VILLAGERS VARY IN what they consider nature to be. Some connect it with a spirit they call God, others with God-like ideas they call "balance," "goodness," and "purpose." Most do a bit of both. But virtually all the villagers use the framework of pastoralism—the idea of a gradient between ways of living close to nature and ways far from nature—to apply nature to life. Through pastoralism, they connect the country and country people with nature and the natural. Through pastoralism, they discover the natural goodness of the way some people live, at least ideally. Through pastoralism, they find nature's relevant difference.

The villagers' ideas do not offer perfect solutions. Although it was not my business to point out the problems as I saw them, many Childerleyans were well aware of potential holes in their arguments. Ann and I laughed over the possibility of providing a perfect answer to the question of nature.

"We've cracked it!" she said with a shout.

"Right here in your living room!" I answered.

Charles was a bit more defensive.

"I hope I've been logical in what I said. I hope I haven't contradicted myself too much."

"I don't think you really have at all," I assured him. "I think nobody has got all this stuff worked out, do they?"

"No, no. They haven't, have they. But I just hope it makes sense from the point of view of one particular person. That's all."

The sense nature makes to each particular Childerleyan may not be perfect, not even to them. But, like Charles and Ann, they have hope that it could be.

SEVEN

The Natural Conscience

O man, whatever country you may come from, whatever your opinions may be, listen: here is your history as I believe it to read, not in the books of your fellowmen, which are liars, but in nature, which never lies.

Jean-Jacques Rousseau, 1755

I

JOHN BONE LIVES in an unremarkable house. It's a small bungalow, built in the early sixties, with a somewhat weedy, pebble driveway and a small expanse of (by local standards) scruffy grass in front. A couple of high, wild-looking hedges bound the property. The front gate is reddened with rust. No front door, grandly presented, faces the road. (You enter by a side door, which leads directly into a small mud room, and then the kitchen.) There are no rose bushes or finely trained topiary to admire. The passerby's eye, in search of more picturesque pleasures, passes on quickly to the next house and next scene.

Yet this is the house of someone utterly committed to country life, as he sees it. And as long as his health permits (he's sixty-seven now), John intends to continue living here, in the house he built in Childerley, some five miles from the village in which he was raised.

"I live here because I like it," says John. "I've got no ties to anyone, you see. I'm a single person, so I haven't got a family. . . . I think probably why it is, I know this part of Hampshire very, very well. I've lived here all my life. I know all the woods, the fields, and it's part of me."

Another time, John put it this way:

"I've got a completely wonderful life. Because I'm out in the country, I'm free."

What is this freedom that John and other villagers feel in country life and in their sense of themselves as country people? It is a freedom that, as they see it, nature alone allows. Through the idea of pastoralism, Childerleyans associate nature with the countryside and find thereby a source of moral contrast they consider to be quite relevant to their modern lives. But there is another important aspect to their conception of nature. The villagers also regard nature as free from social interests—something that stands apart from the selfishness, greed, power, and domination they see in social life. Childerleyans find in nature a kind of moral preserve in a landscape of materialist desire, an alternative region of moral thinking I will call the *natural conscience*. They discover this other moral landscape with the help of their pastoral and interest-free conceptions of what nature is. On this more solid, more fertile inner ground they seek to build their house and plant the garden of their identities.

II

I WILL USE ANOTHER conceptual map drawn up by previous scholars as a guide through this part of village life. Let's take a moment now to look over that map, for much of what I will be trying to point out in this chapter will be in response to what is charted there.

Where do moral judgements—our sense of what we, and others, ought to do in life—come from? The answer, said Emile Durkheim, is through the agency of the *collective conscience*—beliefs and sentiments we gain from our community, our social surround.

George Herbert Mead agreed, noting, moreover, that our moral judgement is linked with our sense of self—our sense of what we ought to do with our sense of who we are. We draw both, said Mead, from our social context.

Mead's view was that a person's sense of *me* ultimately comes from learning to see herself as she believes her society sees her. We do this, Mead argued, by "taking the role" or "attitude" of our society, learning to look back at ourselves as we imagine a *generalized other* might do. By generalized other, Mead meant a kind of mental personification of the collective conscience—the sense we have in our minds of what "society says" or "society believes" or "society thinks." The internal vision a person constructs of how the generalized other sees her is what Mead called the me.°

Mead also suggested that the physical world contributes to the sense

---

° Although it does not concern us here, some readers may be interested to know that the third part of the self, according to Mead, is the *I*, the active agent we sense inside us.

of me. "The essential thing," Mead wrote, "is that the individual, in preparing to grasp the distant object, himself takes the attitude of resisting his own effort in grasping."[1] In this way, "we talk to nature . . . and nature comes back with other responses."[2] Consequently,

> Any thing—any object or set of objects, whether animate or inanimate, human or animal, or merely physical—toward which [a person] acts, or to which he responds, socially, is an element in what for him is the generalized other; by taking the attitudes of which toward himself he becomes conscious of himself as an object or individual, and thus develops a self or personality.[3]

It sometimes takes a couple of passes to understand Mead's sentences. Let me try to clarify. Mead's point: Our sense of self comes in response to both the social world and the nonsocial world, both of which we understand in similar ways. It's a matter of learning to put yourself in the place of others—other people and other physical things. In this way, physical things become part of the generalized other. We only learn to make our way through a forest and down a sidewalk by taking the role of material objects, by imagining their resistance to our actions.

I agree with a lot of what Mead suggested. The concepts of the *me* and the *generalized other* provide a useful language for describing the dynamics of the collective conscience. Mead was also right to point out that the physical world contributes to our sense of *me* through the formation of what Andrew Weigert has recently, and usefully, termed a "generalized environmental other" (with the felicitous acronym of GEO)—a kind of physical parallel to a purely socially derived generalized other.°

But based on what Childerleyans explained to me, I think there is something further, and equally fundamental, going on. The physical world is a matter of both nature and "nature"—nature as a both a material and an ideal, or cultural, phenomenon. The significance of the latter, "nature," is not that it is a parallel to the generalized other, but that it can be an alternative to it.

Nature is a source of self that Childerley's people imagine as external to and therefore truer than the generalized other. What I will be describing first is the villagers' deep suspicion of the collective conscience and

---

° William James, an earlier figure in the same pragmatist tradition as Mead, was perhaps making a related point with his concept of the "material self." See James (1948).

the mental interplay between the generalized other and the me. And second I will be describing their use of the natural conscience for constructing a *natural other* and a *natural me*.

III

ONE OF THE COMMONEST TOPICS of conversation in Childerley, as anywhere, is criticism of the values that underlie the behavior of others. Childerleyans especially level such criticism at those they do not regard as country people.

For these people, living in the country is "like having a smart car," observed Jim Winter. "They want to be seen. And when their friends come down for a party and they see they've got all this land, that's a statement about them."

Statements like these are the very stuff of the generalized other. Here Jim gives it shape by pointing to the values that mark the edge of the community he identifies with, the community of real country people.

And here's another. Ann Martin is a fervent opponent of fox hunting and belongs to an antihunt society. She has considerable antipathy for Colonel Spreadbury, who is very active in the local hunt club. Ann pointed to him as indicative of why fox hunting persists in the face of widespread public opposition to it.

"Because the hunting fraternity is so powerful. . . . As you will probably know Spreadbury is a mighty rich man. We don't have to delude ourselves. [It's not] paranoia. They do influence things a lot."

Ann's comments show the way she locates the moral lines of social life. In contrast, Dorothy Cantelupe is a fervent supporter of fox hunting and a long-time member of the local hunt club. Here's what she had to say about those who protest hunting.

"It's just boys from the university who are paid to come up for the day to make a nuisance. They really don't know what they're doing."

Their justness aside, these criticisms and countercriticisms plainly help mark social boundaries. And more. We should take particular note of the dominant supposition upon which they are based—the suspicion of material motives and social intrigue in the actions of others. This is the basis upon which Jim criticized those moving to the country, Ann the moneyed influence of the "hunting fraternity," and Dorothy the "paid" hunt protesters. The form of all of these everyday comments are, in a sense, critiques of class motivation.

Moreover, villagers level these charges very broadly. They subject even their own community, their own source of a generalized other, to the same form of critique.

Villagers' responses to television are a case in point. Television, of course, is often accused of being something of a dictator of the collective conscience of our day, something people take in uncritically. I was at the home of the Coopers one evening, having a drink with Harriet, Ed, their son David, and his girlfriend Colleen. Someone switched on *Hymns of Praise*, a religious show in which ordinary people describe the importance of Christianity in their lives and conclude with naming their favorite hymn, which a choir then sings for them. A woman on the show was giving an account of how Christ had come into her life in a time of trouble and what a difference that had made. Colleen thought it sounded rather contrived.

"You're just saying that," she said, addressing the screen, "because you're on telly!"

Later in the evening we turned to a news show. Ed leveled one of his favorite words at the local commentator, who was discussing an issue I couldn't follow.

"Rubbish! You're just interested in yourself, aren't you, you silly man!"

Ann Martin was angry that the wealthy villagers always seem to get planning permission to build new houses and convert older structures to dwellings. This is how she described what was really going on at one meeting of the local Parish Council that she attended.

"I will say quite openly I think it's a case of the 'old boys' thing. And they weren't going to turn down the local power. . . . It was very apparent to me and to others. But because those on the Parish Council, . . . all of the little group, they are carefully selected."

This causes her to have a broad suspicion of social life, as she mused to me later.

"Oh dear. I just love sitting on the sidelines and watching the politics of it all. The machinations of humanity are just fascinating."

These "machinations" she described as fundamental to all humans, even children. Not even they are innocent.

"I am not a believer that children are ultimately innocent. Not after four or five, anyway."

"How about young babies, a year old baby?" I asked.

"A year old baby. I'm not knowledgeable enough to be totally sure when the time [is] at which one ceases to be innocent. . . . I think children, in many senses, know that they can manipulate very early on. And manipulation is not innocence, is it? . . . If I smile at this person, you know, they'll give me [what I want]. They will be pleasant to me. And that's essential to all of us. That message gets through quite early. So I don't see that there's an age of innocence as such."

Ann's theory that even children must be manipulative schemers is a minority view among Childerleyans. Everyone else I discussed this point with held that the essence of children is their direct and authentic behavior.

"They're guileless, aren't they," said Frank Steers. "I might say something to please you, but a kid will yawn and say, 'When are we going home, mummy?'"

But no one argued that this guilelessness extends into the world of adult society. Here villagers find instead a realm of manipulation, intrigue, and interest—class, writ small, writ large, writ everywhere. How then, I believe they ask, can we trust the generalized other?

For this reason we should be careful about accepting a kind of totalizing view of the significance of the generalized other for the self. A fault with Mead's theory is that he presented the acquisition of the generalized other and the *me* as unproblematical. As R. S. Perinbayagam has asked, "Is an other arrived at effortlessly, unambiguously, and peacefully?"[4] People are not as easily or as permanently socialized into a community's values as Mead seems to have suggested.*

One danger of ignoring people's common criticisms of even their own community of value is the risk of falling into a version of false-consciousness theory. Let me explain what I mean. Marxist scholars have long taken a special interest in the fact that, apparently, poor people rarely protest their conditions. The reason for this, suggested Marx long ago, is the poor are beseiged by cultural teachings promoted by the powerful to quell such inclinations. People rarely protest because they falsely come to believe what they have been taught to believe, namely that the system is just. "What's good for General Motors . . ."

There is probably some truth to the theory of false consciousness. But only some. As James Scott has pointed out, most unempowered people are actually well aware of their situation. Yet this same situation usually pre-

---

* See Wrong (1976) and Mills (1959). The charge of having an "over-socialized" conception of people has been frequently laid at the door of Durkheim as well. But in his case the charge is only half true. Durkheim did have a heavily socialized view of "primitives" living in a society dominated by what he called "mechanical solidarity." His theory of modern life, however, pivoted around his impression of the anomie that results when "organic solidarity" breaks down the "mechanical" institutions of social integration.

vents them from making visible protests against it. Because of their lack of social power, risks are high and access to media is low.[5]

A similar viewpoint may serve us well with regard to the generalized other. Childerleyans experience a generalized other, but they also experience their own ability to recognize material motivations behind it. They are well aware, and quite suspicious of, at least some aspects of the collective framing of individual lives. Rather than a false consciousness, Childerleyans have a consciousness of the falseness of the generalized other.

We need to incorporate this consciousness into our understanding of Childerleyans' sense of social self. To this task I will now turn.

IV

IN PLACE OF THE MATERIAL motivations and social conventions they see undermining the truthfulness and legitimacy of their community's values, Childerleyans offer a *natural conscience*.

One place to listen in on this natural conscience is in villagers' depictions of the social motives of animals. Several residents compared society's false pride over social standing with the animal world's more honest ways of interacting. John Bone pointed this out in the behavior of dogs, using the example of Lady, his hunting dog and constant companion.

"Lady, being a working dog, she meets lots of other dogs. They get on like a house on fire. They never fight. If she's coming on heat and the dogs start mating, she'll put them in their place. Now, I will be having a sheep dog down here for a week, for a friend of mine, to look after. A great bundling thing, three times the size of Lady. And if it starts messing about, Lady will just tell it off. Put it in its place. And then they get on fine, no trouble at all. There's no resentment. Now human beings, if someone puts you in place some time, you get all up tight about it."

Rachel Wood thinks this same false pride prevents most people from engaging in the kind of unaffected love and touching that is the way of animals.

"Animals love you all the time. Some people are absolutely cold to their animals. And the animals will still give them their loyalty. Real friends will take you whether you're good, bad, or anything. You can do the most awful thing and [animals] will forgive. But, generally, people, if you cross them, then they say, 'Oh. *That* person did so-and-so. Or said that.' You're much more careful with people. You've got to be, when you meet them. You've got to be careful what you say in case you offend them."

Rachel also used the example of dogs.

"Whereas with a dog, you can be totally relaxed with a dog. If you want to cuddle a dog, you can cuddle it. It will accept it. Whereas if you want to cuddle a person, not everybody's like that."

Several villagers felt that human society not only runs counter to the ways of nature revealed in animals but is also a threat to animals. Ann Martin made this point to me in defending her stance against fox hunting. She sees all existence, including humans, as on the same moral plane. Nodding toward her dog, who was sleeping at her feet, she explained that human law, contrived as it is, does not recognize this equality.

"I see everything that lives as being equal. Leave aside the law, which is manmade anyway. To me, this dog feels pain like I do. It missed its mum when it came [here]. It suffers. It is happy. It likes reward. All of it."

The law and other social conventions are all products of human interest. Therefore, Ann points out, hunters "will see the fox as vermin, not realizing they're choosing to give it that label because it suits them. Because then they don't feel guilty about this, you see."

The self-interested ways of society also pose a more general threat to nature, said some Childerleyans. Andy Sparrow blamed corporations and the state.

"The big boys, the I.C.I.'s of this world, well they're some of the major polluters, vandals of our earth. And we're victims of their corporate irresponsibility. . . . They're out to make money. The North Sea, too late! European forests. Chernobyl affected the world's sheep. Bhopal! It's really frightening. . . . And there's a feeling, you know, that money will win in the end. You can protest just as much as you like, but it's whether money will talk [that matters]."

Frank Steers brought the problem down to an individual level. The materialist threat to nature is something for which all Christians like himself are responsible.

"Incredibly impotent about doing anything, really, a lot of Christians are. Just let it happen. Sit back and enjoy what we've got. We're going to have it, chaps. Blow the rest of these fellows. As long as we've got their souls we're O.K. Forget about nature and any kind of thing like this. . . . But then we're bound up in the flaming economy, and you've just got to get on with it, haven't you. You just chop down another tree, make it into a frame for your window, and stick it in. You're just trying to make as much money [as you can]. It's a shame, isn't it."

Charles Goddard-Brown explained the matter somewhat differently. Human greed is a part of nature, he thinks. But when it gets out of control, it becomes contrary to "balance," the purpose he sees in nature. This is how he put it in our discussion of the problem of cars:

"I think what happens is that the human being has got things wrong, become too greedy, and is using an asset [cars] in such an irresponsible way that it becomes a liability. When all is said and done, we are the species that controls the planet—well, not controls it, but has a great say in it. We are the species that has got to control our greed, and all the destructive aspects of [that]. And when we don't, we become contrary to the purpose of nature, which I see as something which has the ideal of being in balance."

I then asked him whether nature could destroy its own balance, as with the series of powerful storms that I had also asked Ann about earlier. Charles said no. The storms were actually the result of greedy human interference with nature's balance.

"The storm is the result, if you pursue a certain type of argument, of the world being put out of balance through excessive use of fossil fuels. So in other words, industrialization has become too bloody greedy. . . . So there again it's our irresponsible use of things."

Charles was pointing to the theory that carbon dioxide and other gases released from the burning of fossil fuels has warmed the global climate. Some commentators have suggested that the recent storms in Britain are a result of the altered climate of a Green House (and, Charles would say, an industrialized and materialistic) world. I tried another topical example.

"But how about the recent earthquake in San Francisco? [That] would be hard to trace to human intentions."

"Well, you could," Charles replied. "[It] was perfectly obvious to anybody with the slightest intelligence that there's been earthquakes in that particular area ad infinitum. So if you're stupid enough, because it is to your financial advantage to build houses, et cetera, then basically it's your stupid fault. The ultimate responsibility must be human."

Charles looked at me with a twinkle.

"Well," he said, "I managed to get out of that one!"

We laughed.

Charles was making a serious point, though, a point that Rachel,

Andy, Ann, and Frank were also making. For them, nature's value is opposed to pride, greed, money, and other social interests. In nature, they find a moral domain clearly free from the pollution of social motives and intrigues. This is the moral contrast that the villagers are ultimately trying to draw through their conceptions of nature.

Nature's innocence of social intrigue gives it a further quality for many villagers. The contrast removes the things of nature from all moral criticism. Childerleyans therefore see nature as somehow more real, more true, more authentic—as something they can trust that is free of society's fickleness and back-stabbing.

"I believe quite strongly," said Andy Sparrow, "that one of the disadvantages of urban living, and most of England's population is an urban population, . . . is that they are divorced from the reality of the land. . . . I have a feeling that to understand where we live, to understand who we are, we need to have a fairly close contact with the earth, nature. And unless people grow things, and understand all those sorts of things, then they're divorced from a lot of realities about themselves."

"I think one of the things about country life," observed Reverend Bill Cazalet, "is you get buried in the ground, and so you start thinking about the world. When you're not buried in it, you don't think about the world. And when you stop thinking about the world, you stop thinking about other people."

"[In the country] one is capable of looking at England in a more objective way than the town person is," said Charles. "I think. Because to start with, you're looking from nature into manmade environments, and you can judge that against nature. Whereas if you live in a town, you're only really dealing with manmade stuff."

Real country people, to Rachael Wood's mind, are therefore more genuine. She has great respect for Harry Roud, a local gamekeeper who, at seventy-four, is one of the oldest lifelong residents of Childerley. Harry has a captivating, thick countryness to him, a rural sophistication unmatched among the villagers. Rachel described him as a "more natural" person because "He doesn't have to put on any airs. He's not pretending to be something that he is not. He's himself. Whereas lots of people you meet, they are one person, but they are pretending they are somebody perhaps up the social scale a little bit higher."

Maybe Nigel Brown put it best. He has become very interested of late in the environmental movement and the defense of nature. This was a big change for him, he felt. He used to be an avid hunter, taking his gun out into his father's fields and "potting at anything that moved."

Earlier, we had talked about his change of heart, but the conversation shifted somehow to politics. Nigel wanted to know what I thought about Northern Ireland, and we found we agreed there was fault on both sides. There was a pause as we reflected to ourselves about the contradictions of the situation there, and then he broke in.

"That's why I think I'm interested in the environment. You *know* what's right. It's clear where one should be standing. It's never that way with politics."

One way to understand what Nigel and other villagers are describing is to consider it as a sort of moral entity in their minds. In addition to the generalized other, they are describing an other uncompromised by social interests and social desires. I will call it the *natural other.*°

The presence of the natural other in villagers' thoughts is intellectual and secondary. By an intellectual presence, I mean the natural other is made possible by resolving the problem of dualism, which in turn allows nature to serve as a moral alternative. By secondary, I mean that it is probably only called into being in response to problems people may come to perceive in the generalized other. I can envision a person, probably a very young one, with a generalized other and no form of natural other. (And let me point out that while Childerleyans stress pastoral nature, there are many other forms of the natural other—some of which Childerleyans also experience, as we shall see.) I find the reverse harder to imagine. But although it is secondary in origin, for some Childerleyans it is primary in importance for it alone offers a source of value they can trust.

V

THIS MAKES NATURE a compelling basis for grounding the self.

"There are lots of places that I've been where there have been no human beings," said Andy Sparrow, "[where] you were yourself, and there was just nature. But on those occasions, one realizes the frailty of the

° Sometimes one encounters in environmental writing the charge that the West regards "nature as Other"—as something foreign, objectified, and hated. (For example, see Shiva [1988], 6). When I say "natural other," I mean something more dialectical—nature as something we come to regard as external yet still relevant, and which we can then, perhaps somewhat paradoxically, incorporate into the self. That other manner of natural otherness is also a frequently used route to self, I suspect. But it is a route through the terrain of negative pastoralism, not the positive pastoralism Childerleyans emphasized to me.

human being without all the trappings of what he created that was unnatural. So I value nature for its beauty. I value nature for the freedom that
it gives me, that when I'm involved in natural sort of circumstances or
places, that brings me back to my roots, in terms of creation. And I have
a spiritual sort of affinity [for that]."

"The countryside gives me the necessary background," said Charles
Goddard-Brown. "Because I feel relaxed and happiest nearest to nature
and the purpose of nature. I mean, I can feel the most at ease, a restful
peace."

As did John Bone at the beginning of this chapter, Andy and Charles
speak the language of identity. "Part of me." "Where you were yourself."
"The necessary background." "My roots, in terms of creation." "Where I
feel at ease, a restful peace." Moreover, this is a self that emerges only
in the absence of society. "Where there have been no human beings."
"In the woods and fields" where "I'm free." "Nearest to nature" and its
"purpose." Away from "unnatural" "trappings." This is the self the natural
other sees, what I will call the *natural me*.

There's a common phrase for this self among the villagers. They call
it the belief, the inner conviction, that one is "a real country person."

And what makes this *me* such a valued basis for the self is its freedom
from the interests that shape the social me. One evening I was chatting
with Margaret and Albert Cook and their old friend Bert Longman in the
Cook's sitting room. That afternoon, the Cooks had treated me to a fine
pheasant dinner using a bird that Bert had shot and given to them. The
three of them got to talking about some of the ways that they differ from
others, something they often discussed together (at least in my presence).
Earlier I had complimented Bert on the pheasant. He turned to me now
and described some of the distinctiveness he felt about country food—that
it represents the community of sharing country people still maintain, the
greater naturalness of a self-sufficient rural life, and that real country
people are proud still to eat poor people's food like rabbit.

"The world has changed, hasn't it?" he said. "But we haven't. We
still eat the rabbit. If we kill a deer, we share it with each other, don't we
Albert? We've always been that way with rabbit and the rest of it."

Bert then drew a parallel between their lives and that of traditional
native Americans, a people whom pastoralism suggests lived as close to
nature as one can.

"They had a program on the telly about the Indians and about the
ceremonies they had when they killed a moose. They shared it all, didn't

waste anyting. And I think we're like that, at least a bit like that. Whereas down in the towns it's all different."

Bert's point, I think, was that he and the Cooks are not motivated by materialist desires for competitive and conspicuous consumption. Real country people like themselves work together and consume only what is necessary. And they are more self-sufficient, less dependent on the greedy industry of the city, which brings them closer to nature at the same time that it demonstrates their lack of competitive materialist motives.

John Bone too finds that his natural *me*, his sense of *myself* as "a countryman bred and born," gives him the moral foundation for freedom from the petty class interests of so much of society. And on this foundation—a foundation, he says, most people don't see—he builds his house of self.

"Other people think that [they're] better than what [you] are," says John. "That chap down there [points down the lane], he's got quite a chip on his shoulder, you see, because [he's got] a big house. It's a lovely house, and he thinks he's so much better than me. He always talks down to me. And there it is. I'm probably far more wealthy than him, because I've got [no mortgage]. Just because I live in a modest home and I don't show it. I'm not at all worried about it. I couldn't care less what people think about me now. But other people do. I'm not worried because I haven't got a lot of rubbish out there. My friends know me, and they're not worried either. It's all keeping up with the Joneses. But I don't keep up with the Joneses. I keep up with myself."

It may sound contradictory that John both says he "couldn't care less what people think" and stresses the importance of his friends' opinions. But the *natural me* is not solipsism. When John says "people," he does not mean that he doesn't care what anyone thinks. He means a generalized concept of "society." He has friends, and that is important to him. John's friends are real country people too, in his estimation. They also follow the natural other in forming a more honest sense of who they are. They too agree that class values are not the true ones. But apart from the companionship they provide, their importance, he thinks, is not that they define who the real John is. What they do is give him some assurance that he is not some idiosyncratic oddball in following nature instead of conventional society. "I'm not a recluse," as he explained to me on another occasion.

Margaret said it best, I think. She is a person who has suffered much at the hands of what the villagers call class. Yet she is also a gregarious, positive woman who prides herself in her ability to transgress the barriers class erects.

"It doesn't mean anything to me. Because I like people of all kinds, period. Perhaps there again I'm fortunate, but I communicate with them from all ranges. . . . This is what [my] stepmother always said. I'd speak to the biggest tramp on the road, which I did. Whoever it was, if they wanted to say good morning, I'd say good morning too. And every person whether they are unfortunate enough to be tramps in the roads or if they are fortunate enough to be a lord or lady, they are still only human beings like we are. And therefore I don't see why I can't speak to them. A lot of people say, oh, you mustn't, you mustn't put yourself [out]. . . . But I don't agree with that. I mean, you're all human beings. You all came in the same way. And you'll all go out the same way, with nothing. So whatever you make in between is immaterial, really."

Margaret was born in a large city but has lived the last fifty years in villages across the south of England. She has no doubt that she is now a country person. And this is how she prefers to think about who she is:

"I've been country since I was sixteen. And there's no way I would go back and live in the town. So I am country as countryfied goes. All the things pertaining to the countryside are mine. I'm not a town person any more. And therefore, what was I going to say, the class system doesn't worry me."

VI

CHILDERLEYANS RECOGNIZE the existence of a social context for their lives. They recognize that they live in a community, indeed communities—of work, leisure, neighborhood, generation, nationality, religion, ethnicity, politics, and other sources of group differentiation. And they recognize that who they are depends on the collective conscience of the social context outside them. The *me* they feel inside depends on the generalized other they also feel inside.

Yet Childerleyans are suspicious of the generalized other in their mind—its values and the me it constructs for them. They suspect that its values are tarnished by the rust of social interests, particularly the materialist desires of class. Were there no alternative for them, villagers might experience the crisis of self Durkheim called "anomie," the sense that one has no sure moral foundations. Childerleyans largely avert this crisis by adopting a different source of values, the natural conscience, which does not have this social tarnish. Through their ideas of nature, they gain a conscience they regard as free of the interests which undermine the validity of the generalized other for them. Villagers have not worked these ideas out perfectly, they admit, but they have some faith that it could be done. This faith is the natural other. Through it they construct an alternative me, a natural me—that of being a country person.

I should hasten to point out that neither I nor the villagers mean "nature" precisely. What is "natural" in the natural conscience is not Aristotle's or Charles Goddard-Brown's conception of the difference between beds and birds or cars and carpenter ants. Let me say it carefully. The natural conscience is the imagination of something—some realm, some agent—apart from the collective conscience that can serve as a disinterested basis for values and the self. For most villagers, one very important route to this conscience is through their ideas of nature, which they see as a realm free of human social intrigue. There are many other routes.

One villager explicitly refused to use the word *nature* for what he found so compelling about living in a place like Childerley. Jim Winter uses a natural conscience, but he bases it on "countryside," not "nature." He took the questions I asked about nature rather differently than other villagers.

"How might you define nature?" I asked. "Have you ever thought about this question. It's a tough one, I know."

Jim was very sympathetic to my project, but he reacted to this question with some hostility, intellectual hostility, as I was to find out.

"I feel like throwing it straight back to you, and saying whether I think you're right or not. It's the strangest question I've ever had on me."

I suggested that we try the series of questions about which are the things of nature and which are not.

"Would you include cities as part of nature?" I asked.

"Yes, of course. . . . A building, once it's been put up by a lot of very active men, it just exists, doesn't it, as a piece of nature. . . ."

"Are manmade objects part of nature?"

"Yes. In the sense that I'm talking about."

Jim grew frustrated with the direction of my inquiries.

"You can't answer these questions," he said. "All life is nature, isn't it. . . . What we're talking about really is just my relationship to these things, isn't it. Not to do with what nature is. It's a question of conscience rather than nature. I mean, I'm making these decisions which to other people are probably inconsistent. I'm making them to some internal consistency of my own, which you could call a conscience."

I was struck by his use of the word *conscience,* and I pressed him on its relationship to nature once more.

"Is nature involved in that, what you consider nature to be? To the extent that any of us have worked it out in our own minds."

"I can't answer that," Jim replied, "because I don't use the word. You're using the word. . . . I think I have just proved to myself that I don't make the same distinction. . . . I think we should be using the word *countryside,* not *nature.* Quite different."

Jim is a man who tries to think things through. And he has concluded (as have many other philosophers) that there is no logical way to separate anything from nature. "All life is nature"—even humans, cities and all. Such a radically holistic conception allows for no separatism, no point of moral contrast, and he abandons it as basis for arriving at an "internal consistency." But Jim thinks a lot about the moral component of what brings him to the countryside. He finds the necessary contrast in the opposition of country and city, although both are, for him, equally part of nature.

"What is the definition of countryside, then?" I asked. "Is that opposed to cities?"

"Well obviously yes. It's the nonurban environment. And the various distinctions of the urban environment, such as roads and everything else of a manmade, civil-engineering nature [encroach] on the countryside. . . . It's relatively crude here, and there's more space between you and your fellow man, isn't there. In the city, you can be just passing along and there's some stranger there who you have nothing to do with. So you haven't got the same space. It may be nothing more than that. Just physical space around one."

Although Jim says it is no more natural than any other place, for him the countryside is a realm whose very definition places it in a gradient leading away from society, from fellow man. In this realm Jim finds his values and what he regards as his true self.

"I think it provides for me a kind of secure emotional base, literally. Just my relationship with the physical countryside. And everything outside that [is] actually . . . a venturing away from that and then a returning to it. That may be exaggerating, but I think that's probably the essence of it. . . . I have had similar feelings when I've been on my own in the city, particularly in certain states of mind. . . . The only thing which is constant is my own relationship with the physical environment, as opposed to the social environment."

On another occasion, he put it this way:

"It's probably no more complicated than I feel safer dealing with things rather than people. . . . And they've got a lot to say to you if you're prepared to listen. They'll speak to you with importance. Whereas people are just a shifting sand, aren't they."

This "secure emotional base" he can always return to is Jim's natural other. Normally he finds it in the physical space of the countryside and, "in certain states of mind," in the physical reality of buildings. In this way he has made a mental place to go that lies outside the insecurities of the social terrain. Here is where he feels safe from the "shifting sand" of social interests.

In this place, Jim sites his self. Yet Jim does not consider himself the "country person" other villagers described. As he discussed earlier, he is suspicious of the status implications of the term.

"A 'country person' embraces all sorts of things, really, doesn't it. . . . It's difficult to describe. It's just that I feel more at home in the country than in the city."

That sense of at-homeness is Jim's *natural me*. For Jim, "country" is no less a source for a natural conscience than "nature" is for others.

VII

DESPITE THE MORAL SECURITY it can provide, a natural conscience is not unproblematical for Childerleyans. The problem of dualism is one source of difficulty. There is a further problem too. The natural conscience often directs villagers to do things that conflict with aspects of their collective conscience, aspects they find hard to reject fully. It is one thing to adopt an inner sense of natural self in opposition to the social me; it is another to act on it.

Andy Sparrow explained the contradiction well. He firmly rejects the greed he sees underlying the economy.

"The idea that we should have at all times a growth economy seems obscene to me. You know, that we should always be getting richer. The idea that one cannot be content unless one is making more money. And that commercial exploitation of human beings. We are being exploited by commercialism all the time, the more to buy, the bigger the better. And we've got to get the video, we've got to get this, we've got to do that. It doesn't add up. . . . There is an ascetic side to my nature that says, you know, that's not all that life's about."

"Do you find that living in the countryside helps you perhaps get away from that?" I asked.

"Well, it's a sop. It's a sop to the idea that you do without it. Because you don't do without it. You're just as bad as the rest. You join the band wagon, you know. You need all these things and you want them and you get after them just as fast as the other guys. But you get an intellectual sort of laugh. And then they'll allow you in the country. I'll grow my own potatoes, sort of thing. So if you're really honest with yourself—"

Ann also spoke of the contradiction between what her natural other and her generalized other suggest as the best course of action. She spoke of it as a problem of what is "convenient."

"Do you ever find," I had asked, "when you're contemplating what you should do in a situation, and you have several courses of action that you could follow, that you choose the one that you finally do because it is the more natural way?"

"I think up to a point. I would like to think that I did and I think up to a point I do. But there is probably a point where that is not as convenient as I would like it to be. Either through the time factor, maybe the cost factor, maybe the emotional expense factor that I would not follow that rule. . . . Despite all my feelings, genuine feelings, and talking of and wanting to be thought of kindly towards animals."

Although Ann is very concerned about cruelty to animals, a principle she derives from her egalitarian view of nature, she went on to give an example of where this natural other conflicted with the petty desire to get to work on time. The week before, there had been heavy rains in the area, and a number of streams went into flood.

"[When I was] going to work about a week ago," Ann said, "there was a deer caught in the floods. It must have been. I knew as I drove past. But I did not stop or call in at a nearby house to do anything about it."

This was only the most recent time she felt this contradiction.

"There have been other occasions when I thought, 'Well, I could have done something there,' and didn't. Because it meant stopping the car, getting out, and it might have been raining. So for my own personal comfort, despite my feelings, I have not followed through. There's also being late for work. Even so. That's my personal convenience, isn't it. I would be disapproved of, being late."

Lucy Pearce, though, is one villager who risked social disapproval in her attempt to accept the guidance of her natural conscience. Six months after she first moved to Childerley, she decided to increase her involvement in the village. Lucy had finally settled her family into their little country cottage, so she had the time. The furniture was in place. The pictures were hung. The antiques were unpacked. She was in the village post office when an advertisement for someone to clean at Church Farm, which has a grand big house, caught her eye.

"It's a lovely house," she told me. "I didn't know anybody in the village. And I thought I would get to know people and what was going on from being involved in the farm."

Lucy was worried a bit about the status implications of being a cleaner. Her father had been raised in a poor family on an estate village, and several of her cousins still live and work on country estates. Cleaning seemed awfully close to that in status. But when she thought about it some more, the idea felt all right to her. It felt natural. It felt country.

"I'd never done cleaning in my life before, except for myself. This didn't bother me, as my cousins have been in service for generations."

So she took the job. The lady of the house was Elizabeth Juleff.

"But when I was there," Lucy continued, "I suddenly felt this class barrier. I was with Elizabeth and she went out one Tuesday to meet the hunt. And she said, 'Lucy, take a few minutes off. Go down and see the hunt [with me]' . . . And when I was introduced, I was introduced as, 'Oh, this is my cleaner . . .'"

This was quite a shock. Lucy had already met a lot of the hunters through the local Conservative Club, which she had just joined.

"And for the first time I felt, 'Blow it, I'm not going around with Elizabeth if I'm her cleaner. I'm me! I'm Lucy!' . . . And then I got people saying to me, 'Oh, I've got a little cleaning job you can have. Would you like to come down and clean my place?' Well, blow it. I'm not the cleaner."

Lucy quit. In so doing she was making a statement, a statement at least to herself, about the pain of her own contradictory feelings, a contradiction between two consciences. One conscience told her there is nothing to be ashamed about in being a cleaner. Cleaning in a big house is one thing real country people have always turned to for employment. It's a part of country life, as she sees it, a natural thing for a country person, such as she sees herself as, to do. Another conscience seemed to relish a potential association with the romance of wealth. There was the "lovely house," the big farm, the chance to mix with the gentry who owned it. But this same part did not want to be identified as a lesser person, as lower class, as Elizabeth Juleff's inferior, as "the cleaner."

The fact is, Childerleyans do need to heed the callings of the collective conscience. Ann Martin needs her job and she can't be late unless she has an excuse her clients would accept. Lucy's social standing, as much as she might prefer it to be otherwise, does have an important influence on her life chances. Even though her family relies on her husband's work for the bulk of their income, his chances for advancement or even keeping his job, should his firm decide to cut back, could well be materially affected by having a wife who was seen as "the cleaner." Status and class in the Weberian sense—that is, social honor and economic power—are indeed closely connected. These are matters villagers must handle with care.

Consequently, Childerleyans often find that they are unable to take the courses of action their natural conscience suggests to them. Of course, the line at which people can honestly say they took another course because of the constraints of the collective conscience (something merely external) and not the desires they may have derived from it (something internal) is difficult to locate, and many villagers are troubled by it. They are troubled because they feel that such an internal *me* is not a true one.

This is how Frank Steers put it:

"I'm an idealist, really. . . . But what actually comes out in life is, of course, a load of hypocritical rubbish. There's a constant conflict within my life between materialism and my love of nature. I'd like to reverence God's nature more than I do. But the fact is I'll go and sell myself short for a bit of materialism. . . . I see that in myself. That here I am, always trying to promote myself, the ego. God's ways are much more humble ways. Our way is the big flashy car way."

A popular economic theory, of course, waves away this conflict, arguing that Frank's self-promotion contributes to economic growth. Frank's material interest thus serves the material interest of us all. And if we all benefit from materialism, why doubt its moral value? Self-interest is not self-serving. As a farmer, as an agricultural businessman with five to ten employees (depending on the season), Frank is quite familiar with this common collective belief.

"You know I'm an entrepreneurial bloke. I'm always going for another angle. And I create employment, create wealth. It's good for the economy, and that's not a bad thing, is it? In amongst it all, I care for the blokes that work for me. And I look after them. Probably in a bit of a paternalistic way, and all that rubbish. [But still] I have a tremendous caring feeling for folk along the way of it all."

Yet when he looks hard at this argument, he ultimately finds personal "vanity" underlying most of it.

"But then I think all this economy stuff is a load of crap. It doesn't make anybody better to have more, to be better off. Sure, it stops us from starving and everything. Over and above shelter, protection, warmth, food, and what have you, there's a hell of a lot of vanity after that, isn't there. I mean, I'm just building for myself a bigger, better little kingdom of me own. And is it really making the world a better place to have all this crap in it?"

Even so, he still can't stop his social me from its consuming vanity.

"The crunch comes down to, will the planet take all this plastic that I need? Am I going to kill myself with the pollution just in order to get the plastic? It's crazy isn't it."

Frank has a strongly theological natural other, a theology he links closely with the nature most other villagers emphasized. For him, God too is a natural other, a basis for a natural conscience.

"Man has always had this vanity, being better than their next door neighbors. And it isn't right. The true value of man is, maybe, who he is. And God loves us because he loves us, and that's the value that we have."

Frank is not alone in this—not alone is his view that the "true value of man" is not the materialism of the collective conscience, but "who he is," the *natural me* that, for Frank, comes ultimately from God. But however they find this sense of a truer *me*, a *me* apart from social interests, Childerleyans still must struggle with the continued presence in their minds of society's *me*.

Although the natural conscience is by no means unproblematical for Frank, Ann, Andy, and other villagers, it does give them an additional mental resource for contending with doubt—an alternative landscape in which to plant an identity. Here Childerleyans find fertile soil for their moral souls.

REFLECTIONS

EIGHT

The Foreground and the Background: Class

Within the mind strong fancies work,
A deep delight the bosom thrills . . .
Where, save the rugged road, we find
No appanage of human kind.

William Wordsworth, 1810

I

BEHIND THE COOKS' council house stands an odd-looking shed.
Salvaged materials make up the central section—mismatched
roofing tiles, scrap lumber, a battered door, scratched-up fiber-
glass siding, and a couple of old windows. Two wings lead off it, with
chicken wire walls and roof. The whole structure is about twenty feet long
and uses up almost half of the space in the Cook's back garden. When I
first saw it, I couldn't imagine what it was for.

That was the day I met the Cooks. I had come over for a chat about
the village with Margaret Cook and two neighbor women. After a brief
handshake, Albert Cook cleared out, leaving the rest of us in the sitting
room with our tea. Margaret excused him, explaining that he needed to
work on his "aviary." After her neighbors left, she asked me if I wanted
to see the aviary. I said sure, but I had little idea what she meant or what
it was she was then leading me into the back garden to see. I expected a
smallish outdoor cage with perhaps a few birds, so my eye soon moved
past what to me was a big, meaningless structure. Just then, an enormous
clattering and chirping swelled up from the shed. I noticed the bright
colors flitting about within.

"There's the aviary," said Margaret. "He built it all himself."

Inside I could see Albert doling out bird seed with an old aluminum
pot from a big burlap bag. With each toss of seed across the feeding table
set up in the shed, another few birds screeched and yammered and dove
in for a beak-full.

During a later visit, Margaret actually took me into the aviary, and I   161 eventually entered it perhaps a half dozen times.° For me, it was definitely something one "entered," a clear break from familiar settings, for inside was a world of swirling sounds, colors, and movement I had never before experienced. To get into this world, Margaret took me around the back, through a screen door, and into a kind of airlock. Then she opened another door, and we stepped inside.

Immediately we were in a cloud of birds. There were about seventy-five in the aviary—a dozen Yorkshire canaries, two pairs of cockatiels, six finches, three parakeets, half a dozen pheasant (including "Old George," a glorious golden cock pheasant), and about fifty budgies in various brilliant shades of blue and yellow. Never still, the smaller birds swooped, hopped, darted, and pecked around the roosts and bird boxes which hung from virtually every available bit of wall and ceiling space. Every perch, shoulder, and outstretched hand was soon alive with their constant little movements. Bigger birds like pheasants move more slowly, and they swaggered along the floor, stalking through the hay.

Although the aviary is quite large, seventy-five birds filled this confined space with a sensual density of aural, visual, and tactile stimulation found nowhere else in Childerley. Margaret plunged into a nonstop, chattering conversation with the birds as soon as we entered, which went more or less like this:

"Come right in. Close the door. There we are. You can talk to them, you know. People think it's crazy, but it's true. Come here Billy! You're a pretty bird. Aren't you, aren't you? Yes you are. Come on Joey! Here Billy, Billy! Sing for me!"

She whistled gaily at the birds.

"There you are Ginny. Come on and sing! Come on Johnnie. You're a pretty one, and you know it."

She pointed out the roosts, nesting boxes, and hay bedding to me.

"It's all natural, you know. There's Bobbie! You think you're something, don't you?"

A finch landed on Old George's tail, but he didn't seem to mind. "He'll ride that way all day sometimes," Margaret observed.

As the birds dipped and dived about us, she went on to describe each bird's personality as it flew by. Periodically all the birds would join together for another great swell of singing, which was quite deafening when

---

° Albert Cook never took me in himself, for reasons I am not at all sure of. Ed Lambton, though, twice took me through his own aviary.

they really got going. We left after about ten minutes. I felt the kind of exhilaration one sometimes feels after standing out in a fierce wind storm, letting it buffet you about for a few minutes.

Aviaries are not common in the village. Only three other families maintain one on anything approaching the scale of Albert Cook's, which is the biggest. Yet I have dwelled on Albert Cook's for what I think is a significant reason. All four households with large aviaries identify them-selves with the working class, the ordinary people. The moneyed residents could certainly afford to keep an aviary (many do keep one or two pet birds inside the house), and probably a much grander and populous one than Albert's. But they choose not to.

There is reason behind this choice, this difference. Childerleyans live in "a different world," as Sarah Weller noted earlier, depending upon their class experience. As in communities everywhere, material circumstances condition the cultural fabric of Childerley, resulting in contrasting habits of feeling across the class divide. The back-door spirit of working-class villagers I described as more informal, group-oriented, interactive, local, and experiential. The front-door spirit of the moneyed people I character-ized as more formal, individualistic, private, far-flung, and distanced.

And what goes on in an aviary, it strikes me, is more a back-door kind of experience. I'll elaborate on that later in this chapter. For now, I'd just like to use this observation to introduce the chapter's central point: That there is a class-based spirit to villagers' natural experience. Childerleyans go into nature through the same door they habitually use for their own home and the homes of their friends and family. A pair of words which I think captures much of the difference (and I intend these only as evocative terms, nothing more) is *background* for the moneyed front-door spirit of nature and *foreground* for the ordinary back-door one. (Yes, background does go with front door and foreground with back door.)

I take this finding (and the findings I will report in the following two chapters) as evidence that the social experience of Childerleyans informs their experience of nature. More precisely, it informs their experience of the nonsocial realms they look to for interest-free value—"nature," ani-mals, plants, the countryside, forces outside human influence—the realms I have been calling the natural other. The villagers have not arrived at these correspondences in a deliberately reasoned way. But neither are they accidental. The previous chapters discussed how Childerleyans use the natural other as a cultural resource for resolving the quandaries of identity and motivation that confront them. Correspondences between social experience and the natural other serve to ground identity and motivation in other less conscious ways.

II

THESE CORRESPONDENCES should interest us because of what is charted on a third conceptual map. The existence of similarities in the way a people think about social and nonsocial realms is a widely observed phenomenon. Along with his student (and nephew) Marcel Mauss, Emile Durkheim made one of the first sustained efforts at explaining why this should be so. They suggested that the fundamental origins of thought stem from the organization of social relations. "The first logical categories were social categories," they wrote.

> Furthermore, the ties which unite things of the same group or different groups to each other are themselves conceived as social ties. . . . They are of "the same flesh," the same family. Logical relations are thus, in a sense, domestic relations. . . . The same sentiments which are the basis of domestic, social, and other kinds of organization have been effective in this logical division of things also.[1]

In other words, kinship in the widest sense of the term—that is, the manner in which we determine not only family ties but social ties of all kinds—gives us the root "sentiments" by which we understand our whole world.

This mental process, Durkheim and Mauss claimed, explained correspondences in the way various peoples think about society and such diverse realms as space, time, fauna, and flora. One could point to many examples of these correspondences in the West: The common projection of human society into the world of animals in children's literature. The ascription of mood and emotion to features of the landscape, like the Mad River of Connecticut, the state where I live. The personification of winter with the character Jack Frost, or a mountain with New Hampshire's Old Man of the Mountain. The association of places with authors, like John Muir and the Sierra Nevada, and William Wordsworth and Britain's Lake District. Perhaps even the association of scientific laws of nature with people, like Planck's Constant, Ohm's Law, and Heisenberg's Uncertainty Principle. Even units of measure—Hertz, Kelvin, Watt, Fahrenheit, Volt(a). Or, to choose another example from science, the use of terms like *class, kingdom,* and *family* in taxonomy. Indeed, perhaps the whole idea of basing taxonomy on kinship. These are all socializations of nature.

Karl Marx and Frederick Engels made much the same point in *The German Ideology*.° Knowledge of anything, they held, cannot be separated from human interests, interests that stem from the way a society organizes its means of material production. Ideas have no "independent existence."

> We set out [our theory] from real, active men, and on the basis of their real life-process we demonstrate the development of the ideological reflexes and echoes of this life-process. The phantoms formed in the human brain are also, necessarily, sublimates of their material life process.... The ruling ideas are nothing more than the ideal expression of the dominant material relationships, the dominant material relationships grasped as ideas.[2]

In other words, people's beliefs closely match in form and feel the pattern of their social relations, a pattern set by the structure of the economy—economic relations "grasped as ideas." The classic example of the materialistic approach applied to concepts of nature is Marx and Engels's analysis of Darwin's theory of natural selection. As Marx wrote to Engels in an 1862 letter,

> It is remarkable how Darwin recognizes among beasts and plants his English society with its division of labour, competition, opening up of new markets, "inventions," and the Malthusian "struggle for existence."[3]

Marx and Engels were concerned about this on theoretical and moral grounds. Theoretically, it seemed to them that Darwin saw not nature, but society. They also worried that Darwin's theory served the ideological end of promoting capitalism and the interests of the wealthy—something Marx and Engels saw as both a theoretical and a moral issue. As Engels observed in 1875,

> The whole Darwinist teaching of the struggle for existence is simply a transference from society to nature of Hobbes's doctrine of "bellum omnium contra omnes" and the bourgeois-economic doctrine of competition together with Malthus's theory of population. When this *conjurer's trick* has been performed ... the same theories are

---

° Marx and Engels (1972). Although written half a century before Durkheim and Mauss's *Primitive Classification* appeared in 1903, *The German Ideology* was not published until 1932. However, Marx and Engels got this idea from what Ludwig Feuerbach called "alienation" in *The Essence of Christianity*, first published in 1841.

transferred back again from organic nature into history and it is now claimed that their validity as eternal laws of human society has been proved.[4]

But the basic idea of the materialist approach is the same as that of Durkheim and Mauss: the origin of ideas lies in the pattern of human social relations. For Marx and Engels, the most important source of the structure of those relations is the economy, not kinship.° But they agree on the fundamental point: that social experience is so important to us that it provides the categories and orientations by which we understand and experience everything—the heuristics of thought itself, one could say. A good metaphor for these heuristics is one that writers in both traditions have used: *reflection*.°° Categories originating in ourselves we find looking back at us from what is outside us. In the words of Raymond Williams,

> In the idea of nature is the idea of man; and this not only generally or in ultimate ways, but the idea of man in society, indeed the ideas of kinds of societies.[5]

Reflection theory, if it is correct, raises a very important issue for the effort—tracing the natural conscience of Childerleyans—of this book. If the natural other reflects social experience, then is it really separate from the generalized other? Does the natural conscience really serve as the interest-free alternative to the collective conscience the villagers hope for? Or does the natural conscience actually reinforce social ideas rather than providing an alternative to them, through what Engels called the "conjurer's trick"? The answer, I believe, is that while it accurately portrays much of the cultural landscape in Childerley, reflection theory is too stark, too literal, too deterministic for what is a largely intuitive and casual mental process.

But that argument must wait for the final chapter.

III

I OFTEN ASKED VILLAGERS what their favorite views and places were both in the village and in Britain. Most moneyed villagers, I discovered, have

---

° Indeed, they largely subsumed kinship into relations of material production, seeing the family as the oldest of economic institutions. See Engels (1968).

°° In the words of Marx (1977), 102, "the ideal is nothing but the material world reflected in the mind of man, and translated into forms of thought." Also, see Engels (1968), 602–3; Hubbard (1982), 21; Levi-Strauss (1963), 96.

a more developed aesthetic language for talking about land as landscape. Charles Goddard-Brown's description of his favorite view, the one behind his house, is an example.

"It changes continually, depending entirely on the weather as to what it is. In the fog, in the mist, when the mist lies low, it's almost like an estuary with the fog and the trees moving about in it. In the snow, it's an entirely different view. And as you go through the seasons, because some of it is grassland and some of it is wheat field, you've got a changing color scheme going through it. And you've got a woodland up top which changes from black to a light green, to dark green, to the golds of autumn."

Jim Winter doesn't limit his aesthetic appreciation to pastoral landscapes. He feels that one of the most "scenically interesting" sights in Britain are the vast heaps of slag and mine waste left over from mining and industry.

"I personally think that a lot of industrial slate and mine waste and so on, such as you find in Wales, or the Peak District, they have a certain magnificence about them. Can do. They can have a scenic value. They're a fairly clear statement because they're usually all one material."

A moneyed visitor to the village walked the fields near my house with me. Over the years farmers have removed many hedges in that section of the parish, creating large grain fields up to eighty acres in size. We talked about the ecological problems of hedge removal, as well as the changes it has brought in the land's appearance. He conceded that the traditional character of the land had been lost but argued that in "the proper slant of light" there was a scenic glory to these big fields.

The use of analogies such as "it's almost like an estuary," the appreciation of the "clear statement," the importance of the "slant of light"—these are aspects of moneyed talk about views that I rarely heard from ordinary villagers. Ordinary villagers typically characterized a view as pleasing because it was "peaceful," "so natural," or because it "has such a history about it," and left it at that. Short responses were most common.

Moreover, moneyed villagers were very critical of the quality of views and very concerned about whose houses have "nice views." Charles takes pride in having one of Childerley's best behind his house, a commanding panorama reaching across a deep valley to a high hill beyond.

"A lot of people reckon it's the best view along this end," he confided, "That's the reason I bought this place. . . . The view has hardly changed at all since we've been here. If you look over there at that light patch where the ground wasn't properly sown, well, just there, there used to be a scruffy little stand of trees. And there was a hedge through that field next to it. But aside from that, it really hasn't changed at all. A lot of people are rather envious of our view, I think."

I play banjo and guitar, and one day the head teacher at the village school, Laura Boman, brought me in to play for the children. Afterwards, I had a cup of tea with the teachers in their lounge, while an aide supervised the children in the school yard. As we settled into our chairs, sipping tea and nibbling McVitie's biscuits, one of the teachers, Jane Grace, asked me if I'd heard about the development proposal for the abandoned farm buildings next to my cottage. I hadn't, and she excitedly described the plans.

"Aha! So you don't read your local paper! You should read the planning application section. They are going to pull down all those barns and build four new houses."

Jane's house was in my end of the village, so Laura thought the development might be visible from her house.

"Will it affect your view?" Laura asked her.

"No. Not ours," Jane replied. "If it did, you can be sure I'd be making a loud noise about it."

"You do have a nice view there," said Laura, commiserating.

Jane then gave an explanation of the value of her house to her, an explanation that rang through the words of many moneyed Childerleyans.

"Yes. It is a nice view. That's why we bought the house. We looked at a lot of places, but when we saw that view, we knew we had to have that house." She turned to me and added, no doubt in part for the benefit of all, "Our view is one of the best around."

Working-class Childerleyans are also happy to have a nice view from their house, but they placed less emphasis on it in our conversations. An extreme example is what Audrey Spencer told me about the view from her tied cottage, which is adjacent to the farm where her husband Ted works. Our car wouldn't start (it rarely did), and I went to the Spencers to borrow Ted's battery charger (again). Ted had forgotten to bring it up from his workshop at the farm, so Audrey offered me a cup of tea in recompense. I accepted, and we chatted in the kitchen while she set about making the tea.

Striking up what I intended to be idle conversation, I asked Audrey about the big hedge that grew across their back garden, visible through the window over the sink. The Spencer's cottage stands near the top of Church Hill, and were it not for the hedge, they would have a sweeping view across a mile of fields out the back, the kind of view for which tens of thousands of pounds have exchanged hands. I assumed the farm manager must have planted the hedge for some reason having to do with the farm. As they lived in a tied house, I supposed, they were not allowed to do anything about it. To my surprise, Audrey said that Ted had put it in.

"Yeah. We wanted to get some shelter from the wind so we could sit in the garden in the sun." She laughed and added, "Not that we ever do. It really hasn't worked that well."

My moneyed mind was horrified at this.

"Too bad it blocks the view," I commented.

Audrey shrugged and said, "You still know what's out there."

This kind of reasoning contrasted strongly with what nearly every moneyed villager I spoke to said about why they prized their homes.

When ordinary villagers do talk at length about the view, it tends to be in more utilitarian terms. Tom Fuller takes pride in having a "sensitive side," as he put it, not apparent to some beneath his weather-worn skin. He tried to oblige me with answers to my questions about landscape, I think in part to try to perform in what he considered a moneyed cultural field. But he could only tell me, "It's quite nice to see a nice view. Something relaxing on the brain. It's quite peaceful." He could, however, speak at length about a more utilitarian image of land and the importance of having "a good look around" whenever he goes someplace new—for bearings and the spatial relations of things. Tom has only lived in Childerley a short while, and this is how he described his first impressions of the parish:

"When you come to a new place, the first thing you start registering is, what's the countryside look like? The lay of the land, as we say. When I first came here, the first three or four months, I thought I'd sort myself out. So I looked around here. Had a good look around. Cause when I drive down the road, my eye's always looking, . . . what it looks like, all the time. I can practically tell if [even] a tree's missing. Or there's something out of place."

He searched his mind for an example.

"I think it's down in Axworth. There's a plow or something at one of the junctions. Now if I pass that junction next year, I'll still remember that plow being in there. And if it ain't, I can turn around and tell you it's been moved."

Tom looks at the village's land, and looks at it with care. He takes pride in his detailed knowledge of it. But like most other ordinary villagers, he has a small vocabulary for describing it as landscape.

Perhaps that's in part because most ordinary Childerleyans have seen the village scenes for so much longer (Tom and some others excepted), and these scenes seem therefore less remarkable to them. What they see around the village is still very important to them. But instead of putting mental picture frames around village views, villagers like Ted Spencer (who has lived in Childerley since he was nine) speak of village places more as where things have happened—as sites of story and memory.

One time I went for a walk across the fields with Ted, and he took great delight in pointing out where notable local events had taken place and where things now gone once were. For example, we spent half an hour retracing some of the path he had taken across the parish the time he set out to find a missing village man—who, it turned out, had committed suicide—where he found some of his belongings, the butt of a last ciga-rette, and finally the body. Similarly, Bert Drake enjoyed telling me about the spot where the rector kept on finding used condoms and eventually caught a young village couple in the act. A number of ordinary villagers pointed out the inconspicuous dry stream valley my house sat in, and how it had flooded many years ago, drowning all the pigs in a nearby barn. It happened at night, and the farmworker who then lived in my cottage first noticed it when he got up to a foot of water around his bed. The stories we tell take place in places, and most ordinary Childerleyans live right in the setting of most of their lifetime's accumulated stories. And that makes a difference in what the parish's lands mean to them.[6]

The possessive, room-with-a-view attitude of moneyed residents to-ward land has a strong element of status in it, of course. A key aspect of the value of the view from their homes for Charles and for Jane is their sense that not everyone has one so good. They value their view partly on the basis of how few other people have it—on the envy they sense in others. To the extent that others look at views in the same social light, this restricts the number of people who can have valued views. The "nice view" becomes a positional good, something in short supply that is widely desired and can be possessed. Limited by this criterion, nice views confer honor upon those who have them. Charles and Jane both take pride in being among those few. It's an example of what Thorstein Veblen called "pecuniary beauty"—the nice view is a symbol of wealth, and it looks beautiful in part because of that.[7]

Working-class villagers have positional goods too, but the nice view is a realm of status they have less access to. For one thing, they can rarely choose a home based on its view. Other considerations necessarily figure more prominently, such as the limited (indeed, the shrinking) supply of council properties, tied cottages, and affordable private houses. For another, ordinary villagers travel less. Their mental slide carousel is not as full, so they are not as able to formulate standardized comparisons for evaluating land as a positional good. Many ordinary residents of Childerley have not been out of Hampshire and adjacent counties in several years, and one man had not been further away than Harchester (just nine miles off) since the midsixties.

Sensitive to the honor at stake, moneyed villagers evaluate views with a critical eye. I think a sense of potential threat to status and value can be heard in the criticism Ed Laws, a moneyed villager, expressed to me about his own view. Ed had some books on local history he thought I might be interested in seeing, and I came over to leaf through them. At one point, he popped into the breakfast room where I was reading to see how I was "getting on." We chatted a bit, and I complimented him on how far one could see out the picture window over the breakfast table. He replied, "Yes. But there's that ghastly dairy out there, which they just put in a few years ago."

When the nearby farm expanded its operations, they had to move the dairy out of the center of the village where it had been for probably hundreds of years. The old brick-and-beam barns were "listed buildings," regulated by preservation orders to maintain the village's character. That meant they could not be taken down for a new, bigger dairy. So a modern installation of sheet aluminum with two big bunker silos and a small standing silo were put up down a side lane out in the middle of the fields. A bunker silo, as those familiar with modern dairy farming will know, consists of a poured concrete box open to the air which is filled with silage and covered over by huge sheets of black plastic, weighted down with old tires. Given general attitudes toward concrete, black plastic, and old tires, they are seldom regarded as a pretty sight. All this is in full view of Ed's picture window. I pointed out that they did try to hide it by planting a screen of trees. But this has not satisfied Ed.

"True, but the problem is the type of trees they used. They're not native to this area, so it isn't at all natural. When they built it, there was such an outcry by the residents along the ridge here that they knew they had to plant something. But they put in those foreign cedars. Besides, several of them have died, which has left big gaps, unfortunately one right in front of that hideous silo."

But to say that moneyed people have only their social interests at heart in their concern for landscape quality would be a gross oversimplification. For this would not answer the important question of why this good, of all the many potential limited goods, should be valued so highly by them. The answer, I believe, is that there is something about the taste and feel associated with the front door that pervades moneyed villagers' experience of land as landscape. They have these tastes and feelings apart from their material implications. When Charles Goddard-Brown, Jane Grace, or Ed Laws gaze on a scene, they are not constantly thinking about how they stand to gain from their attitude toward it. They experience these attitudes inwardly. They simply "know" how they feel about some view.

Nor would it be correct to say that moneyed villagers' more vivid language for landscape is simply a product of their greater schooling. Education is indeed important, I suspect, for landscape appreciation is an aspect of the high cultural tastes most schools stress. But this does not explain why moneyed villagers accept these patterns of feeling (for we commonly reject much of what we are taught), nor why moneyed culture emphasizes these tastes and not others.

There is something about the spirit of land as landscape that feels more right to the moneyed villagers. Formality is part of it. Formality implies adherence to standard forms, and to rank landscape quality one must compare the view against the standards in the mental carousel. Evaluating landscape also requires self distancing, a "standing back" from what is "out there." One must mentally break the seamlessness of the environment which connects out there to here so that the view becomes distinct from the self. In so doing, one turns landscape into an object, separate from the subject who views it, an object one can take for one's own. As the geographer Denis Cosgrove put it, "the landscape idea represents a way of seeing, [a way of] appropriating the world through the objectivity accorded to the faculty of sight."[8] In other words, seeing land as landscape is a bit of a power trip, a mental taking possession of all one sees—something that feels right to the socially powerful.

These are speculative matters. The effects of the different spirits of the front door and back door are clearer in the different kinds of landscape villagers like. The conversation I had with Wallace Turnbull is an example. He held a reception for the local Young Farmers Club, and I was invited. It was an unusually hot day, even for July. The reception was outside in their large garden. I longed for a tree to sit and eat under, and noticed that there wasn't a single one. True, their house was relatively new— perhaps twenty years old—but the adjacent barn dated from the 1840s. It then dawned on me how few trees local people typically kept around their houses. This stood in great contrast to areas of the United States with similar rainfall, like the East and Upper Midwest, that I was familiar with. I asked Wallace about this.

"A lot of people here," he replied, "cut down the trees around their houses. I have one friend in the village who just did that. She said they made her feel too enclosed."

I then explained the contrast with America.

"That's very interesting," I said. "In America people want trees because it gives them shade in our summers, which are much hotter than here, of course, but also because they make people feel more secure."

I had no particular basis for suggesting that trees make Americans feel more secure, but Wallace didn't question it. Instead he offered this resolution:

"That's our British psyche you're getting into now. We all feel so surrounded by people all the time that there's no escape. So we don't like feeling enclosed. We want lots of open space, open views."

Yet Audrey Spencer evidently does not have this same feeling. It was only when I talked with moneyed villagers that I heard about this desire for isolation and for privacy. Charles Goddard-Brown praised the view behind his house precisely because it gave him this sense of aloneness.

"I love this view," he remarked. "I think it's the fact that there's nothing manmade in it. No houses at all, except for that one over there. That's what I like. I'm not very keen on my fellow man, you know. I'd rather I had a place with no houses for miles and miles around. And when I look out here I can imagine that we're all alone."

As with Tom Fuller, the eyes of most moneyed villagers are "always looking," but what they look for is the feeling of privacy the landscape conveys to them. Henry Norkett is a middle-aged architect, some fifteen years in Childerley. He grew up in a village on the other side of London. When he was a teenager, he once tried to draw a map of "different feelings of privacy" in the surrounding countryside, as he laughingly explained.

"I think it was privacy. It's an extremely difficult, rather interesting map to draw."

It was only moneyed villagers who described the virtues of the country in such isolationist terms. Albert Bickley was another, as in the story he told of how he and his wife Mary came to buy their house in Childerley.

"We loved it from the first, went up the road so we could see it from on top. It didn't have too many other houses around. You see, we've always lived in the country and never wanted to live close to other people."

Such isolation is getting harder and harder to achieve in southern England, a number of moneyed villagers explained to me. Andy Sparrow complained that more and more people are using the countryside now, disturbing his experience of it.

"[There]'re not the secluded spots that I used to just get regular pleasure from. . . . For years I've walked this countryside. And it's magic to go out in the countryside where you won't meet anybody."

The prizing of privacy adds to the exclusivity of the rural view and of country life, limiting those who can have access to it. But it is more than a material matter. The "magic" of aloneness Andy describes is how it fits the individualistic and distanced feel of front-door life. This is the "deep delight" which thrilled Wordsworth's bosom, and it still thrills Charles Goddard-Brown's too.

"I like my fellow man," said Charles, qualifying an earlier statement of his, "but only as long as he keeps a certain distance."

Not once did an ordinary villager, in discussing village land and the importance of the countryside, mention the importance of privacy and living far from others. Rather than the silent, empty, unpeopled background of the grand view, their attention is more on the foreground—on things that move, that can be approached and interacted with.

Mary Drake, for example, will sit at her kitchen window for hours watching the common wildlife of her own garden.

"I love to hear the dawn chorus, and the cuckoo. I've got me birds in the garden. I've got a pair of doves come on my wall. Where would you get that [in a town]? They might be down presently. They've got a nest up in the Christmas [spruce] tree. They come down here and look in the window at me. Where would you find that? . . . There's four pairs of robins, two out here and two out the back. And I've got a woodpecker comes down for peanuts. Green finches, coal tits, blue tits, you name it. Thrushes, black birds, everything you can think of. They're all out there. I spend hours [watching]."

Mary has been ill and recently spent a month in the hospital. She's doing better now, but her doctor is trying to convince her to live in town closer to medical care.

"Dr. Wilson said, 'Why don't you go have a flat somewhere?' 'You might as well put me in a box,' I said, 'because that's where I'd be after a few [weeks].' I couldn't live in a flat."

She's afraid that in a town she would lose that close, interactive contact with the countryside she enjoys so much.

"I spend hours in the kitchen watching my birds. And you know, they're so cheeky, they don't fly away when I go and put the peanuts out. They perch right there, looking at me right close. I could pick them, pick them off the branch. They're ever so lovely."

Albert Cook is another example. He will take a chair out into the back garden and watch the territorial battles of a couple of squirrels with all the attention and discernment of a wildlife biologist writing a scientific treatise. Although he appears to be looking only casually, Albert doesn't miss a tail twitch. He observes a lot that other people miss (or, rather, that I at least missed while watching backyard wildlife with him). Albert is less attentive to the view in the moneyed sense, and his aviary almost totally blocks it off. That's not where his interests direct his focus. Although he's read a fair number of books on birds and is extremely interested in them, it would never cross Albert's mind to go deliberately bird watching. Like Mary, he finds a density of interest that easily holds his attention right in his own garden, or wherever his travels happen to take him.

I take ordinary villagers' inclinations toward the approachable and storied foreground of animals, plants, and memory to fit well with their interactive and local *habitus*. Moneyed villagers don't ignore these things, but they do keep their eyes more on the horizon. Nor do ordinary villagers ignore the background and the special attraction of the good view. But they have other, stronger interests, and they give these more of their mind.

IV

THE EMPHASIS ON FORMALITY, distance, and individual privacy in the lives of moneyed villagers is immediately apparent when one steps into the gardens they keep. Most of the villagers show an avid interest in their gardens. But there is a marked contrast between the gardens of the wealthier residents and those of most poorer residents.

Moneyed villagers regard John Lane's as a fine example of what a country garden should be. He has a fairly large lot, perhaps an acre and a half, and he does all the work himself. He likes to take people out into it through his solarium, with its antique leaded glass. The door opens onto the stone patio, with its fountain, Grecian marble statue, and border of boxwood topiary. In the center of the garden is a section of grass, as green as could be imagined, perfectly rolled and edged, smoother and fuller than many an indoor carpet. The grass merges into massed plantings of flowers, scented clouds of carefully harmonized colors. First are the low borders of annuals—marigolds, ageratum, pansies—which round away into such taller perennials as delphinium and iris (to mention only those I recognized).

John also grows a lot of vegetables. His patch is away in the back, discreetly screened from the patio and solarium by a bank of high perennials. He keeps a lot of fruit trees back there too, as well as gooseberries and currants, nestled amid the winding grassy paths he maintains. One of these paths leads unexpectedly to a picture-perfect pool of water flowers, with an arched bridge, another Grecian statue, and a shady bench where one can sit in individual contemplation and seclusion. The rest of the back is devoted to a small wilderness of bushes and fruit trees that John has let go wild for the birds (he's an enthusiastic birdwatcher), his equipment shed, and two large compost piles. The whole serves as a fit setting for the jewel that dominates the scene—his seventeenth-century thatched house with antique varieties of roses round the door. Virtually any view of his house and grounds would do for a calendar or postcard of English country scenes, particularly in June.

Although few gardens of the wealthy in the village come up to moneyed standards as well as John's, the same principles of formal gardening guide most of them. Balance, harmony, massing of plantings, and usually one main focus—the house. Different uses are typically strictly isolated from each other. Outdoor seating is nearly always in the back.

For contrast, take the Lambtons' garden. The Lambtons are a retired and much cherished couple among the villagers. Warm and lively, and usually at home, many villagers pointed them out to me as examples of the real country people whose familiar presence typified what a village should be. Rose still works part-time in the village, although she is sixty-eight, and Ed is a retired mechanic. They live in a ramshackle bungalow they own themselves, having bought it twenty years ago before the local housing market entered the stratosphere. At the time it had a leaky roof, no central heat, and no indoor plumbing—not even a sink. Since then Ed has made a lot of improvements, often with salvaged materials. The result is a completely vernacular place, done up by them just the way they like it, within the constraints of their income. They are proud of its quirks, such as the door off the sitting room that goes nowhere, a relic of the room's layout before Ed expanded it years ago—he never got around to taking it down, and now it suits them to leave it. The house is on an oddly shaped lot, small by the standards of fancier places—perhaps five thousand square feet.

They invited me over for tea one sunny Saturday afternoon. When I arrived, Rose was sitting out in the little patch of lawn in front of the house, mending a dressing gown at an old metal garden table with a big umbrella. Their lawn is shaded by a huge old ash tree, around which they have built a circular bench. As I opened the creaky gate she looked up from her work and welcomed me in. Ed was a little late returning from an errand, so she took me around for a tour of the garden until his arrival, when we would have tea.

Already their garden had presented important contrasts with moneyed places. The principal outdoor seating area was in front of the house, not secluded away in the back garden. The view of their house from the road was obscured by the big ash tree and several smaller ones. In full view in the front garden was an old caravan (a camper to Americans) up on blocks, faded, dented, and somewhat rusty, as well as a retired auto in similar condition.

As Rose showed me around, many more contrasts stood out. In place of controlled formalism, the garden was fairly bursting with a kind of dense activeness. Every bit was not only used, but doing something. Instead of massed plantings separated by wide grassy spaces calculated for the framing of the house, there were many small centers of activity and interest. Here the fish pond (an old bathtub sunk into the ground), there the caravan, here the tea table, there the vegetable garden, here a pile of construction debris, there a flourishing bank of roses. Perhaps the right term for it is "multifocused." In such a garden, there is less emphasis than in moneyed gardens on formal boundaries between uses and carefully planned sight lines pointing toward a grand focus.

And rather than creating a still, silent backdrop for the house, the Lambtons have filled their garden with a foreground of animation and talk. The pond water is alive with tadpoles and goldfish. Clustered about the pond, but also scattered everywhere, are arrays of little statues of dogs, leprechauns, children, kittens, badgers, foxes, an old man, and a pair of smiling boots, all brightly painted. Nearby is Ed's aviary, in which there are about sixty-five birds. In back of the house, there's a run with chickens and ducks, cackling and quacking, filling the air with the sounds of liveness. All told the Lambtons inhabit their bit of ground with two ducks, ten hens, four bantams, four goldfish, perhaps a hundred tadpoles, fifty Yorkshire canaries, two parrots, a dozen other birds, and a dog—in addition to the friendly statues and colorful flowers forever talking. The overall effect is of a swirl of excited life, a moving, buzzing, chirping, squawking social group.

A number of ordinary households do not treat their land as the kind of intentional aesthetic space we call a garden, for many of them do not have the cash or leisure time for it. But Rose and Ed love their place and spend much, maybe even most, of their time working on it. They grow nearly all their own fruit and vegetables—potatoes, swedes, beetroot, beans, peas, lettuce, cabbage, carrots, gooseberries, plums, and pears. Most of the conversation over tea, after Ed arrived, was about their plans for improving it.

Not that there are no ordinary villagers who follow formal gardening principles. Many do. Indeed, formal gardening is the most widespread style among them, and in Britain as a whole.° A particular example is Claude Kemish's little postage stamp of a garden in front of his council bungalow. But Claude is a retired gardener from a local estate. Few other ordinary Childerleyans take formal principles as far as moneyed villagers typically do.

Most moneyed villagers would probably consider the Lambton's garden quaint at best, and at worst vulgar. Yet what the Lambtons display in it are simply different principles of gardening, principles that better fit the back-door way. Their multifocused, animated, moving, talking style gives an interactive, less formal, group-oriented liveness and immediacy to their place, feelings quite unlike the formal distance of John Lane's garden of the background.

V

WHY IS IT, THEN, that it is ordinary villagers who keep the big aviaries? My guess is that it is because aviaries conjure up the same spirit that the Lambtons' garden does—a foreground world of conversation and interaction with an informal group, the social group of animals. Standing inside surrounded by birds and their sounds, smells, droppings, colors, and touch, one gets a feeling of being a part of something larger than one's own self. Amid the flitting movements, there is an immediacy of contact with a sociable entity. It is an intimate group which routinely transgresses

---

° See Green and Lawson (1989). By "formal gardening" I do not mean the regimented gardening favored on the Continent. I mean a careful planning of overall effect, within the "picturesque" language of the English gardening tradition.

conventional boundaries of interpersonal spacing and regions of the public self. The birds, of course, have no sense of human formalities, and they fly through visitors' hair, sit on their shoulders, peck at their hands, and defecate on their clothing. Moneyed villagers do not actively reject such sociable informality. But it may well be something with which they feel less comfortable.

The idea that one can talk to animals and plants I also take to fit with a more interactive outlook. Mary Drake told me that she often talks both to her birds and to the plants in her garden.

"I talk to them all, and the flowers. Always have done. Always told them they can please themselves. I put things in and I say, 'If you don't want to grow, it's up to you. I can't do any more for you.' . . . I went out there yesterday doing a bit, cut round the edges and that. And I said, 'Well I'm sorry, you'll have to have a few weeds this year, because I just can't get down and do it.'"

She knows this is not accepted by the scientific, educated crowd. And she takes pride in that.

"I've always been like that," she said. "I'll tell you I go talk out in the churchyard. . . . I think people look at me and think I'm a bit—but I *am* a bit peculiar! Bit peculiar to a lot of people."

Several wealthier villagers also spoke about animals, plants, and places in this personified and communicative way. Emma Barham was one. She told me stories about her two cats for well over an hour one afternoon—their personalities, their moods, their histories, their tastes. She is also a firm believer in the idea that talking to plants will make them grow better. The division between the experience of nature by moneyed and by ordinary villagers is not everywhere sharp. Indeed, it is no sharper than the divisions in their class experiences. (Childerley is more polarized than most settlements in England, and this is perhaps the dominant feature of community life there. But there are a number of people there whose lives and empathies transcend the axis of class in various ways.) And I often had a hard time determining how to "measure" in the manner of the scientist the differences that, for all the overlap, I think were evident in their stories and responses to my questions. The differences lay mainly, I found, in emphasis, style, language, and social context, not always in the topics themselves.

But there were, when they appeared, some ideas and attitudes associated almost exclusively with one door or the other. One was the belief in ghosts and spirits inhabiting Childerley. Ordinary villagers told me a number of ghost stories which I believe reflected their more animated, experiential, and interactive outlook. Sensitive to the declassé and country bumpkin associations of superstitiousness, moneyed villagers whom I spoke to regarded such stories with the formal and distanced eye of science.

For example, moneyed villagers were very skeptical of stories about a haunted section of wood along the main road or the "magic tree" which came down in a recent storm. But they regarded them as quaint, and several wealthier villagers pointed me in the direction of old "locals" who they thought would tell me these stories. I did ask a few ordinary villagers about them, and it is important to note that when I asked Mary Drake, a lifelong resident, about the "magic tree," she was somewhat insulted. The implication of the backwardness of country folk was something she resented. She denied that there ever was such a tree and wanted to know where I had heard such nonsense. But this ancient idea is still favored by several of the ordinary villagers.

Harriet and Edmund Cooper told me two of these stories late one evening at their home. Harriet began.

"Did I ever tell you about the crinoline lady?" I said no, so she went on.

"I went out in the garden one night and there was this lady all dressed in white crinoline. Other people in the village had seen her over near our house too. I saw her twice and Ed saw her once."

Ed broke in.

"I was laying in bed one night and I felt something cold touch me."

"He gave a big scream," said Harriet, "and we all came running from downstairs. There was father looking white as a sheet."

"It was like a big block of ice came down out of the ceiling right on top of me."

"He wouldn't turn the light off the whole night."

At the time, they were living in a very old tied cottage in a different village. Ed went on to tell another story of the spirits that haunted the cottage.

"The floor boards upstairs used to creak just like there was somebody walking across them. You could see the boards shift and move from the sitting room. One evening we had a friend over and he said, 'Who's upstairs?' I said, 'Nobody.' He said, 'Well there must be a dog up there or a cat.' I said, 'No, there's no one there.' He said, 'There's got to be someone there.' I said, 'No. There's absolutely no one up there—not a person or a cat or a dog or anything.' And he said, 'Well, I'm very sorry, but I shan't be coming here no more.'"

"It was a five hundred year-old house," Harriet added, "and it was bound to have a few spirits after all that time."

Childerley too is a house with many spirits. Despite their ambiguous feelings about the importance class should have in their lives, the habits of class animate the nature villagers experience. Taken together, what the residents said about views, animals, gardens, and ghosts amount to a village with (at least) two natural others—one that some villagers enter through the front door, and one that others enter through the back.

NINE

The Pursuit of the Inedible: Politics

I would like to see the foxes on the horseback.

Tom Fuller, 1988

I

IT WAS A beautiful morning—March 17, last day of the 1989–1990 fox hunting season. A local hunting family owns a small pasture directly adjacent to the village green, and here the hunt assembles at eleven in the morning whenever it meets in Childerley. By ten-thirty, the hunters and curious onlookers (like myself) had already begun to collect. There has been some controversy recently about hunt vehicles obstructing traffic on Childerley's narrow lanes. So the thirty or so hunters were riding in on horseback, having parked their Land Rovers and horse boxes (horse trailers to Americans) somewhat out of the village center. By eleven, there was a crowd of perhaps a hundred—and seemingly as many dogs as people. (Hunt people are dog people). The woman standing next to me commented, "It's quite a sight, isn't it? A real spectacle. This is some of the real England."

Enthusiasts call it a sport. A pack of specially bred and trained dogs sets off across the countryside, sniffing for foxes. If they flush one, they chase after it, braying, and try to corner it. A huntsman (who is usually paid) and two whippers-in (who usually are not) guide the hounds from horseback. After them trails the "field," some ten to twenty (or, occasionally, more) riders who charge along behind. Everyone dresses well, and the horses are beautifully groomed. The stated object is to kill the fox.

Eleven o'clock, and then eleven-thirty came and went. The huntsman and hounds still had not arrived, but the contented chatter of the crowd continued unabated. A few thirsty and impatient riders broke out glasses and bottles for an early stirrup cup, a tradition that usually waits for the arrival of the hounds. Then shortly before twelve, a man in full hunt regalia—red top coat, shiny jodhpurs, and black top hat—came thundering up the road on horseback, pulling up at the home of the chairman of

Childerley's parish council, which happens to face the green. A hush of anticipation quieted the crowd, and the rider's voice rang across the assembled group.

"The opposition has blocked the hounds' lorry."

The crowd knew exactly what that meant, and a swell of dismay and indignation began to well up. The rider cut it off with a wave, and called out to the chairman, who was leaning on his gate watching the scene, "Give the police a call—as chairman of the parish!"

Inside scurried the chairman, and the rider thundered back down the road. The crowd palpably roared. Walkie-talkies were produced. People huddled around them. Frowning faces exchanged scowling sentences.

When the little knots of people loosened somewhat, I went up and asked a group of knowledgeable looking men in tweed caps and Barbour coats what was going on.

"The *anties* have blocked in the hounds' lorry at the bottom of Winter Hill. They should lock them up in a horse box and throw them in the sea until the end of the bloody season!"

"They've got no right to block the road."

"They'll soon be paying their poll taxes, and then we'll have seen the last of them!"

I thanked them for their information and wandered off. I had a black Labrador with me, Rascal, a villager's dog I was taking for a walk. We stopped at the fence bordering the field. A woman walking by stopped and patted Rascal's head. "Lovely dog, aren't you. Do you eat anties?"

As the crowd hummed and seethed, a Volkswagen beetle drove up to the green. Two women and a man got out. "Hunt Saboteurs Association" and "Vegetarian for Life" read the women's tee shirts. The man wore no slogan, but the shoulder-length gray hair fringing his bald pate made the same immediate impression on the crowd: "Anties."

An air battle of sorts began. A number of hunters had ridden over to the Horse and Hound, and supporters were ferrying pints out to them to drink on horseback. Several were taking the opportunity of the delay for a smoke. The anties sat down across the road, and stared pointedly at them. One anti struck up a running patter of loud, sarcastic taunts (with an occasional supporting "That's right" from her associates), that went something like this:

"Where are the hounds? Where are they, I wonder? They must be delayed. They should have been here an hour ago. I hope they come soon. I hope you're enjoying your pints and your cigarettes. Keep that right up. That's good for your body, isn't it? You'll go a long time if you keep that up. And keep eating all that meat too. I love it when they catch the fox, don't you? Especially when they rip his tail off and his fur. Then they tear his head off. I think that's a bit cruel, don't you?"

The hunters jocularly toasted them and flashed saccharine smiles in their direction. A few started to yell back, but were quieted by their fellows.

Tom Manning, a village hunt supporter, offered to give me a lift down to the bottom of Winter Hill to see the blockade. On the way Tom observed, "They really don't know anything about it, do they? It doesn't mean anything to them. They're just a few college students making fifteen bob for the day. It's really just a job for them."

We got there in time to see the police hustling the last of the blockaders back into the two old Land Rovers and rusty van they had come in and used to block the road. We didn't see it, but they must have somehow gotten a vehicle in front of and behind the hounds' lorry, preventing the hunters from either moving the lorry or unloading the hounds from the back. The police were taking names, but not arresting anyone. A few people in hunting clothes were huddled in a knot near the hounds' lorry, waiting for the police to clear things up.

Tom took me back up the hill. Just as I was helping Rascal out of the back of Tom's station wagon, the crowd heaved a collective sigh of relief. A police motorcycle fore and aft, the hounds and the huntsman came trotting up the road. The tense scene at the pub dissolved, and the crowd's attention jubilantly returned to the pasture where the hunters made their final preparations (which mainly consisted of another stirrup cup all round).

The anties weren't through, though. Their two old Land Rovers and van pulled up, and the blockaders piled out—twenty men and women in combat fatigues, boots, tee shirts, and a range of oppositional hair styles, from crew cuts and purple hair to men with pony tails. But before they could organize another blockade, the hunters tossed back their cups and followed the hounds down the lane. Still, the anties made sure that the chorus of shouts they rode through was liberally mixed with boos.

Fox hunting has long been controversial. Years ago Oscar Wilde labeled it "the pursuit of the inedible by the unspeakable," a phrase that still rings in the ears of everyone on all sides of the debate.° For many Childerleyans, it remains a sore point in village life. Although only a few

---

° The actual line is "the unspeakable in full pursuit of the uneatable," from act 1 of *A Woman of No Importance.* But I never heard it that way.

have ever engaged in overt antihunt actions, many vigorously oppose this and other legal "blood sports," such as hare-coursing, pheasant shoots, the otter and stag hunts, ferreting, and even fishing. And many warmly support them.

I discussed blood sports, and particularly the fox hunt, with a great many villagers. An ideological conflict over political values, values closely associated with villagers' class experience, rang through their disagreements about blood sports. Close parallels, I found, exist between the political values of villagers and the meaning of nature they felt hunting demonstrates. The previous chapter explored parallels between Childerleyans' experience of the natural other and their class experience. There is also a political spirit to the natural other each villager sees, spirits I found especially evident in their varying views on the fox hunt.

II

SOME RURAL IMAGES are well settled in the global imagination. The vast grain fields and towering silos of the American Midwest, the canals and windmills of Holland, the upland rice paddies of Indonesia—these are widely recognized rural visions. Another is the English fox hunt. Throughout the Anglo-American world, one encounters prints of English hunting scenes on the walls of libraries, private homes, and corporate conference rooms. A red jacketed huntsman on horseback leaping a hedge; the hounds and field of riders thundering away in "full cry"; a fox poised in the foreground, deciding on an escape route, the hunters and horses in the distance.

"Some of the real England," that woman at the hunt told me, and perhaps she was more right than she knew. For in the real England, the place of the fox hunt is hotly contested, as it was that hunt day in Childerley. It is not hard to see why, at least in part. Fox hunting is an expensive sport, long associated with the aristocracy and wealthy elites. A well-organized hunt requires a pack of dogs, a dog trainer, a huntsman, and a kennel. Hunt participants must pay stiff fees to offset these costs, in addition to paying for their own horse, its stabling costs, a horse trailer, a vehicle to pull it, and other costs like hunt clothing. Few in England are unaware of these class overtones. And in the postwar debate over the place of class in British society, the hunt has become a potent symbol of what all the argument is about.

Childerleyans don't mistake the class dimension of the hunt—the "social" aspect, as several villagers referred to it. Purely on these grounds we might expect more support for the hunt from conservative villagers, and less from the others. And in fact, among the residents I spoke with, hunt supporters were all politically conservative people (although not all conservatives supported the hunt). Villagers on the left were all opposed to it. I encountered no exception to this.°

I pointed this finding out to several villagers. It didn't surprise them, but such consistency is rare in fieldwork. It exists in this case because villagers understand the hunt at more than just a "social" level. The significance of the hunt lies as well in something the villagers are not consciously aware of: The striking parallels that exist between their political philosophies and the way they justify their views on hunting, their natural philosophies of the hunt. As Clifford Geertz said in another context, "it is a story they tell themselves about themselves."°° More precisely, it is a *set of stories* they tell themselves about themselves. What makes the hunt so compelling is that many different stories can be told through it, a quality of many a good tale.

III

WE'LL BEGIN WITH the conservative hunt supporters, and with their politics first.

What do I mean by "conservative"? A simple guide is that of political party and voting record, or membership in organizations like the village Conservative Club. As far as I could determine (people were not always forthcoming about politics with me), all the village hunt supporters qualify as conservative by this measure. But people vote the same way for a variety of reasons, and parties encompass a range of ideologies. More significant are the little tales and statements and questions villagers often offered to me, and I to them, by which we felt out how our moral boundaries corresponded, a feature of small talk everywhere.

° In this the villagers closely match the way their Members of Parliament voted on the Wild Mammals Protection Bill, introduced by Labour M.P. Kevin McNamara on February 14, 1992. The bill sought to ban the hunting of foxes with dogs, and went down by only 12 votes. Every Labour M.P. supported the bill, and the overwhelming majority of Conservatives opposed it, although about 10 percent broke ranks and voted in support. A national poll taken at about that time found 80 percent of the British public supported it as well.

°° In this much-cited passage, Geertz (1973) was speaking about the Balinese enthusiasm for cock fights, a practice whose use of natural metaphors for social understanding bears a surprising resemblance to the English fox hunt, separated though it is by culture and continent.

The conversations I had with Dorothy Cantelupe are a case in point. At eighty-seven, she is one of the oldest residents of the village. Never married, she lives alone in the same gracious house she has lived in since the 1930s. Reputedly a distant cousin of royalty, she carries herself with a grand yet easy grace. All the residents of Childerley hold her in high esteem as one of those who have indeed "got it proper." She is universally known as Miss Cantelupe.

Up until only a very few years ago, Miss Cantelupe rode regularly with the local hunt. She was once a famous horsewoman and stories still circulate of her sidesaddle jumps over hedge and fence. Although she doesn't ride anymore, she still follows the hunt avidly. The first time I met her was on a rotten hunting day in January, 1988, a day of cold, dark, clammy rain. Despite the weather, a small group of supporters walked the lanes and footpaths, following the hunt's progress. I tagged along, cursing. The rain had turned the footpaths into that specialty of England's chalk downs—a deep, grasping mud that relentlessly crawls up the inside of your legs. I slogged up one hill, only to meet Miss Cantelupe at the top, calmly walking her two terriers.

She had heard of my presence in the village, and invited me to tea. At the appointed time, I came by. Her front door opened into a dark hallway, hung with huge canvasses of hunting scenes in gilt frames, the biggest about five feet wide. She led me down the hall into a sunlit sitting room with stiff antique furniture and a grand piano. After the tea was served, she brought out some old books about the history of the hunt, which she thought might interest me, plus a scrap book with pictures of her riding sidesaddle. Although I am no fan of the hunt, I admired the books just the same, concentrating on the aspects I could appreciate along with her, such as the quality of the horses and the personalities of some of the hunt people she has known. Miss Cantelupe's years of participation in the hunt had meant a lot to her and were still central to how she thought about herself. The sidesaddle pictures showed her as active yet feminine. The books reflected her countryness and social graces.

As we talked, she expressed some of her views on a range of topics. The gentility of the past of lord and laborer; the incapacity of blacks in South Africa to govern themselves ("Don't you think?"); the problem of the lack of service in today's society; the passing of tradition and politeness.

Miss Cantelupe is a proponent of what I earlier described as *status conservatism,* real old Tory "blue" conservatism.[1] Other hunt supporters in the village echoed her fears about the threats to ascriptive hierarchies in much of social life. They worried about dual earner couples in the village and about several unmarried couples. They spoke about the importance of "Victorian values" and criticized the debasement of (even conservative) politics by the upwardly mobile. Alice Gilbert, for instance, complained about the U.S. political system for allowing a man like Ronald Reagan into office.

"I think the whole thing [in America] is too much based on money," she said. "Don't you agree? . . . Here is a man who's been in the country for two or three generations at the most, and now [1988] he's got the most powerful and important position in the world. How can one expect to get the best people for president when things are organized that way?"

Most hunt supporters also spoke of the importance of the *economic conservatism* of the free market.[2] They advocated opening up competition, clamping down on the power of unions, and other probusiness policies. And they overwhelmingly supported the poll tax, the Thatcher government's controversial change in local tax collection that introduced an essentially flat, annual charge per adult.°

"Anything I've got," proclaimed John Bone, "I've worked for. And I'm comfortable now . . . But I worked. Lots of people now are too bloody idle to work. I've got no sympathy for them. See, the Lord looks after them that helps themselves. There is that saying, and I think there's a lot in it. And if you don't, you're going to sink in the mire. No one is going to look after you. You've got to live up to yourself. And this is precisely what I did.

"It's like this poll tax business," John Bone continued. "I think it's a marvelous idea. I mean, I'm better off. My [current taxes] here are nearly 500 pounds a year, so I'll save about a hundred and fifty. Which is peanuts in a way. What I think is nice, it means that everybody is having a fair crack at the whip, paying a fair proportion to what they are going to get. Why should I subsidize everybody else?"

"You must be responsible for yourself," said Frank Steers. "Let [industries] feel the edge of the market. Let them be competitive. Let them get rid of all that dead labor. That's how I see the country going, whether you agree with it or not."

What these villagers see is a kind of tough reality to the fair and proper ordering of life. They see an unflinching responsibility in the way

° The system it replaced was known as the "rates," a form of property tax, which was assessed without regard to the number of adults in a property-owning household. Under John Major, the poll tax has been abolished.

the "edge of the market" gets rid of "dead labor," a firmness which benefits everyone in the end by making the economy more efficient and competitive. It works through the egalitarian mode of giving everyone "a fair
crack at the whip," making everyone "live up to yourself." Most hunt
supporters mix economic with status conservatism, some emphasizing one,
some the other.

They see something very similar in the nature revealed in the fox and
the hunt. One of the oldest charges leveled against the hunt is that it is
cruel.[3] But hunt supporters would put quotation marks around the word.
The hunt may seem "cruel," but it is just a part of the inevitable pain-
fulness of life.

"They say, 'It's cruel,'" said Miss Cantelupe. "The whole world is
'cruel.' One animal is always eating another. If a rat ran across this room
to the fireplace I bet we'd be up pretty quick to kill it with the poker. I
know I would. I've even done it. That's just the way life is."

John Bone also saw unavoidable suffering in nature.

"Would you say that nature is cruel?" I had asked. "Or is there cruelty
in nature?"

"Well, life is cruel. No, I wouldn't say nature is."

John paused and considered our words for a moment. There was
something about the spin I'd given them which he didn't agree with. O.K.,
call nature "cruel," he seemed to decide, but only in a certain way.

"I mean," he said, "[the terrible cold] last January was 'cruel.' It's
like, shall we say, partridges eating insects. They're eating those poor
things alive! As an actual fact, insects are a primitive form of life. They
must have some form of feeling. Can't be very nice being picked up and
eaten, can it? . . . It goes right through the whole spectrum, doesn't it?"

Critics and supporters spin the word *cruel* back and forth. (We will
hear more on the spin that critics give it a bit later.) For supporters,
cruelty as hunt critics mean it does not apply to the hunt, as there is
nothing unusual about the pain the hunt causes. In fact, that pain is
actually good for the fox.

Alice Barnes, housewife, mother of two, and ardent admirer of Mrs.
Thatcher, explained the point.

"It really is much the most humane way to control the fox population,"
she said. "Some people don't understand and think the hunt is 'cruel.'
But it is very good for the breed. Each hunt selects out the weakest foxes."

"It's conservation by destruction, if you get what I mean," said Steve
Kidder.

This quasi-economic Darwinist theme came up many times in the words of the village's hunt supporters. Hunting provides the fox, as well as the hounds and horses, with competition, the necessary source of improvement for all species. Without competition, species would decline. With competition, blood lines progressively improve.

Both these issues—cruelty and competition—come together vividly for many Childerleyans in a story I heard over and again from them: the ancient tale of the fox in the chicken coop. Foxes do get in Childerley's chicken coops, of course, as they have long done, but there are many ways to understand their actions. Here are two tellings from village hunt supporters.

"I don't have any sympathy for the fox," said Alice Barnes. "It's a very cruel animal. It kills for pleasure. For example, just this past summer I came out into our duck pen and found that a fox had killed them all but not eaten any. It had bit off their heads, but then, finding it couldn't get them out of the pen, just left them there. It was a shame, a waste. I can't approve of an animal that doesn't kill for food."

"I've been in the situation when I've had a few chickens and the fox's got in," said Tom Manning. "And if it was to take one chicken and eat it, you wouldn't mind. But they get in and kill twenty chickens, and drag one away. They really only kill for the sake of it."

Alice and Tom were trying to make several related points, I think. First, they were arguing that competitive slaughter is a simple fact of nature, and the fox's habits prove it. Second, these stories suggest to them that the fox actually overdoes it. There is a kind of immoral greed in the way the fox exceeds the bounds of necessary killing. And when it exceeds these bounds, the fox can be justly considered "cruel." Third, the hunt actually reduces cruelty, contrary to what critics say. It restores the competitive balance of nature's proper order by trying to control the fox.

There may have been another point, I sometimes speculated. It's the rich who have a full coop of chickens. It's the working-class fox who preys upon its contents. You wouldn't mind if they only took one chicken, but why should we subsidize their lazy greed? What the fox needs is a good chase, like everyone else.

I may well be inventing this unconscious class message. (I am not, after all, sympathetic to fox hunting.) But certainly hunt supporters do see a hierarchy in nature. Despite the egalitarian play of the free, competitive nature they envision (or perhaps because of it), these villagers assign various aspects of creation to different moral levels—nature as status. Frank Booker, who runs one of the largest farms in the village, supports the hunt by giving it access to his land. I encountered him one day "feeding the rats," as he put it, behind an unused shed on his farm. By that he meant poisoning them. I joked amiably with him about it, but he evidently still worried that I might be one of those animal rights types who would not understand the need for rat control.

"I don't think animals can be considered on the same level as humans," he therefore explained. "It was never meant to be that way. So I 'feed' these rats with a clear conscience."

Although no one I talked to made this point explicitly, there does seem to be a clear hierarchy in the hunt. At the bottom is the quarry, the "vermin," as hunt enthusiasts routinely described the fox. Next are the hounds, who do the dirty work of chasing, cornering, and killing the fox. Above them are the horses. And above the horses, humans.

I debated the issue of a hierarchy in nature with John Bone one afternoon. We sat in John's kitchen. Lady, his constant companion, was at his feet.

"Some people I've talked to have spoken about nature as if everything in it was equal," I said. "Their dog is at the same level as people are, people are at the same level as all the animals. They also have equal rights in the world. . . . Would that be your own view . . .?"

"That's something I've never thought about," John replied. "I don't suppose so. Lady and I, we get on well together. But if she misbehaves, she gets a thundering good hiding from me! She knows she's wrong. And we'll have a real set to. As long as she does what she wants and what I want her to, that's all right. If she doesn't, well then she's in for it. I appreciate that we all came into this world in some form of evolution. . . But I don't know if I'd say equal rights."

"People who talk about equal rights extend that into saying we don't have a right to kill animals."

"But what about the fox going in and killing all the chickens? It is survival of the fittest, isn't it? . . . And what's really crueler than that? The people who go and buy their rump steak, which has been reared for that, and sent to an abattoir and killed for them. People say you shouldn't kill, because it's cruel. But it's all the same. [At work], people knew I was from the country . . . They knew I shot, and they said how cruel I was. So I said to them, 'Well, I'll tell you what. You enjoy rump steaks and lamb chops?' 'Oh yes. But that's different.' 'You come to the abattoir with me and see them being slaughtered.' And not one person did. Not one person had the courage."

The story hunt supporters tell is of the necessary pain and hierarchy of nature—"the way life is" in a "survival of the fittest" world. The gutty facts of the abattoir may seem hard-hearted, these villagers argued, but they are truth, however unpleasant. Gordon Ives put it in the most direct human terms, showing the relevance of this hard, hierarchical natural other to social issues. We were relaxing in his living room after a sumptuous post-church Sunday lunch. The subject of international relief efforts came up. Gordon argued that they were in fact pointless.

"We see the plight of these refugees portrayed graphically on our screens," he said. "But there is little we can do individually to alleviate their suffering. . . . The strong will always come out on top—which was the message contained in *The Origin of the Species*. Survival of the fittest. That's the philosophy of the animal kingdom. It's a tragedy now being reenacted in human terms in our so-called modern world."

In their reading of nature, hunt supporters like Gordon Ives, John Bone, and Miss Cantelupe find confirmation for their conception of the moral universe. This universe contains a harsh truth, that life is constituted through struggle and domination. Moreover, that struggle is good. Like the invisible hand of the market, it improves all the participants by forcing them to compete. The natural order, like traditional values, is the product of this age-old struggle. Hence, these villagers seem to be telling themselves, we have hierarchy in nature as in society. The starry-eyed idealism of the left-wing universe fails because, lily-livered, it refuses to confront this reality. It refuses to confront the grim instinctual truth of the fox hunt and the abattoir, of nature's reddened tooth, as it quixotically advocates reforms of these basic principles of life.

IV

VILLAGERS ON THE LEFT tell a different story.

Andy Sparrow, the school teacher, has rarely given the Conservatives his vote. He has often voted Labour in the past, but says he "wouldn't vote Labour now." He calls himself an "armchair socialist." He votes "for the person, not the party," which usually means he goes with the Liberal Democrats these days.

He still worries, though, about "commercial irresponsibility" and the "merciless" capitalist system. "The system just doesn't take account of failure," he says. "It only worships success." He says that capitalism isn't "going to be a valid answer to society's problems very much longer—unless it's modified." But at the same time, he now rejects "socialism as it was practiced in this country." He finds that "it created people who are robbed of the incentive of looking after themselves." Of Mrs. Thatcher, Andy says "whereas I don't like her, I admire her." And he grants that she has "done a lot of good for the country," but cautions that it has only come "at a price." He worries about the continued class polarization of a status-conscious society and prides himself in being "more fluid in my relationships" than most other villagers.

To put it simply, Andy is not a radical, but his politics are far to the left of village hunt supporters'. And Andy strongly disapproves of the hunt.

"I'm not keen on blood sports," he told me. "I can understand that man in his development was a hunting creature, and that was a very essential part of his life style. And that is still quite strong in us, as human beings. But societies have grown increasingly complex and the world has grown increasingly small and the natural world is more and more threatened by human development and the human species. And I see less and less place for that. It's no longer a necessity for life, or as a sport."

Significantly, Andy links the hunt to the human threat to the natural world. Along with many hunt supporters, as well as other opponents, he worries about what villagers often called a "balance." Hunters say that their role is to protect that balance through limiting the fox population. Andy concedes that "a certain amount of hunting is probably necessary to keep a balance." But he also notes that "human beings have destroyed the balance of the world." In addition, what most human beings regard as balance "is only the status quo." He extends this critique of human ascendancy into his experiences traveling in Africa in the sixties and the threat to wildlife there now.

"I used to wander around in the bush and see elk and African elephants and rhinoceroses and all this sort of thing. And they might be extinct! My children may never see the animals that I loved seeing."

Andy did not discuss the issue of cruelty with me, but many other hunt critics in the village did. Reverend William Cazalet was one. The son of a union organizer from the north of England, Bill retains much of his father's sympathy for the condition of ordinary people. While not a socialist, Bill was a strong liberal voice in the village for breaking down the social barriers between the front door and the back door and for bringing affordable housing to the village. Indeed, given his prominent position in the village, his was the strongest voice from the left.

During an interview in his study, which, like his hair, was perennially disheveled, I asked him about the view many hunters expressed that, as the fox is a cruel animal, there needs to be a hunt. "Two wrongs don't make a right," the Rector replied, giving considerable moral ground to the hunt in calling the fox's actions wrong, while still condemning the hunt. He went on to tell a different story of the fox in the chicken coop.

"The fox is a vicious animal. I reckon if a fox only killed for food, we wouldn't have half the problem. The Longs, they had a hundred and fifty chickens, and one fox, and it was only one fox, clobbered eighty of them. And only took five. And they actually went in one end of the barn as it was going out the other end and saw it go chop, chop, chop, chop, down about ten heads. And all the rest were just left. Now that causes great anger against the fox."

A hunt supporter would have said as much. Yet the rector went on to argue that this might not be cruelty.

"But in a way, one of the things people have looked at, psychologists and fox scientists and all this, [is] that it's the flapping of the wings of the chicken that drives this to a blood lust thing. So is it cruel? Is the fox being cruel, or is it some trigger being set off that it just does it as a natural reaction?"

Furthermore, explained the rector, whether the fox is, "cruel or whether it isn't cruel, it should be dealt with in the most humane way you can. With a hunt you can chase a fox for a good couple of hours and he's gone. And you've just frightened the poor thing to death for two hours."

In arguing that the fox dies a quick, humane death when the huntsman throws it to the hounds, hunters avoid mention of the chase, something which hunt critics often brought up. (I confronted one hunt supporter with this point once, and she replied that the fox actually enjoys the chase, supporting this with the observation that the fox sometimes pauses in the chase and waits for the hounds to catch up, teasing the field of hunters. Hunt critics, I suspect, would counter that the exhausted fox is desperately trying to catch its breath.) Bill agrees that sometimes foxes do need to be controlled. And he says that personally he would shoot a fox because then "you know you've got it." But he abhors the cruelty, as he sees it, of the chase. He drew a parallel with the tiger, another "vicious" animal.

"If you get a tiger, and it's a man eater, that's a vicious thing. The thing you've got to do is make sure you kill it. Not go out and chip a bit off around the hump 'til he drops dead of exhaustion. You don't want to go around wounding the thing and making it suffer for all it's done."

Ruth Hill goes further. She began with the same explanation of the merely apparent cruelty of the fox.

"Why should they be cruel?" she argued to me and to her husband, Robert, who was also present. "I don't understand how a wild animal could be cruel. If a fox gets into a pen that's full of chickens, it'll go mad. It'll kill them all because it gets penned in and it gets frightened by the clucking and everything! I think if [pens are left] open, it'll go in and get them one by one. And it won't cause a lot of destruction."

In nature, Ruth went on to say, there is no cruelty. It is humans that bring cruelty into the world.

"There are wild animals everywhere, but whether you can actually say they're cruel, well no one knows. Man, man, man can be cruel! And that's how an animal can have cruelty done to it."

"Some people would not like to watch a lion bring down an antelope," said Robert, goading her.

"But you can't call it 'cruel,'" Ruth responded. "That's the wrong word. That's not being cruel, is it? A man shooting a lion because he wants to take it home and say 'I shot this' perhaps is cruel. Because it's sport. It's not killing for food. Wild animals kill to eat."

Back when he was a hunter, Nigel Brown explained, he used to get a "thrill" and "a bit of a kick" out of shooting, but now he's "seen the darker side of it." He argued that people do get a kind of pleasure out of blood sports, and that it is not a wholesome one.

"I'd never really thought about it before. I accepted blood sports as something that happened in the country, a bit of fun. Now I don't think it's very nice to take life and get fun out of it. Sure, kill an animal for food at a slaughter house. But, I mean, when it comes to taking pleasure in it, it's something different."

Nigel has not voted yet, but he inclines to socially conscious "Christian ideals," as he calls them. He finds little Christianity in blood sports.

"In the recent months, I've been kind of thinking about what should Christian ideals be. It's just a topic that came to mind just a few months ago, just this winter. Should I approve of blood sports? Should I carry on myself mindlessly shooting birds? I mean, what's the point in it? Is it good, is it bad? And that's the conclusion I came to. It's not right.

"As far as I can see, it's a bit of a joke," he continued. "O.K., it's a bit of fun for the people that do it. People go there to be seen with their red coats and their nice horse. It's a social event. [But] I think people could get together for another reason, rather than mindlessly chasing foxes to kill them."

But neither Nigel, Ruth, the Rector, nor Andy advocates actually banning the hunt. And they all expressed reservations about the activities of anties, particularly the most radical of them, the hunt saboteurs or "sabs." As the Rector explained, the hunters "can be very obstreperous, and think they own the whole countryside. In actual fact, some of the local police that have got to stand at the side and be unbiased arbiters sometimes feel they could quite happily clobber some of the hunt people. Quite happily. But on the other side," he went on to point out, "the hunt saboteurs, some of them do go a bit mad. There was one case of a hunt saboteur clobbering the dogs which were doing the hunting. And they're saying we're trying to save the fox, a dog, and they're doing it by injuring the [hunt] dogs! In some cases, actually killing some of the [hunt] dogs, which I found was absolutely ludicrous."

Ann Martin is one of the few villagers who both support banning the fox hunt and publicly protest against it. She even considers herself an anti. Although she has never sabotaged a hunt, she supports most of what the sabs have done. No socialist, she still sharply criticizes the direction in which the Tories have taken Britain. Ann voted for Mrs. Thatcher in 1979 ("it was such a thrill to vote for a woman"), but not since. She describes herself as "sort of a middle liner," and likes to switch her vote from one party to another. "If I have a political belief," she once told me, "it's that there should [always] be a powerful opposition." Recently she has voted Labour and Green.

I dropped over to her house a week before one of the local hunt's meets in Childerley. I mentioned the upcoming meet. She hadn't heard about it, and excitedly thanked me for the news. "I'll be there," she promised, "but with my R.S.P.C.A. buttons." (That's the Royal Society for the Prevention of Cruelty to Animals.)

On the day of the hunt, Ann was there with her buttons and with two friends from the Winford R.S.P.C.A. By the time I arrived, most of the crowd of hunters, support people, and onlookers had already gathered. Ann and her friends were busy photographing traffic violations committed by all the hunt vehicles. Parked along the verges on both sides, they had nearly closed the road. The photographing made Ann and her friends rather unpopular. A hunt supporter turned to Ann and spat out, "Where I come from, they shoot vermin." Ann spat right back, "So how come you're still around?"

One of Ann's R.S.P.C.A. friends, Mary Singleton, then came up to me. (Ann later described her as midforties, a bit of a socialist, and a very active hunt protester who has even gotten herself arrested several times.) Mary asked me what I thought about the hunt. I replied that, as a foreigner, I thought it wasn't my place to say. Mary was not in the mood for neutrality. She hotly demanded, "Not your place to say about cruelty?"

"Well," I then truthfully answered, "I do think the whole thing is a bit extreme."

"That it certainly is," she went on. "It's downright cruel, something out of the dark ages. I hope you see this is not typical of England. It's the worst thing we do. It's absolutely despicable. And the majority of people oppose it. But still it goes on."

I suggested that it also wasn't a very effective means of fox control.

"In fact," said Mary in agreement, "it has just the opposite effect. If the hunt people knew anything about fox ecology, they'd know that killing foxes actually increases their population. Foxes have the most beautiful system for balancing their population naturally that hunting upsets. If there is space for a fox, several will move in from elsewhere. And when the population gets too high, the vixen raises fewer of her cubs. Oh, they are such adorable things, the cubs."

Ann and Mary went on to try to convince me of the barbarism of the hunt. Often the "brush," the fox's tail, is cut off before the fox is thrown to the hounds, when the animal is still alive, so as not to spoil its trophy value.

Mary described one hunt where "someone got a picture of them throwing the fox to the hounds. You could see that the brush had been removed. Anyway, it was shown to a vet who said very definitely that that fox was still alive."

I later had several long conversations with Ann about her antihunt views. In Ann's analysis, the core of hunting are "these people of a strata," the real upper class. "They live by tradition," she observes, "and therefore they are related to traditional activities." But for the bulk of riders, the middle classes, it's merely a social thing.

"There's the belief that [hunters] are the better strata of society, so they [the middle classes] wish to be seen with them. . . . So they can be seen to associate with these people who actually have money and power. . . . So they keep themselves, you know, very much in the category of moving among the moneyed people."

She says it is only a minority of hunters, "ten percent," who do it because they "enjoy killing."

"They are the ones who pursue the fox. They are the ones who tell the terrier man to dig it out of its hole. . . . And so there is that element in a number of human beings, very sadly."

Ann accuses these people of a perverted eroticism.

"If you have the misfortune, as I did once, to actually be down and see this hard core as they're moving in, their faces are drawn. The flesh is drawn in. The bones stand out. It is an orgasm. And this small hard core—and some of the people who come in cars, [who] may be falling over fences, they're so hoping to see it—are desperate to see the creature turn [to the hounds] and then be torn apart. They are desperate to see it."

She compared the eroticism of fox hunting to the Holocaust.

"And it is massively offensive to me that I am a member of a living order who are willing to do this. It is as offensive to me as the Germans and the Holocaust. It is that. It is exactly that. I see these people lining the Jews up and making them take their clothes off and all this sort of thing, and the pleasure they got out of it."

When the hunt comes to Childerley, an almost overcoming outrage possesses Ann, as she described to me a few days before one hunt.

"It so hurts me that I cannot bear it. . . I feel this all day as they're going round. It tears me apart. It beguts me, and I can't bear it! And I'm dominated by it! To think that another human being chooses to do this. . . . Already it's building up in me. Saturday, it's in my mind. . . . It's only Tuesday and already I'm waiting for it. And it can destroy me."

Like some other hunt critics, Ann suggests that the local hunt should instead set up a "drag hunt" or a "mock hunt." In a drag hunt, someone goes out the day before and drags an aniseed-soaked rag through the countryside, and the hounds try to track its lingering scent. In a mock hunt, one rider dresses like a fox, others dress like hounds, and they chase each other with the "field" of other riders following behind, as in a traditional hunt. "You can still wear your killer gear, as I call it," Ann taunts.

Like Ruth and the rector, Ann rejects the argument of hunters that the fox is a cruel animal. She doesn't deny that animals kill each other, and that in a way this is cruel.

"Nature is very cruel, isn't it, in a sense," she said. "But it's only driven to it through its own need. Because without one animal going for another, it wouldn't feed most of them."

"Cruel in what sense?"

"Well, cruel in that the fox will kill the rabbit because it needs food, and sees it as food. And doesn't see it as another creature which has fear and pain and those things. So far as we can tell."

"Does that justify the fox's actions?"

"Yeah. If it has to, in the sense that it has to live. . . . One can't move into a fantasy world where I say all animals will survive eating grass. . . . The fox is only cruel to the creature it needs to eat, if that is cruelty."

Ann agrees that all creatures, including humans, have a quasi-economic need to do what they must to survive. But this is a very different matter from killing for pleasure.

"In the natural order there is a lot of cruelty like foxes eat rabbits. But foxes don't eat rabbits for fun. . . . Every animal is in the food chain, isn't it. But they don't do it for a great, celebrated pleasure."

Moreover, humans are wrong to count themselves in some way superior to the rest of life.

"I consider all living things equal, just as equal to existence. [We're] just another creature. People say, but ah, the great intelligence and the things that human beings have done. [But] how can I say that I'm more intelligent than [a fox]? I couldn't survive like a fox out there in the fields. So it must be intelligent. So all humans are, I suppose, is very smart at being human beings. I mean, is it so clever to get to the moon? It was only dust when they got there."

This is a point that Andy also made.

"I don't really hold at the end of the day," he said, "with the idea that man is especially God-chosen compared with the rest of nature. I don't hold with the premise that man actually necessarily will be here forever, or that we've got any guaranteed right or position as a species on earth."

"Wild animals," Ruth also argued, "like say a fox, have as much right to the countryside as people do."

In all this I think these villagers find powerful parallels with their political views. They do not deny that there is killing and death in nature, although that troubles many of them. But in nature this is never a matter of pleasure. Animals satisfy no inner need for a sense of power in killing each other—just an inner need for food. Power over others is a human pleasure. It is also wrong, they suggest. We are entitled to survival like any other species, but not moral and ecological superiority.

Their story, then, is that the human pleasure of domination corrupts nature's otherwise egalitarian economy.

V

THERE ARE OTHER REASONS Childerleyans object to the hunt.

Charles Goddard-Brown is as conservative a villager as one could expect to find, aristocratic in bearing, background, temperament, and politics. He is a conservative of the old school and he accepts the free market.

"A free market means a free society. That means that those who have managed to acquire the money should therefore dominate."

But only just so far.

"But sometimes the market gets distorted and those who really aren't all that significant get rather too much attention paid to them."

In other words, the market is fine, even essential, as long as it maintains the social structure of "my day," as he says. But Thatcherite social mobility worries him.

Like hunt supporters, Charles sees a kind of necessary hierarchy in nature. Charles, recall, sees nature as a matter of dynamic balance.

"You've spoken of a balance," I asked him. "Does this mean that there is also equality in nature?"

"You can only say there's equality of part. If you have a total equality, then you must eventually have decadence. There's no positive. It comes to a static state. . . . It's a part of the evolution, as I see it. If you had complete equality, it wouldn't last for very long because you've always got somebody wanting to lead, somebody wanting to do something which is just a little bit above. Otherwise you'd never get any initiative anywhere. So you've got to have these strata [to provide] the necessary motivation."

Charles thinks hunting is natural.

"I don't mind going and shooting if I want a pheasant for my meal," he said. He even finds fox hunting a part of nature's way.

"It is a natural way of keeping things in limitation, controlling. It is a natural way, whatever people say, and in some ways a more humane way. It may not be humane in the action, but then no natural thing is humane in the action. . . . By the action of the chase, you are improving the breed, because they don't all get killed. By their skill [some] avoid [it]. They breed and they pass those skills on . . . I know it's 'cruel,' these things. But then so is all life. Always has been. Even mere insect life is exactly the same, spiders and the fly. And it goes on."

Here are all the justifications for hunting supporters use: that it is necessary to control foxes; that it improves the breed; that "cruelty" is an unpleasant but unavoidable part of nature. Charles, in fact, used to go fox hunting, but he doesn't any more.

"Now I can't bear the thought of getting pleasure out of chasing some poor fox. I find it awful, actually. I went to dinner and somebody started to talk about fox hunting, et cetera. I think I was in one of my bloody-minded moods. I'd drunk too much or something. And I said, 'When I was a child I thought as a child, acted as a child. And when I became a man I put away childish things.' And whoever it was never talked to me the rest of dinner."

George and Eliza Frizzell, sixty-two and fifty-nine, say they have always lived in the country. George is a city businessman. As he put it, "I'm a country person who's been forced to go and work in industry in order to make a living." Both he and Liza are very concerned with the "values of country," which they describe as family, closeness to nature, gardening (they have a spectacular one), friendliness, the slower pace, the quiet. As Liza says, "We deliberately brought the children up in the countryside, because we thought the values were right." They are both lifelong Conservative voters.

Like most other conservative villagers, they love the spectacle of the hunt.

"One of the finest sights when we first came here," said Liza, "[was] to see the hunt in full cry streaming across the fields out the back here."

But unlike many, they do not agree with it.

"I think it's time it came to an end," says George, "[took] a new course. . . . I'd much rather see them chasing after aniseed."

"It's a rather out-dated procedure," says Liza.

They do agree with much of what hunters say in support of it.

"There was a good reason for it originally," George was quick to point out to me. "To keep the foxes down."

Liza confirmed this.

"A genuine reason. It was run by the farmers and the local Squire to keep a pest down."

George continued with the touchstone story of the fox in the chicken coop.

"You've only got to see a pen where the fox has been around the other night. All the heads lying around. And you'll be only too glad to get rid of that fox. Or to make sure they're kept down to reasonable numbers. Although there's some doubt about the way it's done, anybody who lives in the country can see that it's got to be done."

Liza supported him, saying, "You see, there isn't any enemy of the fox except man."

I asked them if they agreed with the position of some of those who are antihunt that animals are on the "same level" as people and should be treated that way. Liza was confused by this, and asked, "What do they mean by the same level?" George jumped in before I could reply.

"Well, they mean they have the same feelings, and pain and all the rest of it, exactly the same. It's absolutely ludicrous."

Liza wouldn't go quite that far.

"I don't know about pain. But they haven't got the intellect that people do."

"They don't," George continued. "It's like people who try and put themselves into the position of a dog. A dog is a dog, and a dog has certain instincts. And people try and make believe that dogs are human. But they will never be human."

Along with their acceptance of a hierarchy in nature, they feel that hunting is the proper outgrowth of natural, competitive "hunting instincts" in people. Indeed, George feels that problems in society emerge when we try to deny this gritty truth.

"I don't object to going out and shooting a pheasant, if you shoot it well. And then bring it back and put it in a pot. I have no objections to that at all. And no way am I going to become a vegetarian. . . . Human beings have certain hunting instincts. And if you're going to take away all those hunting instincts, you're going to have trouble from that human being. Because he'll want to do something else. This is part of the trouble with the young today. That they've got nothing that gives them any satisfaction."

Charles, George, and Liza read nature as typical conservative hunt supporters do. Why then do they object to hunting? Because, I think, of their strong adherence to status conservatism. These three villagers accept the market only insofar as it maintains the social structure. In the face of the deep ambiguity of fending off constant criticisms of their "old-fashioned" view, they need some place to take a moral stand against a purely economic society. For them, the country is that place, that boundary. The problem with the hunt today, they think, is that it has been taken over by "jumped-up" city people.

"It used to be a country pastime," said George. "And it isn't. It's a city pastime now. All the hunt, or nearly all the hunt people, come down in their Mercedes pulling their horse boxes from London. A lot of them do. Some stable their horses out here. And it's not a country pastime anymore."

"In days gone by . . . it was the countryside [people]," said Charles, "the landed gentry who were involved with it. In a place like this now, you've got a lot of people coming down from London and they couldn't care less about the countryside. They don't know anything about the countryside. All their interest in the countryside is a large house where they can take their photograph or 'come down to my place in the country' or what. That sort of thing. Half of them can't even ride. . . . It's all bogus. And I've contempt for it."

George feels the same about "shooting," pheasant shooting.

"And shooting," he said, "I've gone off it now simply because the type of person I object to. Where it used to be a country pastime—again where the farmer used to invite friends around, and he'd even [invite] some of his employees—now it isn't. It's been taken over by wealthy people. And I don't like the way they behave in the country. So I don't go shooting any longer."

He even feels that way about fishing.

"It's partly why I don't go fishing nearly as much. . . But that's where I feel that I'm a countryman at heart. I've enjoyed all that sort of thing. [But] I don't enjoy being pushed around by the moneyed city people, basically."

Charles, Liza, and George uphold a harsh, hierarchical philosophy of nature. But in their reading, the hunt represents the threatened boundary of a countryside of status conservatives against the new market meritocracy of the city. Real country people understand the need for controlling foxes, but they also observe that the fox hunt has become more about vulgar material display than true country life.

VI

THUS FAR WE HAVE HEARD mainly from moneyed villagers.° The kind of hunt stories most working-class villagers tell themselves about themselves follow yet other plot lines. These stories lead most of them to condemn the hunt, regardless of how they habitually vote.

Tom Fuller, thirty-eight, is butler, chauffeur, and all around handyman at one of the big houses. He's a big, hearty fellow with a loud, ready laugh. He doesn't vote much, but his views are conservative by any yardstick. "Mrs. T. all the way," he told me in 1988. "Labour is a bunch of looneys. I hate that bastard Ken Livingstone." As for the short-lived

° John Bone, a lower-middle-class man by the villagers' reckoning, is the only ordinary villager whose views on hunting I have thus far described. Strictly speaking, he is an ordinary villager but not a working-class one. (See chapter 3 for details on how I arrived at villagers' class designations.)

alliance of the Liberals and Social Democrats, "The Alliance doesn't know what it's doing." Eighteen years a soldier, the last few as batman for a major, he's a staunch monarchist and nationalist.

And yet he is totally against the hunt.

"I would like to see the foxes on the horseback. That's my answer. . . . I would say I was dead against it."

Mary Drake comes from a village family of longtime Labour voters. "What I can't understand," she says, "someone from the working class voting Conservative." Back in the twenties, her grandfather used to work as a carter for Lord Lefroy, one of the last big landowners in the village whom Childerleyans considered a true squire. Mary is proud of how her grandfather courageously used to thumb his political nose at Lord Lefroy, at a time when this could well have cost her grandfather his job.

"When they were voting, because it's terrible conservative round here, Lord Lefroy would say, 'All of you workmen can go up in a wagon, providing you vote for the Conservatives.' So my granddad—oh, I wish you could have seen him. He was about six-feet-four, a long white beard, and it trailed behind. And he used to mumble. His lips would move, mm, mm, mm. My granny used to say, 'What you on about, Henry?' 'You wait and see,' he said. He'd come up here and vote. And he'd go back. Old Lord Lefroy would say to him, 'I hope you voted the right way.' 'Well, if you thinks I voted Conservative, you're wrong,' he said. 'But I had a ride up!' Just shows you how independent some of them were."

Mary doesn't reject wealth and capital. She thinks "you've got to have a certain amount of rich people to give ordinary people jobs." But "there's too many rich people now. Too many jump-ups."

Tom Fuller may never vote Labour, but Mary agrees with him about the fox hunt. "Ever so cruel. I don't like fox hunting." Here's what she said about the practice of "blooding" riders on their first successful hunt. In this ritual, the huntsman daubs new riders, even children, on the forehead with the bloody end of the fox's brush.

"Years ago when I was little at school, there was a fox killed out here, and they pulled it to bits. And it really put me off. I didn't like it. And then they smeared all the rich children with blood. Blooded them. And I said to my mum, 'I don't like that.' She said, 'They've no right to do that outside of school.' It's cruel."

Abel Harrowell's politics are closer to Tom's, although he's more of an economic conservative. Vehemently antiunion, he says they "crippled Great Britain." He loudly applauded Mrs. Thatcher when we spoke in

1988. "She's turned the country back round today." He is as firm a supporter of capitalist principles as I met in the village.

"If somebody has worked hard enough for what they get, then fair game. . . . That's freedom of choice. That's democracy. Free society. . . . I would most probably say that I'm a rank capitalist. Not being bloody-minded or anything, I see nothing wrong with people being able to go out and get what they can, and to operate in a free society as free as they can."

Yet he calls himself "absolutely antihunt. I could very easily join the hunt saboteurs."

Working-class Childerleyans, whatever party they side with, are, with few exceptions, united in opposing the fox hunt. Why? Despite their party differences, they have a common political outlook. That outlook is the egalitarian spirit of the back door. Whether from a free-market point of view or from a prounion, prowelfare, prointervention point of view, ordinary villagers see a world that is supposed to be fair—"fair game," as Abel put it—but isn't.

They find that outlook in their reading of the nature the fox hunt reveals. Unlike most moneyed villagers, they agree that nature is unabashedly cruel. Mary, an ardent Labour supporter, explained:

"I know nature is cruel. I mean, we got a stupid black bird here that won't let the others eat. Now what makes it like that? It don't want to eat it all itself, but it won't let the others eat. It chases them away. . . . I don't like to see it. [Nor do I] like my cats killing the birds. They get a smacked bottom with a newspaper if they do. . . . But I don't think they're hungry. They like chasing them."

Abel Harrowell, from the political other side, agrees.

"Way of life. That's what a fox does. That's an instinct. I mean, a mink will go and kill and not eat. That's an instinct. I mean, why does a bird fly? That's instinct. Why does a cat hunt a mouse? Can they breed it out of cats? I expect they could if they wanted to. But in nature, genetics, they just carry on and on and on. . . . Oh yeah. Nature's cruel."

But Abel doesn't think nature's cruelty justifies fox hunting. The problem with fox hunting is that it just isn't fair.

"I would say the fox is a cunning animal. Yeah? And I would say that like the cat with the mouse, if you actually get the fox you're more cunning than what the fox was. But with the help of two thousand dogs and twenty-five riders and people who go around the day before stopping up the dens, the 'earths,' and all that, I think that [the hunters] have a little bit more know-how than what the fox does. Therefore it's not a fair contest. Because in the majority of fair contests the fox gets away."

Neither does Tom object to the notion of cruelty in nature, or even in the hunt. Like Abel, for Tom it's a matter of fair play. And blocking up fox holes, "earths"—a common practice before a hunt sets out—isn't. Nor is digging foxes out, if they make it to their holes.

"When they block up the holes for them to be chased, they can't go back to their own hole. Or [when] they dig them out. That's what gets me. Alright. Every animal's got to have a fair chance of getting away. That's what seems to me unfair. You block the animal's escape hole. He's not got a chance."

Tom is no hunt saboteur. We got to talking about some local sabs who went out to the houses of hunters and scratched their cars, slashed their tires, and splattered red paint on the outside of their homes.

"They ought to be charged," Tom said, vigorously. "I don't believe in them. It's a free country. You can do what you like. You don't have to follow the sheep. When people do that, they ought to be bloody horse-whipped."

He says he "wouldn't go and upset the hunt." But in the name of fair play, he said, "If I had a chance and the fox hid in a shed, I'd lock the door on him. So he couldn't get caught."

Mary did not use the phrases "fair chance" or "fair play." But she supported the idea of quiet collusion behind the scenes.

"There used to be [a fox] down our end near us. Some hunters come down after it and said, 'Have you seen a fox?' 'No way would I tell you.' I couldn't do it. And when they come with the beagles hunting for the hares, poor old hares sitting in the road, great big brown eyes. I'd drive them over in the field, and I'd say, 'You go, and I shan't tell them where you're gone.'"

For all these Childerleyans, conservative and socialist alike, the hunt represents the unfair advantage of class. Abel and Tom think a true free market could correct that; Mary didn't say. Yet they all agree that society as currently constituted is far from even-handed. It is time to end the traditional privileges of the merely wealthy.

"For a way to hunt foxes," said Abel, "I would say it's barbaric. I think that it should have gone out in the dark ages. Maybe it's nice to have a little bit of the dark ages to know what it was all about. But I mean, no, we don't want to go back to being peasants."

In true nature, these villagers see a fair contest. And in a fair contest the fox usually gets away. But wealthy hunters rig the natural system to keep the ordinary fox down, to try to turn the fox back into a peasant. Unbeknownst to the fox, they tinker with the rules of the game. They block the fox's escape holes. If the fox still gets to its haven, they dig it out. Or they send in the dogs—the police, the bureaucrats, the courts, the politicians—to do their dirty work.

Harry Roud doesn't object to the hunt, though. I learned the basics of fox hunting from him the day I followed the hunt in the rain. Harry is retired now, and he still follows the hunt whenever he can. In deep Hampshire broad accent, he told me with admiration that "there's a lot of rich people out here, look." He explained the social structure of the hunt. The red-coated riders in front—"those are the rich ones"—put a lot of money into the hunt. The "field" of riders in back have only paid twenty-five pounds for the day. A conservative of the old deferential school, Harry seems to relish his association with hunt wealth. And the hunt wealthy return the flattery. At a fund-raising meeting for the village Conservative Club hosted by a leading hunting family, Harry was the only guest invited from the working class villagers. The natural philosophy Harry reads from the hunt is the hierarchical one of the fox as "vermin" with fewer rights and privileges than more noble animals, such as horses, dogs, and people.

Harry used to work for the hunt as a kennel keeper and dog trainer, so it is not surprising that he regards it so favorably. In fact, all other working-class villagers who supported the hunt work from time to time for blood-sports groups (or their spouses do). Most common is beating for local pheasant shoots, another aristocratic sport. In a pheasant shoot, the keeper hires several people (usually men, but not always) to sweep or "beat" through the woods and fields toward the "guns"—those who have paid for the day's shoot. The beaters scare the pheasants up into the air and the guns shoot at the birds, always taking care to fire well over the heads of the advancing beaters.

But the beaters take some heat for this from other ordinary villagers, including their own friends and family members. I was at a small evening party at the Cooks' house, and they had invited in a couple from across the road, Dick and Nancy Morris. Dick used to be a farm worker, but now he and Nancy run a small retail business together. During the evening, the subject of the pheasant shoot came up somehow.

"Like our fox hunting," Nancy observed, "I think it's cruel, really. You know, the birds are almost tame. The keeper down the road here, he feeds them all the year round in their cages. And then they release them. And they won't even fly. So they get the beaters in to make them fly. So they can shoot them. Cruel, isn't it?"

Dick asked me if we had pheasant shooting in America. "We have this image of people in America going out and shooting everything that moves." I explained that Americans mostly shoot ducks, deer, and geese, and that the numbers of these animals are kept high by improving their habitat, not by feeding in cages for later release. Dick found support in my words for his condemnation of the shoot.

"But they're not tame, then, are they? Here we're shooting tame birds. These blokes come up from London and shoot birds for two, even three thousand pounds for a day. Incredible, really." He paused, and then added, "It isn't fair."

Dick and Nancy's moral reading of blood sports, then, is of rich people tinkering with the legitimate rules of the natural system through making the birds tame before shooting them. But in the meantime, Albert Cook was suffering in silence. Although I didn't realize it then, Albert is himself a beater, and that weekend went out to work a shoot with his close friend Bert Longman. I was upset when I was told this, as Albert must have been to have heard our conversation in his own living room. He graciously accepted my apology, saying, "I don't let what other people think worry me." I never did find out if Dick and Nancy knew he was a beater.

On another occasion I dropped by Fred Weller's house one Sunday after he had come back from beating. We chatted about the shoot, which had been a successful one—they got almost a hundred and fifty birds. His daughter Katie came in with a beer for him (I had declined one), and chipped in, "I think it's cruel. They're only tame birds." She looked point-edly at Fred. Fred rolled his eyes and looked uncomfortable, but did not respond. We all laughed, and the tension passed.

Fred is a quiet man who usually avoids confrontation. He refuses to talk about politics, and apparently never votes. "You won't get very much from me about politics," he told me with a wave of the hand one evening in his kitchen. He has no objections to "cruelty" and the like in fox hunting and other blood sports. Nor does he object to hunting foxes in itself. But even Fred—quiet, deferential, a beater—finds something unfair in how the hunt is sometimes carried out.

"I don't mind fox hunting, as fox hunting. . . . If they's chasing a fox out on a field, that's it. Fair game."

In an open fight on a level playing field, out in a clear pasture, that is a fair contest as far as Fred is concerned. But not when the hunters dig him out of his hole after he's "gone to ground."

"They go around and block the holes before they start. Or else if [the foxes] go to ground they dig them out. . . . But when a fox goes to ground, they should leave it. He's beat them. They should leave him be."

But they don't. Foxes have no choice but to live as best they can with what resources they have in a cruel world they have little control over.

VII

THE FOX HUNT then, is a kind of cultural lens for villagers, something that brings a morally fuzzy world into focus. Among the blurry ambiguities that the fox hunt helps villagers envision are the problems of power and dominance, of class, of social interest. Through this lens conservative moneyed villagers, hunt supporters and critics alike, see a realm of harsh truth about the unavoidable necessity for hierarchy and competition. Moneyed residents from the village left see an egalitarian realm corrupted by the cruel pleasure some humans get out of dominating others. Working-class villagers see a tough world that, were it not for the manipulations of the wealthy, would be a fair one too. Thus the visions the lens brings into focus closely resemble villagers' own political beliefs and social circumstances. Looking out, they see in.

TEN

The Mouse in the Sprinkler Pipe: Gender

"The devotion of this little creature that was shouting at the
top of its voice! . . . That to me is a very powerful sort of
thing, you know, that that might happen."

Ann Martin, 1988

"You see, I think that when we were made, we were made
with instincts to defend our tribe."

Frank Steers, 1988

I

NICK PRIOR IS a great fan of "all-wheeling," off-road riding in four-wheel drive vehicles. He proudly maintains a gleaming white, top-of-the-line Land Rover, which can often be seen parked outside his family's council house. I was over at the house for tea one Sunday in March—tea in the traditional sense of a small late afternoon meal, with lots of cut sandwiches, a sweet, and (of course) copious tea. As we ate, Nick spoke enthusiastically about the up-coming all-wheeling "trials."

I asked him what went on at typical trials, more out of politeness than anything else. I was, after all, living in Childerley to study the social experience of nature—not the kind of mechanized terror I imagined all-wheeling trials to be. Nick described it a little bit. Much as fox hunters do, enthusiasts schedule a series of practice races around the region, revisiting each site maybe twice a year. Each trial race is organized like a skiers' slalom, with a course of paired gates laid out through difficult terrain, which the vehicles have to pass through. Mud flies. Engines roar. Trees and brush get overrun. The local all-wheeling club had set up trials for the following Saturday on some Ministry of Defense land about fifteen miles from Childerley. Nick asked if I wanted to go.

I didn't give him an answer that evening. I didn't want to be rude, but neither did I want to participate in what seemed to me a very unnatural (and destructive) practice. Yet the more I thought about it over the next few days, the more I came to see that it must not seem so unnatural to Nick. In fact, as Nick had told me, the opportunity to spend time out in the countryside, riding along back lanes and over open land, is part of the premise of all-wheeling and its pleasures. Certainly, it seemed as much a part of it for him as for many of the fox hunters I knew.

To my surprise, I decided to go. And as it turns out, I had another surprise in store.

We drove down in Nick's Land Rover. Sometimes Nick races, but that day we just went to watch and to drive around the course, laid out in a patch of ground used by the military to practice "tank recovery." In this quaint ritual, some soldiers half-bury a tank or other large vehicle in the ground, and then another team of soldiers tries to pull it out somehow. Where they had succeeded, large ruts scarred the land. Where they had not, rusty tanks and armored personnel carriers lay wallowing in some of the biggest mud holes I had ever seen. Here and there were deep gashes and high mounds gouged out and pushed up by bulldozers to make the grounds more challenging. Remnants of the pine forest that once blanketed the underlying Folkstone beds stood out like little islands in a sea of brown mud. Everywhere the all-wheel vehicles of club members were rushing about, trying out the topography, ducking around the scattered military hardware. It had rained the day before, and the all-wheelers were making the best of what were for them near-perfect conditions.

All-wheelers sometimes race in conventional vehicles like Nick's, and also in various categories of specialized machines. Nick works in an auto shop that welds together these specialized all-wheelers, and repairs them after races and trials. So he knew quite a bit about the goings on and was an informative companion.

We watched the "experts trials." Much of the course had been laid out through the patchy pine woods, and we spent a long time watching at a particularly difficult wooded spot. Vehicle after vehicle went catapulting over a very steep ten-foot-high hump, on the other side of which was a sharp turn through the remaining pines. The track was awash in mud, and great sheets of it hurtled through the air with each passing all-wheeler. Regardless of this, people crowded as close as three feet from the track (and sometimes closer), as the all-wheelers spun by.

Once I was there, I too got caught up in the visceral excitement of the pressing crowd, the partially out-of-control vehicles, the noise, and the resistance of nature to it all. Rather than the distanced object of landscape appreciation, in all-wheeling the natural other talks directly back in the language of flying mud.

All-wheeling's experiential, interactive natu.e corresponds with the dominant class background of the participants, at least as far as I could judge from Nick's description of his all-wheeling friends. These were not Hampshire's poorest people, of course. You need a good job to afford an all-wheeler—to buy it, maintain it, and repair it after each race. Indeed, the chance to display this wealth a little bit is, as in the fox hunt, no doubt a part of all-wheeling's lure. Neither were they rich. Nick pointed out no professional or upper managerial people to me. I got the sense that these were hard working folks who, although they were making some money, still liked to use the back door. While there is a staged formalism inherent in an organized race, this is not the main message of the mud-splattered vehicles, racing engines, and tightly pressed crowds.

Given what Nick had told me over tea, I was prepared for the mainly back-door feel to the natural experience of the trials. But I was not prepared for the surprise I felt in the middle of the afternoon as I stood with the rest of the crowd at another tight spot. The driver of the on-coming all-wheeler was a woman. I suddenly realized that this was the only woman driver I had seen.

A large proportion of the crowd consisted of women, perhaps a third. Yet out of the hundred or so contestants, only this woman and (as I later learned) another competed that day. Women do often ride in the vehicles, accompanying men, but rarely drive themselves. The two women drivers were well-known to Nick, and he mentioned that their husbands were also competing. Apparently, it is almost unheard of for a woman to show up alone to the trials with her own all-wheeler.

I tell this story as an introduction to what I think is an important point. Thus far in the book I have emphasized the significance of the class experience of Childerleyans in shaping both how they experience the natural other, as well as why they look for one. This was largely the case even when I discussed villagers' politics, dominated as they are by class considerations. But if class experience has this influence, then why not other central aspects of the villagers' social lives? In this chapter, I hint at this wider range of experience by discussing another such aspect: their lives as men and women. For in a place like Childerley, most of the inhabitants take pride in their adherence to traditional (or, strictly speaking, what they see as traditional) patterns of family life. Consequently, men and women in the village lead substantially different lives. And these differences, I will try to show, have some parallels in the ways villagers interact with and talk about the natural other.

II

THE ECONOMIC AND DOMESTIC situations of village men and women reflect the distinct gender divisions of the kinds of work Childerleyans typically do in support of family life. Twice as many village men as women are in the paid labor force, and most of the women only work for wages part-time. Significantly, the paid work that most village women find—as shop assistants, secretaries, seamstresses, and cleaners—is, in most cases, for lower wages. Consequently, their monetary power is considerably less than that of the men. There are some women in the village who hold professional jobs, particularly younger women. Ellen Brambley is a school teacher. Joanna Oakley is a dentist. Ann Steers is a real estate broker.

But there is much critical talk about these "yuppy" women, as well as about young professional couples more generally. As a resident described one such couple, who were not married, "They're, shall we say, 'partners.' And that's not the village way." Most residents apparently agree, and only thirteen of the village's hundred and eighty-five households are set up in other than the traditionally accepted arrangements of married couples, bachelors, spinsters (no young women live alone in the village), widows, and widowers. These thirteen include five unmarried couples, several separations, several divorced men and women living alone, and one couple of gay men.

In Childerley, as elsewhere, along with traditionally accepted living arrangements and the lower monetary power women wield goes the greater involvement of women in child rearing, cooking, cleaning, and other domestic duties. And as can only be expected, the different social situations of men and women in the village influences how they experience life, day-to-day.

This shows up in many small ways. Take the way villagers mark the changing times and circumstances of their lives. In their conversations with me, the village's women were much more apt to divide their lives by the ages of their children—"when Patsy was still at home," "when I was at home with Barry," "while Elizabeth was still in her nappies." The men marked the passage of their years more often with references to their employment situation at the time. The women also sometimes used jobs as a time marker, but it was usually their husband's jobs.

Or take the ways Childerley women and men interact with nature in the village. There's the matter of outdoor dirt, for example. One of the things that happens in playing Skirmish, the paint-warfare game popular with a number of villagers, is you get very dirty. Crawling through the woods on your stomach as you sneak up on an opponent, getting splotched with the bright orange paint balls, tearing through the woods with wild abandon as your opponents chase you—actions like these mean it is a gloriously dirty crew that returns to the Fox for a pint after a Skirmish match. Much the same is true of a good day's mud-splattering all-wheeling. As the Skirmish and all-wheeling are dominantly male pursuits, it is the men who come back displaying most of this dirty outdoor glory.°

Men in the village also do the bulk of the dirty, outdoor, physical work, not just the dirty leisure. It is the men who dig the big holes, repair the roof, haul the rocks, and mix the cement. Consequently, the sight of a dirty man coming back from outside work is relatively common in Childerley. These tasks are, of course, all well within the capabilities of women, although many women might take a bit longer at it, go for a pair of helping hands a bit sooner, or set up the mechanical advantage of the job a bit more carefully. And indeed, the majority of hard physical labor around the world is done by women—pounding grain, weeding fields, hauling fuel wood, beating laundry, carrying young children around (and giving birth to them).[1] But in Childerley, it is usually the men who can be found up the ladders and walking the wheel-barrows.

What does this mean to villagers? They never spoke directly about it to me, but my guess is that this kind of dirt of outdoor work and leisure (and not of poverty) is a complex emblem for them. It is, I suspect, a sign of mental toughness, for it shows an ability to overcome fear of the outdoor threat to physical comfort. It is probably also a sign of physical toughness, for it presents evidence that the dirty man has tried his bodily prowess against the outdoors. The willfully chosen mud, paint, and dirt gives the wearer a badge of competence amid tough outdoor conditions. And it may also speak to Childerleyans about village men's more public experience of self—connecting men with the tough, dirty, outdoor side of the natural

---

° The premise of Skirmish is described in chapter IV. Some women play Skirmish too, but not many. Tony Vincent, the farmer who runs it, told me that "on a good day" it's about a third women. I have no numbers on this, but based on the games I played, that sounds rather high. Three women out of about thirty-five players was the most I saw. I suspect Tony was deflecting the well-known criticism of the Skirmish as instigating male aggressiveness. I would be surprised if there have been many good days like those he described.

other. Village women's relative lack of involvement with dirty outdoor work may correspond to women's more domestic experience of self, an association most villagers make.

These are speculative matters. What is certain, though, is that village men often amplify their outdoor power with outdoor machines.° In Childerley, as elsewhere, it is the men who overwhelmingly shoot the guns, run the lawn mowers, "rev" the chain saws, and drive the tractors. Village women run machines too, of course, but mainly the machines of the indoors—stoves, hoovers, irons, washing machines. Perhaps it's a matter of the greater upper body strength most village men undeniably have. But most modern outdoor machines do not require big biceps to run them (that usually being the point of such machines). A machine like a power lawn mower requires only the strength to pull the cord on a well-tuned engine. A tractor or sit-down mower, with their electric starts, require even less. Even operating a chain saw, if it is not one of those giant ones, is well within the physical capacities of many village women. (And I suspect even a few, and maybe most, village men are frightened of the big ones—I know I am.) But Childerley women rarely use these powerful machines of the out-of-doors.

It may be significant that killing outdoor animals is also predominantly a male activity in Childerley. Rabbit shooting, bird shooting, ferreting (using a ferret to flush rabbits from their warrens)—these are mainly pursuits for men and their sons. The participants in the local pheasant shoot are also mainly male. Women do often ride in the hunt, but it is nearly always the male huntsman who throws the fox to the hounds. Some women fish, but almost always in the company of their husband or boyfriend; no Childerley woman that I heard from ever goes fishing by herself or with other women. Women do set out traps and poison for mice and other small unwanted animals around the house. Yet killing game and tougher, larger, outdoor "vermin" is something the men usually take on.

III

BUT MORE IMPORTANT for understanding differences in the natural experiences of village men and women is what they say about it themselves. I think it is significant to note that village men often spoke of the enjoyment

---

° It might be argued that the need for mechanized means of amplification makes the men less tough. But I don't think that is how most Childerley men usually see it.

they got out of their outdoor country work. Like several other moneyed village men, Jim Winter explained that, when he gets home from a frustrating day or wants a break from tensions in his own home, he likes to go out and unwind by clearing brush in the woods of the "Community." Fred Hatt is on call with the local council to drive a snowplow when there is a bad winter storm. He relished the story he told me about the time he drove forty-eight hours straight, clearing country roads during the big storm of the 1986–87 winter. That was an incredible feat, to be sure, one that Fred must have found painful to some degree. But it was not something he said he resented having to do. Rather, the active, visible alteration of outdoor nature through the power of machines is something many village men take pride and pleasure in. No village woman described comparable pleasures.

Moreover, like the tanks and armored vehicle carriers scattered amid the mud and pine trees where the all-wheelers held their trials, there is a tone of militarism to the way many village men spoke about their outdoor activities.

Tom Fuller's favorite magazine is *Survival,* a slim glossy monthly with articles on jungle fighting, the kill factors of different types of hardware, and survival techniques in different environments. The issue he showed me, as I recall, had something about how to survive for thirty days in the desert with no water, should you be forced to parachute out over the Sahara. "Good magazine, right?" Tom proddingly asked me. "Survival. That's the most important thing—looking out for number one." Coming from a singularly gregarious man, this militaristic Darwinism seemed a bit cold-hearted, so I asked, "Well, but what about the number twos?"

"Oh sure," he responded, "you've got to look after your mates. But number one is most important. That's what survival is all about."

Tom thinks about land with this same military imagination. In our conversation where he described his photographic memory for "the lay of the land," he went on to say, "I quite often go down the back of the woods in our place. And I just have a walk around, and that. Quite often I stand there and think, well, this is a good tank position. It's all clicking in." He pointed to his head. "You know, I need to move that wood a bit or put a hedge in there, like [to make it perfect]. You can go from A to B there. I always look at it from a fighting position."

What Tom experiences here in looking at land is the "clicking in" of what he describes almost as an instinct, an instinct for fighting, for positions, for survival.

Tom served for many years in Cyprus, Northern Ireland, and Algeria, which certainly explains much of why he experiences land and life this way. No other man I spoke to in the village used militaristic imagery so widely in discussing the countryside. As he said himself, "Eighteen years in the bloody tanks, you got to look at these positions. . . . It's bred into us. Bullied into us, you might want to call it. You know, you still look at the land like that."

But except in degree, Tom is not alone among village men in his mixing of militaristic images with those of pastoral nature. The military remains a dominantly male pursuit, and its language—its repertoire of feelings—was prominent in the talk of many village men. Certainly, no village woman described land in terms anything like Tom's.

The militarism of men is nothing new, of course. Indeed, villagers often criticize it—women and men both—particularly with regard to Skirmish. Even several Skirmish players in the village lamented men's militarism. Bert Drake was one among the ordinary villagers. Bert, who is in his forties, was proud to describe himself as a former hippy. He still wears a pony tail, and he still identifies with the peace movement and the flower-power years.

"What's wrong with flowers?" he said to me once. "Flowers never hurt anything."

But Bert loves the Skirmish and always signs up for the village team when the list goes up in the Fox.

"I remember the last time. I didn't settle down for two days afterwards, it was so exciting."

Still, as a former hippy, he is sensitive to the charge that the Skirmish might encourage violence among the players. He defends it this way:

"It's not a violent thing. I would say more that it prevents violence. Sort of releases it."

Frank Steers, who is one of several Skirmish enthusiasts among the moneyed villagers, agrees.

"When I play it, it's like playing a game of football. I know it doesn't make *me* a more aggressive sort of bloke." He does grant a little ground to the other side, though, saying, "You've got to think about it a little bit. . . . I think that there might be one or two psychopaths out there who are made worse. Whether it does for some of the other fellows, I don't know—whether they get a glimpse of small violence and it sort of drives it, moves it to big ones. I personally don't think so."

But for all this pacifism, both Frank and Burt simultaneously argue for a militaristic conception of maleness. Underlying both their views of Skirmish—that it doesn't make one "more aggressive," that if anything it just "releases" a little steam—is the notion that there is something aggressive there, something there to be released, something that has to be released.

"You see," Frank explained, "I think that when we were made, we were made with instincts to defend our tribe. Or to react against a lion taking one from the flock, or a bear coming in and taking something. These instincts never get an airing. We sit in our office desks [isolated] from that danger, save-the-family type situation. And they're totally— they're just laid into a dusty attic, and left alone, as it were."

And in outdoor nature, running through the woods playing Skirmish, the reality of this aggressive thing in men, "these instincts" that "never get an airing," becomes clear.

"But when you go out there playing this game . . . ," Frank continued, "it's like a dog that's been cooped up forever and then one day it's taken for a walk in the woods and it sees a rabbit. It sniffs it and all its primitive instincts come alive. And I think that's what this does."

Frank explained that hunting and shooting do this too, but that the Skirmish does it "much more so."

"I've done a bit of that and I thought this game would be quite tame [compared to] some of the things I've done in the past. But in actual fact it's quite exciting when a ton of people are coming at you with a gun. And you know the worst you're going to get is a bruise."

IV

AND WHAT DID WOMEN SAY about the natural other? Many things, of course, most of which corresponded closely to what men with similar class experiences and political values said. But many village women also put an emphasis on a domestic value that I found in the talk of no village man—nurturing. A story Ann Martin told me is an example.

"I went out about six in the morning. It was June. You know how beautiful mornings can be. And I heard this immense squeaking. And I thought to myself, 'Squeaking. Right, so there was a squeaking.' It was a Sunday and I went through my various activities. It nearly got to midday and I was having some coffee out there in the courtyard. I still heard the squeaking. I thought, 'I must locate that squeaking.' We've got a little [sprinkler system for the garden], and the turn-off, the stop-cock is down about an arm's length of pipe. And the squeaking was where a mouse, a little mouse, had fallen down the pipe—arm's-length down the pipe—and landed on the stop-cock. And of course it couldn't get out, because it's plastic pipe."

The mouse apparently kept slithering back down every time it tried to escape.

"There were two lots of squeaking, actually. The other squeaking was coming from a little mouse that was just back under the leaves. It was desperate because its offspring or its parent had gone down the pipe, and couldn't get out. So I put a rope down the pipe, and within seconds the little thing shot up and went to its mum or its whatever. And so all was well." Ann paused, and then found these words. "The devotion of this little creature that was shouting at the top of its voice! Either its encouragement or its wish to help, or to draw attention. O.K.? Anything that's got that devotion and care! Because a mouse is a small thing. They've got to eat fairly comfortably to get on. It had already, I knew, been squeaking non-stop for well over six hours. And probably for much longer than that. Probably since the last night. Twelve hours even. So that to me is a very powerful sort of thing, you know, that that might happen."

Ann's interpretation of the significance of this tale of nature in terms of "devotion and care" also came through in a story Harriet Cooper told me. Incredibly enough, the Coopers once had a cat that helped raise two ducklings.

"We had a cat [Suzy]," said Harriet. "We always had lots of cats. And this particular time I went to Harchester, and there were two little ducklings in the pet shop window. And like a fool I thought, well, the kids will like them. And I brought them home, didn't I? And Suzy became a mother and she got kittens, at this particular time. And of course she took the two little ducklings over, didn't she? So wherever she went with the kittens, the ducklings followed. And they used to sleep together in this cardboard box. The cat and the ducklings!"

I somewhat skeptically mentioned that one would think the cat would eat the ducklings.

"There's a picture somewhere isn't there," she responded, "and there's a newspaper cutting. I said to the Vicar's wife, 'Come and look at this.' And the next thing I knew we had a flipping reporter out. She rung them up and made them come out and have a look at it! Of course that was all splashed in the paper, wasn't it? But the article was full of junk. He put words in our mouths. Said things we never said."

I think she mentioned her problems with the reporter in part to instruct me to make sure I got the story straight, if I planned to repeat it. I ventured that it was an amazing story.

"It's completely true," she continued. "She would wash and cuddle the ducklings, just like they were her own. It's the mothering instinct, I suppose, because you know they were just ducklings."

Harriet found in this incident, like the care and devotion Ann described in nature, evidence of a "mothering instinct" in females to wash, cuddle, and look after babies—even ducklings—like "they were her own." She found more evidence in another remarkable story she told me about a family dog who took on the care of the kittens of a cat (not Suzy) who died. Apparently, Harriet said, the kittens even "suckled the bitch. They will do that."

Of course, Harriet's husband Ed knows these stories as well as Harriet. He has heard Harriet tell them a dozen times at least, I'm sure. And these are amazing stories. But they are her stories, not his, and he does not tell them. At least he didn't tell them to me. (This is a point I'll take up again in a few pages.) On the contrary, his tales of nature were mainly about difficult weather he has had to contend with and unusual outdoor work he has done—local floods and particularly bad winters; the year he worked as a logger back before the days of chainsaws, when the wood was still hauled by horse-drawn wagons and loaded by winch and muscle; how for a while he used to commute between his home and job twenty-five miles by foot (as did Albert Cook).

Harriet's experience of nature as a realm of mothering and nurturing also came up in an alternative definition of "nature" she gave me after the conversation I reported in chapter 6. After that interview, we were chatting in the kitchen while she fixed me a little bundle of lemon squares to take home. She abruptly changed the topic and broke in, "Do you want to know what nature is, to me? Nature is caring. It's taking care of others." No man spoke in this way.

This difference is something at least one village woman seemed quite aware of. None mentioned it directly, but Rachel Wood did tell me several stories about the caring approach she tries to take with nature, using men as a point of contrast.

"I couldn't live without animals. The earth wouldn't be a place of beauty. . . . I mean, when my bantam died, I can remember sitting there and absolutely howling. The chap next door, he just couldn't get over somebody who could cry about a bird. But we've got such a relationship with them."

I'm not sure how deliberately Rachel was trying to connect a man with cold rationalism, but the association is certainly there in the story of her bantam's death. (It may also have been there in Harriet Cooper's stories, with me serving as a representative of the cold male ear which is skeptical about caring.) It was also there in the following story Rachel told me later on in the same conversation.

We talked a lot about Rachel's experiences with animals, and eventually I raised the (perhaps somewhat male) question of whether animals have feelings. "I think so," she said, and pointed to Admiral Bird, her pet cockatiel. Before he went off to college, Rachel's son Steve used to have a ritual of feeding the Admiral a bran flake in the morning, and a ginger biscuit with bread and jam when he came home from school in the afternoon. The Admiral thrived on this unusual diet. But when Steve moved out, Admiral Bird stopped singing and became very ill.

"He was suddenly so quiet, dreadful. And we thought he was going to die. I rang the vet. And he said, 'Well, we don't normally treat birds. But if you want to bring him in, you can. But I can't say that we'll find a cure.' To think that he was part of our family and we were going to lose him!

"I rang up this chap who keeps an aviary and said, 'I've got this cockatiel. And he's gone very quiet. And he's sulking and his wings are down.' And I said, 'It's not like him. He's normally chirpy and chattery.' And [this chap] said, 'My goodness! You're giving human feelings to a bird. It's only a bird. They don't feel like that!' And I came off the phone and thought, he's kept birds for years. I thought he was an expert, and he doesn't understand the bird at all."

She tried to think what was different since Steve had left home, and then she remembered the loud music he always used to play in his room, where he kept Admiral Bird.

"And we realized that he didn't have this music going," she went on. "So we put him in another room and put the radio on."

And she remembered the special treats Steve would regularly give him—the bread and jam, the ginger biscuits, and bran flake in the morning.

"Now that's silly," she said. "But that's the way things are. Once we gave him all the silly things, the rubbish, that Steve put in there, [he was fine]."

What was Rachel telling me? Part of the sense I got was the importance she thinks one ought to place on caring and empathy in interactions with nature. True, it may not be purely a woman's empathy of which she speaks. She did talk about how "we realized" the source of Admiral Bird's unhappiness, and how "we gave him" what he needed, probably referring either to Steve or her husband. But it was only women who told me about such a nurturing approach to the natural other.

Moreover, a topic a number of women (and no men) brought up in their hunt stories was the hunt's particular cruelty toward the vixen and her young. Ann Martin was particularly upset about late season hunts because they interfere with the breeding season.

"This year it will be even worse," she told me, "because I know the vixens are breeding. They won't be able to run . . . and the pups will take about a week to starve."

She went on to point out this same domestic cruelty in human treatment of spring lambs, with a wave toward the gamboling in the pasture down the road.

"But of course human beings are slaughtering things all the time. These dear little lambs will be carted off at six weeks, I might tell you, while their mothers are still emotionally deeply in need of their presence. Let alone what happens to the lambs."

Here again was a woman seeing in the natural other something Childerley men never described: love, family life, and the plight of mothers and children in an uncaring world.

V

WHAT ARE WE TO MAKE of these contrasts in the natural experience of Childerley men and women? To begin with, let me make a few points about the character of the evidence.

First, there is far more correspondence than difference between the natural experiences of Childerley's men and women. The preceding chapters make this clear, I think. Moreover, there is considerable overlap even in those matters that seem to pertain to gender experience. Some women do indeed participate in the Skirmish and come home dirty. Some men do engage in nurturing activities with nature. Albert Cook and Ed Lambton raise young birds for their aviaries and take great care in this. Steve Wood used to take the time each morning to give Admiral Bird his bran flakes. Many women did confirm the existence of uncaring, competitive slaughter in nature—what Mary Drake, Alice Barnes, and Miss Cantelupe said about cats, blackbirds, and foxes—as quoted in chapter 8—are examples. Differences only clearly emerged in their most extreme manifestations, like Tom Fuller's military experience of views or Harriet Cooper's story about the mother cat who took over the care of the two ducklings, and in emphasis and preponderance, like the fact that men are in the vast majority among Skirmish players and all-wheel racers.

Second, most Childerleyans practice sharper differences in the kinds of things men and women do than, I believe, is the case in many other communities in England. Thus it is likely that what they said about pastoral nature and their experiences in it are, with regard to gender, far from representative of some other groups of people. I do not doubt that there may be men elsewhere who say and do the kinds of things Childerley women say and do, and similarly for women elsewhere and Childerley men. (In fact, I know of many examples from my own personal encounters.)

And third, although the villagers usually did, I think, see me as largely classless (as I describe in chapter 3), I very much doubt they saw me as genderless. It would be unreasonable to assume that that made no difference in what the villagers said to me. It may even have influenced (although probably considerably less so) the kinds of things I observed men and women doing in the village landscape. Most readers, I suspect, are well aware that, in most places in the world, women and men experience constraints in what they feel allowed to say and do in the presence of someone of the other gender. They also feel constraints—different ones, generally—in the presence of those of the same gender.

To take an example, Ed Cooper might well appreciate the story of the mother cat and the ducklings as much as Harriet. But he may also think it somehow inappropriate for him to stress his appreciation for its nurturing values to another man. Similarly, Harriet may have thought it appropriate that she include such a story in presenting her views about village nature to me. These differences in the natural experience of village men and women, after all, correspond closely with some well-known cultural understandings of what men and women should be and do.

In other words, it is important to consider whether the differences in natural experience I observed among Childerley men and women (remembering those first two points about the evidence) are matters they inwardly agree with, or only things they feel they should outwardly express. It's the same question I asked of their class experience. With regard to class, though, I feel it's clear that some of those matters are things the villagers do inwardly agree with—often to their considerable distress. I did not hear much evidence of a similar moral ambiguity over gender among Childerleyans (as I have indeed heard elsewhere in my travels), but that doesn't mean it wasn't there.

Yet other scholars have seen similar patterns of gender difference in other contexts. In a famous study, Carol Gilligan described the young women she interviewed as speaking their life's experiences in "a different voice" than that of men, a voice that emphasizes "an ethic of care, the tie between relationship and responsibility, and the origins of aggression in the failure of connection."[2] That does indeed sound like the voice Childerley women use sometimes when they talk both about their social lives, and about nature and the countryside.

The real question is why. Gilligan and Nancy Chodorow both suggest these differences are rooted in patterns of early psychological development.[3] Some would go deeper.[4]

Now, I am not in the position to evaluate these theories. Without detailed knowledge of villagers' childhoods, what I saw in Childerley does not bear on them. (Moreover, I think we would do well to remember that however important our past may be, neither anatomy nor childhood are destiny.)

But for the point I'm trying to establish, I don't think it matters. Even if villagers regard these gender differences in natural experience as products of social constraint, they must then feel these same constraints in their collective conscience—despite the good possibility that they may reject this constraining presence in their lives and minds, at least to some degree. It is important to remember, as I argued earlier with regard to class, that people may morally reject much of what the collective conscience suggests to them, even while living and feeling according to those same suggestions.

Which allows me to return to the point I want to establish. And that is, there are indeed some parallels in the ways Childerley women and men, as women and men, experience their generalized others and the ways they experience a natural other. Here too, in nature's many-doored realm, villagers reenter their social lives.

RESONANCE

ELEVEN

The View from the Bell Tower

Ring out, wild bells, to the wild sky . . .
Ring out the false, ring in the true.

Alfred Tennyson, 1850

By the English method of ringing with rope and wheel, each
several bell gives forth her fullest and noblest note.

Dorothy Sayers, 1934

I

THE BEST VIEW in the parish, by everyone's account, is the one from the church bell tower.

The entrance to the tower is behind the organ at the back of the nave, and leads first into the ringing room, a cold square of stone. The red and white spiralled "sallies" (the brightly colored handles of bell ropes) swing gently here in the draft. The ladder up is rusty but secure. Two handholds and a dusty hoist of the body lead to the clockworks in the room above. A flight of rude stairs rises finally to the top level and the bells, arrayed on their woodworks—a great spinning wheel for each bell. Through the belfry walls, slatted to let the tidal rings of treble and tenor surge out across the village, there is a view of virtually the whole of Childerley, from Winter Hill to Holt Hill. Topographically, Holt Hill does rise higher even than the bell tower. But here, from the top of the highest structure on the central hill of the parish, Church Hill, the sense of height—and of centrality—is far greater.

Looking out from the center at the parish boundaries, the villagers see in the arc of countryside evidence of both nature and the threats to it. There are fields and hedges, copses and cattle; there are also houses and cars, burglar alarm boxes and traffic signs. Keeping this boundary of nature is of central importance to the villagers, as we have heard. Upon it they formulate a natural conscience, the moral source of motivation and identity they sometimes use as an alternative to the interest-laden conflicts

227

they find in collective values—conflicts of class and other material desires. They find this conscience by conceiving of a realm free of social interests, a realm Childerleyans discover in what they see as the real country. Others may locate this realm elsewhere, but the country is where Childerleyans mainly encounter it. Here they uncover, beneath the *me* their generalized other sees, the *natural me* their natural other sees. For them, this *me* is the *me* of a country person, the basis of social self upon which Childerleyans prefer to stand.

But how separate are these others and these *mes*? Is there really a boundary between nature and society, between the experience of a natural other and a generalized other, and thus ultimately between country people and city people? This is a crucial matter for solving the sociological question of how the natural conscience comes to be—and also the philosophical question of whether there really is what John Stuart Mill called "an external criterion" for moral value.[1] It is not my intention here to speak to the latter issue. I will leave that for the reader to ponder. (Mill, at any rate, was dubious that such a criterion could be found in "nature.") But I do hope to give the sociological perspective necessary, I feel, for assessing that old question of the moral mind. Let us climb up the bell tower for a final, panoramic view where we may debate the adequacy of the conceptual map I labeled reflection theory.

II

CLEARLY THERE ARE MANY correspondences between the natural and generalized others Childerleyans find in their lives. To use William Burch's apt phrase, the villagers' "vocabulary of nature" closely resembles their vocabulary of society, a vocabulary of class, politics, and gender (among other things).[2]

The back-door spirit of ordinary villagers—a local spirit of informality, group orientation, interactiveness, and the experiential—tends to discover nature in an approachable and animated foreground, a nature personified by an immediate liveness. Moneyed villagers encounter their front-door spirit—a far-flung spirit that puts more stress on the formality of private and distanced individuals—in their greater language for the formality and distance required for discussing land as landscape. Moreover, their taste for nature stresses the privacy of the individual.

The political spirits of moneyed and ordinary villagers also infuse the natural others they conceive. Conservative moneyed villagers tend to see a nature unavoidably red in tooth and claw. The hierarchies that result are harsh but necessary. In these "partial evils" they, like Alexander Pope, find "universal good."[3] Moneyed residents of the village left conceive nature as a realm of moral equality, corrupted by the cruel, hierarchical pleasures of some humans. Most working-class villagers, regardless of their voting habits, see something different again. Nature for them is a tough, even cruel realm, but it is a fair one too. The problem is, human manipulation diverts nature's free workings to the advantage of elites.

There are correspondences too with their sensibilities as women and men. For the most part, Childerleyans follow traditionally sharp gender divisions of labor, with the women consigned overwhelmingly to the concerns of the private sphere and the men to those of the public. The habitual ways in which Childerley's men and women think about their social and economic circumstances appear as well in their experience of village nature. When village women look at nature, they are more likely than the men to find domestic values there, such as a mother's care, self-sacrifice, and nurturing. The language and experience of the men, on the other hand, emphasizes militarism, aggressiveness, toughness, and the visible alteration of nature's outdoor economy.

These summaries of village vocabularies of nature are (perhaps unavoidably) neater than real village talk. But even so, it sounds like pretty good evidence for reflection theory. And it is. Reflection theory suggests that our social experience is so important to us that it provides the categories, the turn of mind, by which we understand everything. Therefore we will likely see these same categories in other realms of experience like "nature," and Childerleyans to a large extent do.

Moreover, argues reflection theory, finding these categories elsewhere helps confirm these originally social ideas in our minds, contributing to ideological stability and entrenchment. This will be particularly true for the natural other, that realm the villagers argue is by definition free of social intrigue and interest. If it appears in the natural other, then, in one's mind, a category must really be truly above the imposition of personal desires for social gain—the "conjurer's trick," as Engels called it, of transferring social ideas back from nature to prove "their validity as eternal laws of human society."[4]

This is a disturbing charge, for it suggests that Childerleyans' hopes for building a natural conscience upon a natural other which is free of social interest is probably a Quixotic project. The natural other, then, may only be the generalized other in sheep's clothing.

III

BUT I DON'T THINK SO. At least, I don't think it is so simple. There are three problems with reflection theory's account which I'd like to point out: its rationalism, its reference problem, and (the biggest difficulty) its sociocentrism.

First, its rationalism. Engel's conjurer's trick, when I try to work it out, seems to me to be inviting us to think about social and natural parallels as a matter of calculated argument. Maybe I'm not doing him justice. But we do need to recognize that these parallels are usually not the product of some deliberate ideological effort.

I have a little evidence from Childerley to offer in support of this. On one of my return trips to Childerley, after I'd been home thinking about the village for a while, I pointed out the existence of the parallels I'd come to see to a few residents. I think it is quite significant (although unsurprising) that this was a new idea to them. Most found the idea intriguing and accurate—but novel—when I explained to them the point. Of course, as sociologists have often shown, many things go on in social life that even the participants are largely unaware of. Still, it makes a big difference in our interpretation of what underlies a social situation to distinguish those aspects people know about from those they do not.

This does not mean that the existence of parallels between the generalized and natural others are ideologically unimportant. Not at all. As I will argue, they do indeed reinforce social categories. But it does suggest something about the process of how these correspondences come about. When Childerleyans describe (or just experience) the fox hunt, the gardens they like, the scenery they admire, their favorite activities outdoors, and memorable moments of interaction with things natural, they are not simultaneously thinking about the ideological implications. It is not so hard and meditated a matter. It is something gentler, less forced— something more intuitive.

That point can be defended more strongly. But before I do so, let me turn to the second problem with reflection theory, its reference problem.

This is a bit hard to explain. Perhaps the best way to put the crux of the problem is to ask, What category of society is any one category of nature to reflect? Reflection theory, if it is right, requires a literal, one-to-one correspondence between the natural and the social. But that's not possible where social ideas contradict one another, as they often do.

The contradiction Childerleyans have spoken most about in this book is their ambiguous feelings about class and material motivations. So what

determines when villagers will experience proclass sentiments in the natural other, and what determines when they experience anticlass ones? Andy
Sparrow, a villager on the left, disapproves of the fox hunt, probably (or
so reflection theory would suggest) because he sees nature in more egalitarian terms. But Andy, recall, also spoke about the importance of solitude
in natural experience, something that could make a class-based positional
good out of the landscape. Ruth Hill, as another example, disagreed that
moneyed people are at fault for driving ordinary locals out of the village.
But that's not how she always thinks about the natural other. When I
asked her about the fox hunt, she vehemently argued that foxes have as
much right to the countryside as any other creature. Maybe it's not so
determined after all.

Moreover, if all knowledge is social in origin, life indeed becomes
little more than a hall of mirrors. In raising the issue of relativism, I am
not asking us to join the objectivist's creed—what Mark Johnson has justly
criticized as a belief in the existence of "one correct 'God's-Eye-View'
about what the world is really like." It is not necessary for us to adopt the
objectivist's faith that (in Johnson's words again) "there is a rational structure to reality, independent of the beliefs of any particular people."[5] The
issue of relativism confronts us here for another reason.

The relativist problem that reflection theory slips into is what we
might call "social solipsism," as opposed to the "object relativism" an
objectivist might worry about. At issue is not that social experience influences what we make of the world (the objectivist's fear), but that social
experience is the sole source of how we think about what we see and feel.
For reflection theory presumes a purely sociocentric origin of the categories by which we make sense of our experience. Therefore all categories
must stem from social experience alone, trapping us, in a way, within
ourselves.

This leads to the final problem I want to raise. Reflection theory's
map leaves unanswered the crucially important question of where our
social ideas come from in the first place. As Barry Schwartz put it, "the
existence of society in the mind presumes the existence in the mind of
the categories by which society is known."[6] Reflection theory does not tell
us where these categories come from.*

* Some readers might object that historical materialism's version of reflection
theory does provide an answer. If categories are, as Marx and Engels suggested,
relations of production "grasped" as ideas, then these relations serve as their
origin. But relations of production, as Marx himself was at pains to point out, are

Claude Lévi-Strauss claimed to have solved this problem. He argued that the answer lies beneath society in "the constraining structures of the mind."[7] According to Lévi-Strauss, there is something about how our minds work, rooted in biological nature, that determines how we think. In his detailed studies of totems and myths, he saw a hidden logic—the tendency to pose knowledge in binary opposites, in dualities and contrasting pairs. Good requires bad, down requires up, raw requires cooked, and nature requires society. In all these cases, the "image is projected, not received," projected from the mind's structures into our knowledge of the world.[8] Our minds are thereby programmed to find order in the world around us, said Lévi-Strauss, a programming necessary to creatures for whom so much else is left open.

Certainly there is a very pronounced tendency to think in dualities. Male, female. Light, dark. Day, night. We also think in trinities. Father, Son, and Holy Ghost. Up, down, and sideways. The primary colors, red, yellow, and blue. He, she, it. We, you, they. Id, ego, super-ego. And quadrinities—north, south, east, and west. And . . .

But perhaps dualities are more important. Perhaps oppositions with greater numbers of elements are only some kind of elaboration of binaries. Certainly, at some point we do have to return to the realm of things labeled "nature" and "biology." Yet even if Lévi-Strauss was right about the constraining structures of the mind, he still did not answer the question of the origin of social categories. He still did not explain why people like Childerleyans should experience life through the categories that they do—only that they need to have categories in order to think, and that binaries are perhaps the most important way they manage this feat.

And without an answer to this question, reflection theory is left with nothing to reflect.

IV

ALL OF THESE ISSUES can be cleared away, I believe, if we consider what recent studies tell us about how we think. New work in linguistics, sociology, philosophy, and psychology has challenged a number of our older ideas. "The traditional view," the linguist George Lakoff has written, "sees reason as literal."[9] Reason is based on propositions about the world which

---

themselves social relations, social categories. Marxists sometimes over-stress the inner logic of the material side of these relations, not seeing (as Weber did) that material logic itself has an origin.

can be objectively verified as to whether they accurately portray reality. Moreover, the symbols we choose to represent these propositions in our minds are essentially arbitrary and inconsequential. Reason has an abstract quality that transcends a local issue like the name I happen to choose for the raised, flat surface upon which I write this sentence.

Not so, say an increasing number of scholars. Reason depends on who is doing the thinking. Specifically, it depends on its imaginative embodiment in people—on the mental imagery and life experiences of thinking individuals. Furthermore, our thinking has "gestalt properties," overall structures that leap beyond the rules for manipulating abstractions. We commonly achieve this with "cognitive models"—metaphors, images, theories—we derive from our life's experiences. "Experiential realism," as Lakoff has summed it up. The point is, reason for us is always human reason.

Thus far this may sound in perfect accordance with reflection theory. If reason, and therefore knowledge, is human-centered, then it must perforce be socially centered, as we are social beings.

But society is not the only aspect of our experience which is of such vital importance to us. We also have bodies and exist in a physical environment. Bodily experience in the physical world, like social experience, is inescapable for human beings. Physical experience pervades our thoughts. There is a "body in the mind," as Mark Johnson argues in his book by that title.[10] In Lakoff's words, "the core of our conceptual systems is directly grounded in perception, body movement, and experience of a physical and social character."[11] Is there any basis for privileging one aspect of our basic life experiences, like society, over another? Barry Schwartz, a sociologist himself, answers no. Rather, we should conceive of knowledge as deriving from a range of what Schwartz calls "experiential prototypes" based on all of life's experiences.[12] In other words, knowledge depends in a fundamental way on that characteristic of the mind we sometimes, rather vaguely, refer to as intuition.

The psychologist Eleanor Rosch makes an important observation regarding how we put prototypes to work. We do not really fill our categories with members that all share a set of common properties, as has been traditionally believed. In fact, for each category there is usually a "best example"—the prototype—and a gradient of better and worse examples away from it.[13] For instance, most Childerleyans would likely judge a robin as more representative of the category "bird" than an ostrich or a penguin. Similarly, there has never been any doubt that a fox is a "mammal," while there has long been ambiguity about the egg-laying monotremes—the platypus and the spiny anteaters. Robins and foxes lie closer to the central zone of their prototypes. Based on prototypes, we order our realms of thought with metaphors and other mental models that capture life into almost ecological wholes.

Why, then, do we see such remarkable parallels between realms of thought like nature and society in Childerley? Are these parallels only the happenstance selection of the same mental models? How, then, do Childerleyans select which prototype to use? Do they just pick up the most convenient mental wrench their social, bodily, and physical experience has given them and apply it to the nuts and bolts of life? Moreover, how do they choose which aspect of experience will be the best example, the prototypes with which they build their mental house? And perhaps even more importantly, now that we have shattered reflection theory's mirror, is there no ideological reinforcement involved?

There is a meeting ground here, I believe, that can explain the parallels and also how villagers select prototypes. It suggests that the parallels and prototypes are far from accidental, and also that there can be social reinforcement even when there is no social reflection.

The point I would like to make is that there is something else about how we think which is missing from the new theories of human understanding. Not only do we think from prototypes to wholes, but *we tend to think a thing more true when we can find it in a range of experience.* Indeed, the more diverse the range the better. An apt metaphor for the process is *resonance.*°

To explain what I mean, let me describe what Childerleyans strive for when they ring the bells of the village tower.

° Here I am pirating (and, I believe, widening) a concept from Northrop Frye (1981, 217), which I learned through Neil Postman (1985, 17–18). Frye described as "resonance" the way certain phrases or statements from ancient sources such as the Bible have acquired much wider significance than they had in their original context. Examples might be the grapes of wrath of Isaiah 63 or the "still small voice" of I Kings 19:12. These compelling phrases have "first, an original context, and, second, a power of expanding away from that context" (Frye, 1985, 218). Postman (1985, 18), in his analysis of communication media, took the concept further, claiming that each medium has resonance "because of the way it directs us to organize our minds and integrate our experience of the world." It is in this sense of directing our minds that I mean the resonance of experiential prototypes. Indeed, the migration of Frye's concept from biblical to media studies and now to the sociology of nature is a perfect illustration of resonance. Readers of Luhmann (1989) should note that I am using the term resonance in a different way than he does.

There are eight bells in the tower, each with its own rope and sally, and eight people are needed to ring them properly. Each bell gives the deep sonorous tone for which English bells are famous, for Childerley's is a good set of bells. But the real beauty comes when they ring together. In the English style known as "change-ringing," the bells are not used for tunes. Instead, the bells ring in a complex pattern using all the bells in rapid sequence—a sequence that "changes" each time through the full set of bells. Change-ringers keep track by giving each bell a number, 1-2-3-4-5-6-7-8, corresponding to *do-ti-la-sol-fa-me-re-do*. (The lowest number refers to the highest pitched bell.) For example, the first sequence or "change" might be

1-2-3-4-5-6-7-8.

The next change,

2-1-3-5-4-7-6-8.

The next,

1-2-5-3-7-4-8-6.

The next,

2-1-5-7-3-8-4-6.°

And so on. The effect is that the bells ring as a chorus, their tones overlapping and combining and intermingling in a kind of deep, steady jangle.

Ringers will speak of the bells in some towers as being "a good ring," and others less so. What gives a tower like Childerley's a good ring is that the bells are well-made and well-tuned, and they *resonate*—not only in themselves, but with each other. There is a fullness to the sound of a tower like Childerley's that has an intuitive goodness about it.

Now, as any change-ringer knows, some bells in the same ring sound better than others. What makes those bells sound so good, apart from their own construction, is the resonance they set off in the other bells, which adds to the fullness of their own ring. In Childerley (as in most other towers), the favorite bell is the "tenor," the low *do*, the deepest bell. As the key of the whole set of bells is based on it, the tenor's pitch is harmonically the best placed for resonance. When it rings, there is a swell, faint and almost unidentifiable to the ear, that would not be heard were it not for reverberations touched off in the other bells.°° Favorite bells do that.

° These are the opening changes of the Major ring "London Surprise."
°° Change-ringers will know that this is most evident when the bells have been "rung down" into their storage position and hang open-face to the ground. In this position, the clapper dangles freely in the middle air of the bell and does

And so it is with good prototypes. Think of each bell as the prototype for a separate realm. What makes a good prototype is, in large measure, the integrity of its own construction—how well it sounds rung by itself. But our sense of its goodness is added to in a deep, almost intuitive way by the fullness of its resonance with the bells of other realms. The more bells—the more realms—among which resonance can be achieved, the greater the truthful fullness of the whole ring.

Not only is knowledge embodied in physical and social beings. Not only does it tend to gestalts—realms of understanding—built out of the mental models prototypes provide. This is what makes a bell sound full by itself. But when people experience something in one realm that fits with their experience in another realm they regard as separate, the general pattern or prototype is likely to make greater intuitive sense to them. I think we cannot doubt that it is deeply reassuring to find one's sense of order, one's categories of understanding, there in what one takes to be a different realm. What I am suggesting is that villagers actively seek this out. They seek, probably largely nonconsciously, to have their prototypes resonate with each other, and they feel more convinced by those that do.

This, then, is how Childerleyans select their prototypes. The best prototypes and mental models are those that can be made to touch off reverberations across the varied realms of our understanding. At the risk of over-drawing the metaphor, the villagers constantly retune, rehang, reject, and otherwise reconstruct the ring of bells. This is a heavy and arduous task, one they do not undertake casually. But constant playing seems to wear the bells out a bit, and the bells must periodically be taken down and tinkered with to bring back the fullness of the ring. Sometimes, however, a bell is too far off from the others, and it must be rejected and recast entirely.

How is the metaphor of resonance an improvement over social reflection? It suggests that our most basic ideas are formulated out of their fit across the full ring of realms, not society alone. The origin of social categories, in other words, depends on more than social experience. Our further experience of other realms such as the natural other can by itself lead us to retune our social thoughts by changing the overall tonality of the ring of bells with which our social categories should, we intuitively feel, correspond. Of course, it could work the other way too. Rather than retuning the social bell, should we sense a lack of resonance with it, we may decide

---

not rest against the side where it would dampen the reverberations of resonance from other bells.

to tinker with the tuning of all our other bells instead. Usually, I imagine, we do a bit of both.

But the bells of thought are not constructed out of air. Each bell is cast from the weighty metal of experience, and this places real constraints on the pitch, timbre, and wider resonance among bells achievable through retuning. No Childerleyan ever observed a fox to enter a chicken house, daintily lick and groom the birds, and leave without harming any of them. Neither has any villager heard a fox laugh cruelly as it killed every bird in a coop. What the villagers try to do is bring these observations and experiences of the realm they regard as nature into some kind of correspondence with those they have of society, leading to their understanding of both realms.

Furthermore, resonance does not require the kind of deliberate one-for-one correspondence between society and other realms that social reflection suggests. (As I'll discuss in a moment, it wouldn't work if this were what always happens.) Resonance does not exclude the possibility that people can make such calculated, literal readings between realms. But it proposes that people will usually arrive at correspondences through finding parallels in the experiential sound of different bells. In most instances, this will be a largely nonconscious process, a kind of a *habitus* of the mental ear that knows a good ring when it hears one, without really knowing why.

Moreover, it is an active process. In many instances, Childerleyans will fail to find that good sound in things. When their ideas conflict, reference problems abound. It is hard to know which bell is the one to retune, and which is the bell to tune the other, or others, to. Consequently, what they hear is the duller sound of partial resonances, and not the full swell of the entire ring. But villagers seek—they tinker and adjust the categories they apply in different realms—to hear that clearer music. They listen for the resonance of categories which are in tune, yet different.

In fact, the correspondence between categories, between realms like the natural and collective consciences, is never perfect. Nor would Childerleyans want it to be. The birds in Albert Cook's aviary may surround him with a close-packed activity of talk and chatter, much like his own back-door style of life, but their talk is not human talk. Foxes may or may not be cruel, depending on villagers' perspectives, but they do not really live as we do. Ann Martin may have seen caring commitment in the mouse that squeaked for help in her back garden, but a mouse is not a human.

These differences are banal but not trivial. If resonance across categories is to provide the intuitive support to our understanding which we desire, these differences must be there. To return to the metaphor of sight, we seek resemblance, not reflection. We do not want perfect dupli-cates, for then there could be no basis for the separation of realms of thought. We need this separation, this difference. We need to regard the natural other and society as at least somewhat separate. It is only by believing that we do not live in a hall of mirrors, mirrors which reflect only ourselves, that we escape solipsism and find a realm we regard as free of interests. When we see resemblance and not reflection, when we hear resonance and not a mere echo, we can convince ourselves that our categories are more than our own delusions.

But are some bells more significant than the others in establishing the tonality of experience? I am inclined to say yes, there is a bell, a tenor bell, upon which the harmonics of the whole set is most closely based. I am also inclined to say that society is the tenor. Although society is by no means the soul source of our experience, it is, I feel, the most central one in forming our overall outlook on the world. As it is the biggest bell, the tenor is the most difficult to retune or even recast. The tendency in English bell towers is to fuss with the other, smaller bells to bring back a full ring, should the tenor go out of tune. Unfortunately, the size of the clapper on a big bell is such that these tend to go out of tune the fastest. I think it is safe to say that the fastest changes occur in the bell (really, the bells) of society. Still, our tendency is to try to keep all the bells in tune with each other, no matter the original source of change.°

In this way, social relations and the interests that derive from them help shape our understanding of all mental realms, such as that of the natural other. In striving for resonance across our categories, in building this kind of larger ecology, the sounds we listen for in other bells are indeed influenced by what we hear in the social. It seems reasonable to expect that people feel the most ideological comfort when they find their categories work across the realms of their experience—across realms of

---

° It may be important to remind some readers here that my argument throughout remains at the level of the kinds of experience we draw on to derive our categories of knowledge. I say nothing about the human need to derive catego-ries in the first place. I do mean to say that nonsocial experience likely has a major influence in the categories we ultimately come up with, adding "nature" (among other things) into the soup of basic experience. Yet I believe I still remain clear of questions of human biology, such as those considered by Lévi-Strauss. Obvi-ously, at some level these questions are appropriate and must be raised. But it is not my purpose to do so here.

the natural other, the generalized (that is, social) other, machines, the body, and more.

Resonance is a (deliberately) complex metaphor. Let me conclude this section by stating as clearly as I can what I mean by it.

We tend to think a thing more true when we can hear it—think it, see it—in a range of experience. If a way of hearing and experiencing suits different realms, that way seems intuitively and ideologically more sensible to us. Indeed, it would be surprising if this were not so. But the direction of how that agreement comes to be—from the generalized other to the natural other, from the natural other to the generalized, or from an interplay between these and other realms of thought and experience— is not significant to us. As long as we get there.

V

For all its difference, a natural conscience is thus something Childerleyans find very relevant to their lives. In it they find a powerful source of motivation and identity—the natural other—a source they consider to be free of the social interests that undermine the moral security class formerly held in English society. The most common way villagers envision the natural other is through their pastoral conception of country life. Upon this conception they construct a sense of a *natural me,* the true *me* the natural other sees, the *me* of being a country person. The search for this pastoral truth is a large part of what brings people to places like Childerley, or causes those already there to stay. And for those who do not seek to live in Childerley, I suspect something of the same desire shapes their love for the pastoral landscape of the village, a love daily pronounced among all the peoples of England.

Paradoxically, the natural other, for all its secure power in the lives of Childerleyans, is an extremely variable and adaptable idea among them. Villagers adapt it through a process that makes it readily applicable to their social context—the intuitive correspondences of resonance. Through resonance, the natural other appears to villagers in categories with a social sound to them. Without this sound, it would probably not seem so reasonable to them to follow the directives of the natural conscience. Resonance is ultimately what makes pastoral nature seem such a relevant source of social understanding to them.

The natural other is not infinitely adaptable. The need for resonance with categories that work across the range of Childerleyans' experience does constrain what the villages think about the natural other—and, for that matter, the generalized other. *Need* may be too strong a word. But there is a kind of intuitive pleasure, an intellectual state of ease, which comes from achieving the adjustments in understanding that bring out a resonance in life. In this way, the natural other does speak back to some degree and help shape the social ideas which in turn shape it. The resonant correspondence that results reinforces the ideological shape the whole takes on.

There is an adjustable permanence to the truths Childerleyans thereby find in pastoral nature. This adaptable sense of fixity is precisely what they—and others—find so hard to find elsewhere in a world whose moorings of self have been cut by the knife of nominalism. "A world without stable points of reference," as Kai Erikson put it, "is a world in ruins for those who find themselves without the personal resources or the good luck to navigate effectively in it."[14]

To their great fortune, Childerleyans have at least one resource. Suspicions of social interest have undermined many bases for a natural conscience, making them merely aspects of the collective conscience—and in this book I have emphasized the undermining of class, but the same could probably be said of religion, gender, and race, at least in some places. Childerleyans' pastoral conception of the natural other gives them someplace else to rest. It gives them what they regard as a secure harbor from the storm of accusations of social interest behind any assertion of permanence and truth. And because of resonance, it is a harbor in which they can all find a place to anchor. All Childerleyans can, within some limits of argument, gain an inner sense of entitlement to this natural me. This is the special grace of their pastoral understanding of the natural conscience.

Childerleyans are not the only people who have discovered this grace. The existence of a pastoral natural conscience apart from the collective conscience is today one of the most widespread of collective ideas. It is increasingly people's chosen source of resistance to directives they have come to doubt in what they regard as the collective conscience. This, I believe, is part of the bedrock underlying environmentalism in the West, a stratum of deep rock of which the organized environmental movement only constitutes the most visible outcropping. This, I believe, is much of what people are talking about when they speak of the importance of preserving country places, wild species, and wilderness areas. The conscience pastoral nature gives is one of nature's most precious resources.

But that does not mean we cannot be critical of the manner by which people become acquainted with the natural other. There are a number of important grounds on which I believe we should question the manner of Childerleyans, at least. They often appeared to me beguiled by the prized other. Consequently, they showed too little sensitivity to the chauvinism of being a country person—a chauvinism that on the part of individual villagers seemed at times to overlap dangerously with class, ethnic, and other forms of exclusivity. They showed too little interest in the ecological condition of cities, perhaps the greatest unaddressed environmental problem of an urban country like England, for that is where most people in England live. They showed too little concern for how their automobile-dependent lifestyle and use of country identity as an alternative language of material acquisitiveness increases the environmental and social impact of their own lives. Despite resonance, the natural other often does not challenge villagers' understanding of social life.

But it can. All propositions about truth are, in the end, propositions about the character of the natural other—that hoped-for realm free of social interest, but not of social relevance. And it is very human to have such a hope, very human indeed to seek a place to stand whereby the free truths outside us can be brought within. Like Childerleyans, we all seek a vantage point for the social self. We find it in a tower of bells we each build out of the materials of life's circumstances. Here we listen, listen for a ring of truth.

METHODS

I

WHY AN ETHNOGRAPHIC study?
Most of the limited sociological work on the experience of nature in the West has drawn upon large-scale surveys.° There is nothing wrong with this approach, of course. The large social survey is one of the most powerful tools available to social studies, and indeed it has become a fixture of contemporary Western society. But as the data are necessarily abstracted from the people described, interpretation of a survey's meaning sometimes takes place from dizzying heights. The overall patterns that are so plain from on high may, like Martian canals, disappear when one is on the ground. The best understanding usually requires a combination of both vantages. I sought to balance our overall perspective with a view from the field.

Not that there aren't problems interpreting ethnographic evidence—as well as ethnographic writing. Three methodological issues in particular have been much discussed of late. First, there is always the possibility, even the unavoidability, that ethnographers' own politics, social interests, and personalities may creep into the accounts they give of the people they studied. Second, any attempt to represent in narrative form the life of a society, a people, a community, necessarily entails some distortion as real life is too ongoing, complex, and ambiguous for the neatness a convincing scholarly argument requires. (Moreover, ethnographers often use the techniques of good storytelling to their rhetorical advantage.) Third, we need to recognize that ethnographers by their very presence in the field help construct the social contexts they observe.[1]

Although ethnography has recently been singled out in these regards, the first and second problems, while real enough, probably pertain to all writing. I encourage readers to be as critical of what I have written here

---

° I am not alone in complaining about the almost exclusive use of survey methods in research on the sociology of nature and environment; see Lowe and Rüdig (1986).

as they are of anything else they may read. But the third problem is perhaps especially salient in ethnography. So it is important to consider how I must have looked to Childerleyans. I encourage readers to keep this in mind in evaluating my report of how they looked to me.

They saw me, of course, as an American, something which was readily apparent with every word I spoke. They saw me as a white male Westerner. Given my last name, they also saw me as Christian and as British in origin. My wife, Diane Mayerfeld, lived in the village with me during the fieldwork, commuting to a job in her own profession in the city, much like many villagers. Consequently, they saw me as a good family man as well, an important mark of decency among most Childerleyans.

But in fact, although I do have some British ancestry (not on the Bell side), I'm Jewish. Furthermore, Diane and I have views on family life that I believe few other Childerleyans shared. For example, we both retain our family names in marriage. Yet I did not attempt to dissuade the residents of these interpretations of me, and Diane responded to "Mrs. Bell" throughout our stay in the village.

There may have been some slight deceit in this, and these are issues I wrestled with throughout the fieldwork. I was well aware that these assumptions on the part of the villagers contributed to my acceptability, something which I stood to benefit from. Yet aside from once early on when I prevaricated, I never denied my religious background, when asked. Nor did we deny what Diane prefers to be called, when someone inquired. Few did. Although I often worried about these issues, they rarely came up, making for an awkward moment in only a couple of instances.

Consequently, I think most villagers saw me as in part an outsider and in part an insider, both a Stranger and an Us. I saw them much the same way. As a result, I believe I was often able to stand at the margins of the village, seeing life there in part through the eyes of a Childerleyan and in part through the eyes of a stranger. Ecologists speak of the margins of lakes as the "littoral zone." My position on the margin of the village gives me some hope that I can give the closest we may ever come in ethnography to literal truth—*littoral* truth. Indeed, it may be that we should aim to come no closer.

The common use in ethnography of a pseudonym for the place under study raises still other issues. Such a practice can distance a study from the compelling specificity that is the essence of place. Furthermore, readers may suspect a hidden case for the generalizability of the findings in the use of a pseudonym—the sense of "everywoman" and "everyman" that such a practice can connote. Although I reluctantly decided to use a pseudonym, let me make plain that Childerley *is* a specific place. Where possible, I tried to convey that specificity here, as I think it important to do. The findings *do* have more general significance, I believe, but I would like to make that claim based on the arguments herein, not the use of a pseudonym. Still, the problems remain.

I could not avoid them due to another over-riding consideration—the need to protect the confidentiality of the residents who speak in these pages. For such a small place, changing the names of the individuals (as I have done) would not have been, by itself, enough to maintain their confidentiality. Moreover, in addition to using pseudonyms throughout, I have slightly altered some minor details of Childerley's demographic profile and local parish boundaries so that a sleuth with a Hampshire census and map could not immediately pick the area out. As well, I have changed a few characteristics of individual villagers in cases where I thought it prudent to give them a little anonymity from each other.

Throughout the study I assured the villagers of these confidences, and I have no intention of betraying their trust. These are necessary fictions. The power of a text to get back to those described in it was already apparent to Alexis de Tocqueville in 1848. Along with him, "I would rather let my comments suffer than add my name to the list of those travelers who repay generous hospitality with worries and embarrassments."[2]

II

WHY CHILDERLEY?

From the thousands of English exurban villages, I decided to look at those in the orbit of the original "Great Wen," urban Hell, and "great cesspool": London.° Here, in the shadow of Britain's capital city, I hoped the exurban question would be very much on the lips of the residents. Thinking that the best insights would come from being able to compare experiences of nature and country life across groups within the village, I

° London has seldom elicited neutral reactions. It was Cobbett who called London the "Great Wen." In Shelley's words (from *Peter Bell the Third*),

Hell is a city much like London—
A populous and smoky city.

In *A Study in Scarlet*, Sir Arthur Conan Doyle described it as "that great cesspool into which all the loungers of the Empire are irresistibly drained."

sought a village with a reasonably diverse class composition. I also felt it essential for the village to be visually rural, although within London's influence—essential for raising the exurban problem of nature. In addition, given the intensive character of the ethnographic methods used in the study and the limited time available for it, I needed a small village.

After two months of poring over maps, site visits, and talking to local government officials and university researchers, I eventually narrowed my search to six villages, two in Surrey and four in Hampshire. But I still had two other factors to deal with. First, I needed a place to stay. Privately rented accommodation is very scarce in the English countryside, so the availability of a suitable flat or small house was a significant limitation. Second, I wanted to make sure, as best I could, that the residents were informed of my intention to study their village and that they had a chance to object to my planned intrusion into their lives. So I decided to approach the rector of each village, and to ask them to inquire of their parishioners both about their enthusiasm for an American come to study them and about a place for him to stay. The rector is still a central individual in small English villages large enough to retain one, and I thought such a person would be best placed to be an intermediary for me. I also hoped the additional request of a place to stay would give people an easy way to say politely no.

I was eventually able to meet with four rectors. One never responded. Another wrote back and said the village was interested, but there was no place available for me to live. Two others said their village was willing, even excited about the project, and that there was a place to stay. I settled on the smaller village, and in December 1987 moved into a somewhat rundown farm workers' bungalow, previously vacant for several years, in Childerley.*

III

AND HOW WAS THE EVIDENCE GATHERED?

Childerley's rector made most of my initial introductions for me, which was very helpful in the first stages of the work. I eventually met other villagers on my own, as well as taking introductions from those I had met earlier. But it was often a slow process. Unlike the village of

---

* Although I did not realize it at the time, it turned out to be very significant for my rapport with working-class Childerleyans that the place I took over had been long vacant and that therefore I had not competed with any of them or their relations for a house.

yore, Childerley has no community well where all the villagers are likely to come during the day. The shop, the church, and the pubs serve this function to some extent. But any one of these attracts only a minority of villagers, and even then usually on an occasional basis. Realizing that waiting for invitations to dinner and tea and inclusion in drinking parties at the pubs would take time (as well as somewhat falsely representing me as a village member), I decided to push things a little bit.

So I made up a short survey of general questions, and let it be known that I wanted to administer it to as great a cross-section of the village as I could. People then found they had a much better reason to invite me over, show me around, and introduce me to their friends and neighbors. Several residents made particular efforts to introduce me to as wide a range of villagers as they could. A few approached me directly and offered to do the survey. I think in some village circles there was even a certain competitiveness about being a part of the survey. (One woman virtually demanded that I include her.) Because of my public and exotic status, I believe these Childerleyans regarded me as a bit of a celebrity. The survey made me a more approachable one.

In all, I conducted first interviews with 109 adult villagers, second interviews with 28, and a series of repeated in-depth interviews with 10 others. This amounted to 81 hours of recorded material, in addition to my field notes. Invitations to dinner parties, tea, nights out drinking, evenings watching telly, walks, idle kitchen chat, days out at the seashore, rides through the countryside, and the like did come in time. These informal exchanges provided a valuable social context for interpreting the content of the formal interviews, and greatly added to the pleasure of my stays in the village. I estimate that by the end of my last stay I had come into direct social contact with roughly half of Childerley's residents. All told, 95 different Childerleyans appear at some point in the text of this book. I remain in touch with a number of the villagers.

In practice, I followed my survey only loosely, usually pretty much abandoning use of it as soon as possible, depending on whether the obvious presence of formal papers in my hands made the person ill-at-ease (as it did some) or initially more comfortable (as it did others). Many villagers, it seemed clear, did not expect a formal survey, just a social call by an interested visitor. For them I did not produce my survey at all. But in any case, I tried to ensure that the same ground was covered in all these conversations, however various the social situation and the order of topics, while at the same time providing space for other conversational ground the residents thought significant. When the person appeared comfortable with taping, I did so. For others, I took notes afterward. Although I think I sometimes guessed wrong about which was best, I believe this variable method of recording (as well as of interviewing) came the closest to getting the villagers' true voices.* And by the word *true,* I mean nothing more than voices from situations in which villagers felt relatively at ease in talking about personally significant topics.

I also took notes on conversations I had in informal settings. I did not do this lightly, for the ethical boundary between friend (as I hope I was to many villagers, and as they were to me) and ethnographer is a very real one. Friends hear things and give their advice on things that ethnographers do not and should not.

Although decency required that I sometimes put it on hold, I never hid my purpose in being in the village. It was common knowledge that I was there "to study country life in an English village." Where it was not, I made sure it became known. Villagers were generally pleased to tell me about their impressions of this life, something they think and talk about virtually every day among themselves. And people often said things they clearly intended for my mental tape recorder, even when the mechanical one was off or at home.

Thus readers will note many quotations from informal situations in which I likely did not have a tape recorder going. As well, I have included a number of passages from interviews which I did not tape. Most of these are short quotations of a few sentences or less, put together later that day or, rarely, the next day from my memory of key phrases. (The passages in chapter 3 from my conversation with Sir Harold, which he asked that I not tape, are long exceptions. Harriet and Ed Cooper's ghost stories in chapter 8 are others.) The overwhelming majority, more than 75 percent, of all the quoted material is from tape.

IV

IT HAD BEEN A TWO-HOUR INTERVIEW, and both Abel Harrowell and I were getting tired. I still had a couple of questions I wanted to ask that night, but I thought better of it.

"I should probably let you get to the pub," I said.

"It is interesting [being interviewed]," Abel graciously responded. "Yeah, I don't mind."

---

* Of the 109 first interviews, portions of 69 were recorded. Of the 28 second interviews, portions of 24 were recorded. Eight of ten villagers with whom I conducted a series of in-depth interviews also consented to some taping.

"Well, good. I'm glad you've enjoyed it."

He smiled broadly in agreement.

"It's a bit of self-analysis as well, isn't it," he said, "really when you think about it. Because you never talk to people, do you really, as such like this."

"I guess not. I mean, not in the pubs? You don't get together with farm workers and say, well, what do you think about tied houses, and stuff like that?"

"Put me on the spot, that did. No. I wouldn't say so. I think you talk about more mundane things, quite honestly. My wife can't understand me when I come back from the pub. She asks me, 'What did you talk about?' You talked about tractors."

We both laughed. Abel does all the field work for a local farm, and, like most tractor drivers, is well known for his unending enthusiasm for these great machines.

"No," he said, "we don't touch on what I would call '*these* sort of topics.' I think these are much more interesting. You talk to a level, you know, don't you. In the company you're in. You must find that you do it a lot."

I thought, but did not respond immediately. Abel continued to probe.

"You talk to the level you know you're dealing with. Come on . . ."

Finally, I answered.

"Well, sometimes I'm pretty surprised, but yeah, you've got to," I said. "You try to fit to who you're talking to. I wouldn't say—it's the word *level* that I didn't want to go with. I try not to look at the world in levels."

"No. No. Alright. Maybe it's a bad word."

"I know what you mean."

"I don't say you talk down or you talk up or anything like that," he added, "but I still maintain that you use your knowledge to, to—"

I broke in with an example to support Abel's point.

"Oh yeah. When I talk to Mrs. Westbrook-Thorp, someone like that who owns a farm," I said, "anybody with a name like Westbrook-dash-Thorp—you know what kind of background she's from. We don't talk about quite the same topics we're talking about right now."

"Yup. That's right."

"And you choose. Of course you fit. You've got to. But I think that's part of trying to see if you really are communicating in talking to some-body. Because if you can't sort of adapt to who the other person is, or whatever, that means that you don't understand what they're about."

"Right."

"You're just going at different levels."

Abel heard my words better than I spoke them, and observed, "You're using levels, see."

I tried to respond.

"No, I mean, different levels in the conversation. You know, you're sort of missing like two planes in the night."

Abel gave me a little support.

"Alright, alright. You want repartee."

"That's right. If you say something, and you get a response—Whoo! That's not what I was expecting. Then you know you were coming at it from the wrong kind of thing. So not only do you do it, but it's not a bad thing. In fact, it's essential if you're really going to find out where somebody else is coming from. No. I think it's certainly true."

I let my mind catch up with itself. Then I added quietly, "You're right. I did use levels. I did use it in that way. Oh well."

The conversation paused. I finished off the can of beer I'd been nursing as I sat on the old green couch in Abel's sitting room. Then Abel spoke—broadly, gently, and wisely.

"No. We're all born into a little sphere somewhere along the line. We take that as we go. The one man, he might be a cowman, and he'll talk about his cows all night. The other man, he'll be a tractor driver and he'll talk about his tractor all night. Another man might be a sprayer operator and he'll talk about his sprayer all night. Another man will be a professor of physics and he'll talk about Newton all night. Which is, as far as I'm concerned, great. Great, because the bigger cross-section you can talk to, the more you learn about the world."

And here the tape ended.

NOTES

Chapter 1: The View from Winter Hill

1. Horace, *Epistle* 1.10 (Raffel [1983]).

2. See Wie-Ming (1989), Cook (1989), and Black Elk and Lyon (1990).

3. Glacken (1967), xv.

4. Durkheim (1964), 79, defined collective conscience as "the totality of beliefs and sentiments common to average citizens of the same society."

5. Plato's *Gorgias* (Lamb, trans. [1933]), 483B.

6. Lovejoy (1961), xi.

7. Lovejoy and Boas (1935).

8. Williams (1976), 184.

9. Swidler (1986).

10. Howkins (1986).

Chapter 2: A Parish on the Fringe

1. On chalk geography and Saxon land use patterns, see Hoskins (1955) and Coones and Patten (1986).

2. In order to protect the village's identity, I cannot give the citation for this quotation.

3. These figures are from the mid-1980s. See Phillips and Williams (1984), 112; and Champion and Townsend (1990), figure 7.3.

4. Harper (1987). Her study also covered Staffordshire villages, but I report only her Hampshire figures.

5. On "occupational" villages, see Newby (1977 and 1979). On "traditional" villages, see Crichton (1964). On "working-class" villages, see Pahl (1965).

6. For more on "metropolitan" villages, see Ambrose (1974) and Connell (1978).

7. Pahl (1965).

8. Newby (1977 and 1979).

9. Hampshire County Planning Department (1986).

10. Gibbs (1983), 1.

11. Pahl (1965), Russell (1986), Harper (1987), and Hart (1991).

12. Hundreds of studies have documented these changes. For an overview, see Phillips and Williams (1984) and Champion and Watkins (1991).

13. For the United States, Johnson (1989); for West Germany, Kontuly et al. (1986); for France, Ogden and Winchester (1988); and for Denmark, Court (1988).

14. For samples of such structural explanations, see Pahl (1965) and Frisbie and Kasarda (1988). For a more balanced view, see Harper (1991).

15. Pahl (1965), 21; and Connell (1978), 4–8.

16. Mackinder (1902).

17. Hunter (1987).

Chapter 3: A "Slightly Feudal" Village

1. Hobsbawm (1981), Kitchin (1968), Lukes (1984), Perkin (1989).

2. Berger et al. (1973), Cohen (1986), Erikson (1976), Giddens (1991), Habermas (1975).

3. Priestly (1973), 20.

4. *Daily Mail*, June 18, 1990, 23.

5. Calvocoressi (1978), 10.

6. Halsey (1978), 43.

7. Hobsbawm (1981). See also Lukes (1984) and, for an earlier statement, Kitchin (1960), quoted in Dyer (1986).

8. Gorz (1982).

9. Thatcher (1992), 37.

10. Goldthorpe et al. (1980) and (1987).

11. Marshall et al. (1988).

12. Goldthorpe et al. (1980), 252.

13. Erikson (1982) and Grusky and Hauser (1989).

14. Goldthorpe et al. (1987).

15. Erikson and Goldthorpe (1985) and Kerckhoff et al. (1985).

16. Lipset (1963).

17. Kerckhoff et al. (1989).

18. Kerckhoff et al. (1989) did not, however, find support for Ralph Turner's (1960) view that schooling in America operates on the meritocratic principles of

"contest mobility," versus the "sponsored mobility" of Britain, in which a child's class background determines access to good schools and resultant prestige.

19. Weber (1967), 926–40.

20. Marshall et al. (1988), table 6.3, reports that their respondents used much the same criteria.

21. Here I am following the practice of Marshall et al. (1988). For readers interested in more details on the scales, their book is the place to start.

22. This scale is also commonly known as the Hope-Goldthorpe scale. For details, see Goldthorpe and Hope (1974).

23. Marshall et al. (1988), table 6.1; Marwick (1982) for the 1948 poll; and Young and Willmott (1973, 12) for the 1970 London survey.

24. Marshall et al. (1988), 148.

25. Western (1992).

26. Champion and Townsend (1990), 44–46.

27. Derived from Hunter (1991).

Chapter 4: The Front Door and the Back Door

1. Williams (1981), 11.

2. Bourdieu (1984).

3. Goffman (1959).

4. See Pahl (1965).

5. See Fussell (1983) and Brazelton (1990).

6. Fleming (1979).

7. The literature on the stratification of cultural forms is vast. Some works that I have found informative include Hoggart (1970), Willis (1977), Willmott and Young (1960) and Young and Willmott (1957) for Britain; DiMaggio and Mohr (1985), Labov (1973), and Veblen (1967) for America; and Bourdieu (1984) for France. My perspective has been largely guided by Bakhtin (1984).

8. Marx (1972 [1859]), 4. My emphasis.

9. Durkheim and Mauss (1963) and Durkheim (1965).

10. *The Sun*, May 20, 1988.

11. BBC 4's *Today* show, May 21, 1988.

12. Newby (1979) and Russell (1986).

13. Champion and Townsend (1990), figure 7.3.

14. Scott (1985), 350.

15. See Blythe (1969) and Newby (1977).

16. Newby (1977).

17. Marshall et al. (1988), 143.

18. Veblen (1967).

19. Schama (1988), 609.

Chapter 5: Country People and City People

1. See Coleman (1990), Dewey (1960), Fischer (1982), Gans (1962a, 1962b, and 1967), Hillery (1955 and 1963), Pahl (1965, 1966), and Webber (1963). The next section reviews this work in detail.

2. Thomas (1951), 81. By "men" Thomas meant all people.

3. Hegel (1952); Weber (1967 [1922]), 212–301; Durkheim (1964).

4. On the stagnant and vegetative quality of rural life, see Marx (1972), 582. On rural idiocy, see Marx and Engels (1968).

5. Simmel (1950).

6. Tönnies (1940).

7. It is significant in part because many scholars have missed this. See Abercrombie et al. (1988), 45.

8. Tönnies (1940), 18.

9. Sorokin and Zimmerman (1929) are often credited with founding this perspective in American sociology.

10. Wirth (1938).

11. Redfield (1947), 293 and 297. Miner (1939) is an exemplary study in this scholarly tradition. Avila (1969) offered a similar argument from a modernization perspective.

12. Whyte (1955), Suttles (1968), Gans (1962a, 1962b, and 1967), Young and Willmott (1957), Willmott and Young (1960), Liebow (1967).

13. Gusfield (1975), Lewis (1951), Miner (1952).

14. Pahl (1965).

15. Dewey (1960).

16. Pahl (1966).

17. Hillery (1963).

18. Stacey (1969).

19. Abercrombie et al. (1988), 44.

20. See Smelser (1988) and Coleman (1990).

21. Friedland (1989).

22. Griswold (1992).

23. Williams (1976).

24. See Howkins (1986) and Lowenthal (1991).

25. Cited in Lowenthal (1991).

26. Williams (1985), 104.

27. For overviews of the effects of modern agricultural practices on the land-scape and the political conflicts they have engendered in Britain, see Shoard (1981), Pye-Smith and Rose (1984), and Lowe et al. (1986).

28. Erikson (1965), 13, 27.

29. Williams (1985).

30. Cohen (1986).

31. Hirsch (1977). Newby (1979) and Lowe and Goyder (1983) were among the first to apply the positional-goods argument to the politics of the countryside.

32. Shucksmith (1991).

33. As Newby at times in his work appears to suggest. See Newby (1979), especially pages 13–24 and 201–259.

34. Blythe (1983).

Chapter 6: Finding Nature

1. *Epistle* 1.10. Raffel (1983).

2. All quotations from Berger (1981), 14–15, 172.

3. See Glacken (1967); Kelsen (1943), vii; Mill (1961 [1874]); Sidgwick (1907), 81; Williams (1976).

4. Mill (1961), 449.

5. *Physics* 185b:15–25, Ackrill (1987), ed.

6. Glacken (1967), x.

7. Mill (1961), 463.

8. Sidgwick (1907), 81.

9. Marx (1980 [1964]). Glacken (1967) dates pastoralism to the poetry of Bion and Moschus in the third century B.C.E.

10. Lovejoy and Boas (1935) and Williams (1985). Williams calls these two readings "pastoral" and "counter-pastoral."

11. See Buttel and Newby (1980), Friedland (1982), Mingey (1989), Newby (1979), Williams (1985).

12. *The Republic,* Book 6, 509d, in Sterling and Scott (1985). *Timaeus,* 29E–30A, in Archer-Hind (1888).

13. *Physics,* 2.1, 192b:9–15 and 2.8, 199b:15–20, in Ackrill (1987).

14. Ibid., 2.8, 199a:15-20.

15. See *Parts of Animals*, 1.1, 639b:20 and *Politics*, 1.1, 1252a:0-5, in Ackrill (1987).

16. *Politics*, 1.2, 1253a:5-10, in Ackrill (1987).

17. See, for example, Oelschlaeger (1991).

Chapter 7: The Natural Conscience

1. Mead (1938), 109-110.

2. Mead (1934), 184-185.

3. Ibid., 154n.

4. Perinbanayagam (1985), 155.

5. Scott (1990).

Chapter 8: The Foreground and the Background

1. Durkheim and Mauss (1963), 82-85.

2. Marx and Engels (1972), 118, 136-137.

3. Meek, ed. (1971), 195.

4. From a letter to P. L. Lavrov, November 1875; cited in Schmidt (1971), 47. A very similar passage, although not so well phrased, appears in Engel's *The Dialectics of Nature* (1940), 208. My emphasis.

5. Williams (1980), 70-71.

6. I am indebted to Ronald Blythe for pointing this out to me.

7. Veblen (1967), 138.

8. Cosgrove (1984), 1, 9.

Chapter 9: The Pursuit of the Inedible

1. See chapter 4 for an explanation of status conservatism.

2. See chapter 4 for an explanation of economic conservatism.

3. See Pine (1966).

Chapter 10: The Mouse in the Sprinkler Pipe

1. See Dankelman and Davidson (1988), 3-4.

2. Gilligan (1982), 173.

3. Chodorow (1978) and Gilligan and Wiggins (1988).

4. See Paglia (1990) and Shiva (1988).

Chapter 11: The View From the Bell Tower

1. Mill (1961), 452. Also see Béteille (1983).

2. Burch (1971).

3. Pope (1951).

4. See passage quoted in chapter 8.

5. Johnson (1987), x.

6. Schwartz (1981), 171.

7. Lévi-Strauss (1970), 10.

8. Ibid., 104.

9. Lakoff (1987), xi.

10. Johnson (1987).

11. Lakoff (1987), xiv.

12. Schwartz (1981).

13. Rosch (1978).

14. Erikson (1976), 257.

Methods

1. Some of the central books in this debate are Fabian (1983), Clifford and Marcus (1986), and Geertz (1988).

2. De Tocqueville (1969), 20.

REFERENCES

Abercrombie, Nicholas, Steven Hill, and Bryan S. Turner. 1988. *The Penguin Dictionary of Sociology.* Harmondsworth, UK: Penguin.

Ackrill, J. L., ed. 1987. *A New Aristotle Reader.* Princeton: Princeton University.

Ambrose, P. 1974. *The Quiet Revolution: Social Change in a Sussex Village, 1871–1971.* London: Chatto and Windus.

Anderson, Benedict. 1983. *Imagined Communities.* London: Verso.

Archer-Hind, R. D., ed. 1888. *The Timaeus of Plato.* London: Macmillan.

Aslet, Clive, editor. 1988. *Buying a Country House.* London: Country Life Magazine and Knight, Frank and Rutley.

Avila, Manuel. 1969. *Tradition and Growth.* Chicago: University of Chicago Press.

Bakhtin, Mikhail. 1984 (1965). *Rabelais and His World.* Bloomington, IN: Indiana University Press.

Berger, Bennett M. 1981. *The Survival of a Counterculture.* Berkeley: University of California Press.

Berger, Peter, Brigitte Berger, and Hansfried Kellner. 1973. *The Homeless Mind.* New York: Vintage.

Béteille, André. 1983. *The Idea of Natural Inequality.* Delhi: Oxford University Press.

Black Elk, Wallace, and William S. Lyon. 1990. *Black Elk: The Sacred Ways of a Lakota.* San Francisco: Harper and Row.

Blythe, Ronald. 1969. *Akenfield.* London: Alan Lane.

———. 1983. *Characters and Their Landscapes.* San Diego: Harcourt, Brace, Jovanovich.

Bourdieu, Pierre. 1984. *Distinction.* Richard Nice, trans. Cambridge, MA: Harvard University Press.

Brazelton, Berry T. 1990. "Why Is America Failing Its Children?" *New York Times Magazine,* September 9th, pp. 40–43, 50, 90.

Burch, William R. 1971. *Daydreams and Nightmares.* New York: Harper and Row.

Buttel, Frederick, and Howard Newby. 1980. *The Rural Sociology of the Advanced Societies: Critical Perspectives.* London and Montclair, NY: Croom Helm and Allanheld and Osmun.

Calvocoressi, Peter. 1978. *The British Experience, 1945–1975.* New York: Pantheon.

Cannadine, David. 1992. "Cutting Classes." *New York Review of Books* 39(21): 52–57.

Champion, A. G., and A. R. Townsend. 1990. *Contemporary Britain: A Geographical Perspective.* London: Edward Arnold.

Champion, A. G., and Charles Watkins, eds. 1991. *People in the Countryside.* London: Paul Chapman.

Chodorow, Nancy. 1978. *The Reproduction of Mothering: Psychoanalysis and the Sociology of Gender.* Berkeley, CA: University of California Press.

Clifford, James, and George Marcus, eds. 1986. *Writing Culture.* Berkeley: University of California Press.

Cohen, Anthony, ed. 1986. *Symbolizing Boundaries: Identity and Diversity in British Culture.* Manchester: Manchester University Press.

Coleman, James S. 1990. *Foundations of Social Theory.* Cambridge, MA: Belknap.

Connell, John. 1978. *The End of Tradition.* London: Routledge and Kegan Paul.

Cook, Francis H. 1989. "The Jewel Net of Indra." In *Nature in Asian Traditions of Thought,* J. Baird Callicott and Roger T. Ames, eds. Albany, NY: State University of New York Press.

Coones, Paul, and John Patten. 1986. *The Penguin Guide to the Landscape of England and Wales.* Harmondsworth, UK: Penguin.

Cosgrove, Dennis. 1984. *Social Formation and Symbolic Landscape.* London: Croom Helm.

Court, Yvonne. 1988. "Population Distribution in Denmark: The Beginning of a Return to Large Urban Places?" Paper presented at the Annual Meeting of the Institute of British Geographers, Loughborough, England.

Cowley, Abraham. 1949. *Poetry and Prose.* Oxford, UK: Clarendon.

Crichton, Ruth. 1964. *Commuter's Village.* London: MacDonald.

Czikszentmihalyi, Mihalyi, and Eugene Rochberg-Halton. 1981. *The Meaning of Things: Domestic Symbols and the Self.* New York: Cambridge University Press.

Dankelman, Irene and Joan Davidson. 1988. *Women and the Environment in the Third World: Alliance for the Future.* London: Earthscan.

de Tocqueville, Alexis. 1969 (1848). *Democracy in America.* George Lawrence, trans. Garden City, NY: Anchor.

Dewey, Richard. 1960. "The Rural-Urban Continuum: Real but Relatively Unimportant." *American Journal of Sociology* 66:60–66.

DiMaggio, Paul, and John Mohr. 1985. "Cultural Capital, Educational Attainment, and Marital Selection." *American Journal of Sociology* 90(6):1231–1261.

Durkheim, Emile. 1964 (1893). *The Division of Labor in Society.* George Simpson, trans. New York: The Free Press.

———. 1965 (1915). *The Elementary Forms of the Religious Life.* New York: Free Press.

Durkheim, Emile, and Marcel Mauss. 1963 (1903). *Primitive Classification.* Rodney Needham, trans. Chicago: University of Chicago Press.

Dyer, Geoff. 1986. *Ways of Telling: The Work of John Berger*. London: Pluto.

Engels, Friedrich. 1940. *The Dialectics of Nature*. Clemens Dutt, trans. New York: International Publishers.

————. 1968 (1888). *The Origin of the Family, Private Property, and the State*. Reprinted in *Karl Marx and Frederick Engels: Selected Works*. New York: International Publishers.

Erikson, Kai T. 1965. *Wayward Puritans*. New York: Wiley.

———— 1976. *Everything in Its Path*. New York: Simon and Schuster.

Erikson, Robert. 1982. "Social Fluidity in Industrial Nations." *British Journal of Sociology* 30:415–441.

Erikson, Robert, and John H. Goldthorpe. 1985. "Are American Rates of Social Mobility Exceptionally High? New Evidence on an Old Issue." *European Sociological Review* 1:1–22.

Fabian, Johannes. 1983. *Time and the Other: How Anthropology Makes Its Object*. New York: Columbia University Press.

Feuerbach, Ludwig. 1957 (1841). *The Essence of Christianity*. George Elliot, trans. (This translation first published 1854.) New York: Harper and Brothers.

Fischer, Claude. 1982. *To Dwell among Friends*. Chicago: University of Chicago Press.

Fleming, Patricia Harvey. 1979. *Villagers and Strangers*. Cambridge, MA: Schenkman.

Friedland, William H. 1982. "The End of Rural Society and the Future of Rural Sociology." *Rural Sociology,* 47(4):589–608.

————. 1989. "Is Rural Sociology Worth Saving?" and "An Answer to Three Responses." *Rural Sociologist* 9(1):3–5, 12–13.

Frisbie, W. Parker, and John D. Kasarda. 1988. "Spatial Processes." In *Handbook of Sociology,* Neil Smelser, ed., pp. 629–666. Newbury Park, CA: Sage.

Frye, Northrop. 1981. *The Great Code*. New York: Harcourt, Brace, Jovanovich.

Fussell, Paul. 1983. *Class*. New York: Balantine.

Gans, Herbert J. 1962a. "Urbanism and Suburbanism as Ways of Life." In Arthur Rose, ed., *Human Behavior and Social Processes*. London: Routledge.

———— 1962b. *Urban Villagers*. New York: Free Press.

————. 1967. *The Levittowners*. New York: Pantheon.

Geertz, Clifford. 1973. "Notes on the Balinese Cockfight." In Clifford Geertz, *The Interpretation of Cultures*. New York: Basic.

————. 1988. *Works and Lives*. Stanford, CA: Stanford University Press.

Gibbs, J. Arthur. 1983 (1898). *A Cotswold Village*. London: Breslich and Foss.

Giddens, Anthony. 1991. *Modernity and Self-Identity: Self and Society in the Late Modern Age*. Stanford, CA: Stanford University Press.

Gilligan, Carol. 1982. *In a Different Voice*. Cambridge, MA: Harvard University Press.

Gilligan, Carol, and Grant Wiggins. 1988. "The Origins of Morality in Early Childhood Relationships." In *Mapping the Moral Domain*. Carol Gilligan, Janie Victoria Ward, and Jill McLean Taylor, eds. Cambridge, MA: Harvard University Press.

Glacken, Clarence. 1967. *Traces on the Rhodian Shore*. Berkeley: University of California Press.

Goffman, Erving. 1959. *The Presentation of Self in Everyday Life*. Garden City, NY: Doubleday.

Goldthorpe, John H., and Keith Hope. 1974. *The Social Grading of Occupations*. Oxford: Clarendon.

Goldthorpe, John H., Catriona Llewellyn, and Clive Payne. 1980. *Social Mobility and Class Structure in Modern Britain*. Oxford: Clarendon.

———. 1987. *Social Mobility and Class Structure in Modern Britain*. 2nd edition. Oxford: Clarendon.

Gorz, Andre. 1982. *Farewell to the Working Class*. London: Pluto.

Green, Candida Lycett, and Andrew Lawson. 1989. *Brilliant Gardens: A Celebration of English Gardening*. London: Chatto and Windus.

Griswold, Wendy, 1992. "The Writing on the Mud Wall: Nigerian Novels and the Imaginary Village." *American Sociological Review* 57(6):709–724.

Grusky, David B., and Robert M. Hauser. 1989. "Comparative Social Mobility Revisited: Models of Convergence and Divergence in 16 Countries." *American Sociological Review* 49:19–38.

Gusfield, Joseph. 1975. *Community: A Critical Response*. Oxford: Basil Blackwell.

Habermas, Jürgen. 1975. *Legitimation Crisis*. Boston: Beacon Press.

Hacker, Andrew. 1992. *Two Nations: Black and White, Separate, Hostile, Unequal*. New York: Charles Scribner's Sons.

Halsey, A. H. 1978. *Change in British Society*. Oxford: Oxford University Press.

Hampshire County Planning Department. 1986. *Hampshire's Rural Settlements Past, Present, and Future*. Winchester: Hampshire County Planning Department.

Harper, Sarah. 1987. "The Rural-Urban Interface in England: A Framework of Analysis." *Trans. Inst. Br. Geog.*, N.S. 12:284–302.

———. 1991. "People Moving to the Countryside: Case Studies of Decision-Making." In Tony Champion and Charles Watkins, eds. *People in the Countryside*. London: Paul Chapman. Pp. 22–37.

Hart, John Fraser. 1991. "The Perimetropolitan Bow Wave." *Geographical Review* 81(1):35–51.

Hegel, Fredrich. 1952 (1821). *Philosophy of Right*. T. M. Knox, ed. Oxford: Clarendon.

Hillery, George A., Jr. 1955. "Definitions of Community: Areas of Agreement." *Rural Sociology*, 20:111–123.

———. 1963. "Villages, Cities, and Total Institutions." *American Sociological Review* 28:779–791.

Hirsch, Fred. 1977. *Social Limits to Growth*. London: Routledge.

Hobsbawm, Eric. 1981. "Observations on the debate," in *The Forward March of Labour Halted?* Martin Jacques and Francis Mulhern, eds. London: New Left Books. Pp. 167–182.

Hoggart, Richard. 1970. *The Uses of Literacy.* New York: Oxford University Press.

Hoskins, W. G. 1955. *The Making of the English Countryside.* Harmondsworth, UK: Penguin.

Howkins, Alun. 1986. "The Discovery of Rural England." In R. Colls and P. Dodds, eds., *Englishness: Politics and Culture 1880–1920.* Beckenham, Kent: Croom Helm.

Hubbard, Ruth. 1982. "Have Only Men Evolved?" In *Biological Woman: The Convenient Myth,* Ruth Hubbard, Sue Henifin, and Barbara Fried, eds. Cambridge, MA: Schenkman.

Hunter, Albert. 1987. "The Symbolic Ecology of Suburbia." In *Neighborhood and Community Environments,* Irwin Altman and Abraham Wandersman, eds., pp. 191–221.

Hunter, Brian, 1991. *The Statesman's Year-Book.* New York: St. Martin's.

James, William. 1948 (1892). *Psychology (Briefer Course).* Cleveland and New York: World Publishing.

Johnson, Kenneth M. 1989. "The Nonmetropolitan Turnaround in the 1980s." *Rural Sociology* 54(3):301–326.

Johnson, Mark. 1987. *The Body in the Mind.* Chicago: University of Chicago Press.

Kelsen, Hans. 1943. *Society and Nature: A Sociological Inquiry.* Chicago: University of Chicago Press.

Kerckhoff, Alan C., Richard T. Campbell, Jerry M. Trotty, and Vaered Kraus. 1989. "The Transmission of Socioeconomic Status and Prestige in Great Britain and the United States." *Sociological Forum* 4(2):155–177.

Kerckhoff, Alan C., Richard T. Campbell, and Idee Winfied-Laird. 1985. "Social Mobility in Great Britain and the United States." *American Journal of Sociology* 91(2):281–308.

Kontuly, Thomas, Susan Wiard, and Roland Vogelsang. 1986. "Counterurbanization in the Federal Republic of Germany." *Professional Geographer* 38(2): 170–181.

Labov, William. 1973. *Language in the Inner City.* Philadelphia: University of Philadelphia Press.

Lakoff, George. 1987. *Women, Fire and Dangerous Things: What Categories Reveal about the Mind.* Chicago: University of Chicago Press.

Lamb, W. R. M. 1933. *Plato, III: Lysis, Symposium, Gorgias.* Loeb Classical Library. Cambridge, MA: Harvard University Press.

Lévi-Strauss, Claude. 1963. *Totemism.* Rodney Needham, trans. Boston: Beacon.
———. 1970. *The Raw and the Cooked.* John Weightman and Doreen Weightman, trans. New York: Harper and Row.

Lewis, Oscar. 1951. *Life in a Mexican Village: Tepoztlán Restudied.* Urbana: University of Illinois Press.

Liebow, Elliot. 1967. *Tally's Corner*. Boston: Little, Brown.

Lipset, Seymour Martin. 1963. "The Value Patterns of Democracy: A Case Study in Comparative Analysis." *American Sociological Review* 28:515–531.

Lovejoy, Arthur O. 1961. *The Reason, the Understanding, and Time*. Baltimore: Johns Hopkins University Press.

Lovejoy, Arthur O., and George Boas. 1935. *Primitivism and Related Ideas in Antiquity*. Baltimore: Johns Hopkins University Press.

Lowe, Philip, Graham Cox, Malcolm MacEwen, Tim O'Riordan, and Michael Winter. 1986. *Countryside Conflicts*. Aldershot, UK: Gower.

Lowe, Philip, and Jane Goyder. 1983. *Environmental Groups in Politics*. London: George Allen and Unwin.

Lowe, Philip, and Wolfgang Rüdig. 1986. "Political Ecology and the Social Sciences: The State of the Art." *Political Studies* 16:223–260.

Lowenthal, David. 1991. "British National Identity and the English Landscape." *Rural History* 2(2):205–230.

Luhmann, Nicholas. 1989. *Ecological Communication*. Chicago: University of Chicago Press.

Lukes, Steven. 1984. "The Future of British Socialism?" In *Fabian Essays in Socialist Thought*, Ben Pimlott, ed. London: Heinemann.

Mabey, Richard. 1980. *The Common Ground*. London: Hutchinson.

Mackinder, Halford J. 1902. *Britain and the British Seas*. London: William Heinemann.

Marshall, Gordon, David Rose, Howard Newby, and Carolyn Vogler. 1988. *Social Class in Modern Britain*. London: Unwin Hyman.

Marwick, Arthur. 1982. *British Society Since 1945*. London: Allen Lane and Penguin.

Marx, Karl. 1972 (1853), "The British Rule in India." In *The Marx-Engles Reader*, Robert Tucker, ed. New York: Norton.

———. 1972 (1859). "Preface to 'A Contribution to the Critique of Political Economy.'" In *The Marx-Engels Reader*, Robert C. Tucker, ed. New York: Norton.

———. 1977 (1873), *Capital*, vol. 1. Ben Fowkes, trans. New York: Vintage.

Marx, Karl, and Friedrich Engels. 1972 (1846). "The German Ideology." In *The Marx-Engels Reader*, Robert C. Tucker, ed. New York: Norton.

———. 1968 (1847). "Manifesto of the Communist Party." In *Karl Marx and Frederick Engels: Selected Works*. New York: International.

Marx, Leo. 1980 (1964). *The Machine in the Garden: Technology and the Pastoral Ideal in America*. London: Oxford University Press.

Mead, George Herbert. 1934. *Mind, Self, and Society*. Charles W. Morris, ed. Chicago: University of Chicago Press.

———. 1938. *The Philosophy of the Act*. Charles W. Morris, ed. Chicago: University of Chicago Press.

Meek, Ronald L., ed. 1971. *Marx and Engels on the Population Bomb.* Berkeley: Ramparts.

Mill, John Stuart. 1961 (1874). "Nature." In *The Philosophy of John Stuart Mill,* Marshall Cohen, ed. New York: Modern Library.

Mills, C. Wright. 1959. *The Sociological Imagination.* New York: Grove.

Miner, Horace. 1939. *St. Denis: A French-Canadian Parish.* Chicago: University of Chicago Press.

———. 1952. "The Folk-Urban Continuum." *American Sociological Review* 17:529–537.

Mingey, G. E., ed. 1989. *The Vanishing Countryside.* London: Routledge.

Naipaul, V. S. 1987. *The Enigma of Arrival.* New York: Knopf.

Newby, Howard. 1977. *The Deferential Worker.* London: Allen Lane.

———. 1979. *Green and Pleasant Land?* London: Wildwood House.

Oelschlaeger, Max. 1991. *The Idea of Wilderness.* New Haven and London: Yale University Press.

Ogden, P. E., and H. P. M. Winchester. 1988. "Counterurbanization in France." Paper presented at the Annual Meeting of the Institute of British Geographers, Loughborough, England.

Paglia, Camille, 1990. *Sexual Personae: Art and Decadence from Nefertiti to Emily Dickinson.* New Haven, CT: Yale University Press.

Pahl, Raymond E. 1965. *Urbs in Rure.* London School of Economics and Political Science Geographical Papers no. 2.

——— 1966. "The Rural-Urban Continuum," *Sociologia Ruralis,* 6:299–329.

Perinbanayagam, R. S. 1985. *Signifying Acts.* Carbondale, IL: Southern Illinois University Press.

Perkin, Harold. 1989. *The Rise of Professional Society.* London: Routledge.

Phillips, David, and Allan Williams. 1984. *Rural Britain: A Social Geography.* Oxford: Basil Blackwell.

Pine, Leslie G. 1966. *After Their Blood: A Survey of Blood Sports in Britain.* London: William Kimber.

Pope, Alexander. 1951 (1733–34). *An Essay on Man.* Maynard Mack, ed. London: Methuen.

Postman, Neil. 1985. *Amusing Ourselves to Death.* New York and London: Elizabeth Sifton and Penguin.

Powers, Ron. 1991. *Far From Home: Life and Loss in Two American Towns.* New York: Random House.

Priestly, David. 1973. *The English.* New York: Viking.

Pye-Smith, Charlie and Chris Rose. 1984. *Crisis and Conservation: Conflict in the British Countryside.* Harmondsworth, Middlesex: Penguin.

Raffel, Burton, trans. 1983. *The Essential Horace.* San Francisco: North Point Press.

Redfield, Robert. 1947. "The Folk Society." *American Journal of Sociology,* 52:293–308.

Rosch, Eleanor. 1978. "Principles of Categorization." In *Cognition and Categorization.* Eleanor Rosch and Barbara B. Lloyd, eds. Hillsdale, NJ: Lawrence Erlbaum.

Rousseau, Jean-Jacques. 1964 (1754). *Rousseau's First and Second Discourses.* Roger D. Masters, ed. New York: St. Martin's.

Russell, Anthony. 1986. *The Country Parish.* London: S.P.C.K.

Sayers, Dorothy L. 1962 (1934). *The Nine Tailors.* New York: Harcourt, Brace, Jovanovich.

Schama, Simon. 1988. *The Embarrassment of Riches.* New York, Alfred A. Knopf.

Schmidt, Alfred. 1971. *The Concept of Nature in Marx.* Ben Foukes, trans. London: New Left Books.

Schwartz Barry. 1981. *Vertical Classification.* Chicago: University of Chicago Press.

Scott, James. 1985. *Weapons of the Weak.* New Haven: Yale University Press.

———. 1990. *Domination and the Arts of Resistance: Hidden Transcripts.* New Haven, CT: Yale University Press.

Shiva, Vandana. 1988. *Staying Alive: Women, Ecology, and Development.* London: Zed Books.

Shoard, Marion. 1981. *The Theft of the Countryside.* London: Temple Smith.

Shucksmith, Mark. 1991. "Still No Homes for Locals? Affordable Housing and Planning Controls in Rural Areas." In *People in the Countryside,* A. G. Champion and Charles Watkins, eds. London: Paul Chapman.

Sidgwick, Henry. 1907. *The Method of Ethics.* London: Macmillan.

Simmel, Georg. 1950 (1903). "The Metropolis and Mental Life." In *The Sociology of Georg Simmel,* Kurt Wolff, ed. Glencoe, IL: Free Press.

Smelser, Neil, ed. 1988. *Handbook of Sociology.* Newbury Park, CA: Sage.

Sorokin, Pitirim, and Carle C. Zimmerman, 1929. *Principles of Rural-Urban Society.* New York: Henry Holt.

Stacey, Margaret, 1969, "The Myth of Community Studies." *British Journal of Sociology,* 20:134–47.

Sterling, Richard W., and William C. Scott, trans. 1985. *Plato: The Republic.* New York: Norton.

Strathern, Marilyn. 1981. *Kinship at the Core.* Cambridge: Cambridge University Press.

Suttles, Gerald. 1968. *The Social Order of the Slum.* Chicago: University of Chicago Press.

Swidler, Ann. 1986. "Culture in Action: Symbols and Strategies." *American Sociological Review* 51:273–286.

Tennyson, Alfred, Lord. 1982 (1850). *In Memoriam.* Susan Shatto and Marion Shaw, eds. Oxford, UK: Clarendon.

Thatcher, Margaret. 1992. "Don't Undo My Work," *Newsweek,* April 27, p. 37.

Thomas, William I. 1951. *Social Behavior and Personality.* Edmund H. Volkart, ed. New York: Social Science Research Council.

Tönnies, Ferdinand. 1940 (1887). *Fundamental Concepts of Sociology (Gemeinschaft and Gesellschaft).* Charles P. Loomis, trans. New York: American Book Company.

Turner, Ralph H. 1960. "Sponsored and Contest Mobility and the School System." *American Sociological Review* 25:855–867.

Veblen, Thorstein. 1967 (1899). *The Theory of the Leisure Class.* New York: Funk and Wagnalls.

Waplington, Nick. 1991. *Living Room.* New York: Apeture.

Warner, Lloyd W., Marchia Meeker, and Kenneth Eells. 1960 (1949). *Social Class in America: The Evaluation of Status.* New York: Harper.

Webber, Melvin. 1963. "Order in Diversity: Community without Propinquity." In Lowdon Wingo, ed., *Cities and Space.* Baltimore, MD: Johns Hopkins University Press.

Weber, Max. 1967 (1922). *Economy and Society,* vols. 1 and 2. Guenther Roth and Claus Wittich, eds. Berkeley: University of California Press.

Weigert, Andrew J. 1991. "Transverse Interaction: A Pragmatic Perspective on Environment as Other." *Symbolic Interaction* 14(3):353–363.

Wei-Ming, Tu. 1989. "The Continuity of Being: Chinese Visions of Nature." In *Nature in Asian Traditions of Thought,* J. Baird Callicott and Roger T. Ames, eds. Albany, NY: State University of New York Press.

Western, John. 1992. *A Passage to England: Barbadian Londoners Speak of Home.* Minneapolis, MN: University of Minnesota.

Whyte, William F. 1955. *Street Corner Society.* Chicago: University of Chicago Press.

Wiener, Martin. 1981. *English Culture and the Decline of the Industrial Spirit, 1850–1980.* Cambridge: Cambridge University Press.

Williams, Raymond. 1976. *Keywords: A Vocabulary of Culture and Society.* London: Fontana/Croom Helm.

———. 1980. "Ideas of Nature." In *Problems in Materialism and Culture.* London: Verso.

———. 1981. *The Sociology of Culture.* New York: Schocken.

———. 1985. *The Country and the City.* London: Hogarth.

Willis, Paul. 1977. *Learning to Labor.* New York: Columbia University Press.

Willmott, Peter, and Michael Young. 1960. *Family and Class in a London Suburb.* London: Routledge and Kegan Paul.

Wirth, Louis. 1938. "Urbanism as a Way of Life," *American Journal of Sociology,* 44:1–24.

Wordsworth, William. 1948 (1810). *A Guide Through the District of the Lakes in the North of England.* Malvern, UK: Tantivy.

Wrong, Dennis. 1976. "The Over-Socialized Conception of Man in Modern Sociology." In *Skeptical Sociology*, pp. 31–46. New York: Columbia University Press.

Young, Michael, and Peter Willmott. 1957. *Family and Kinship in East London.* London: Routledge and Kegan Paul.

———. 1973. *The Symmetrical Family*. New York: Pantheon.

INDEX

achievement
  defined, 32
  tensions with ascription, 32–33,
    40–42
  See also ascription; class; social mo-
    bility
agriculture
  employment in Childerley, 13–15,
    69–70, 99–100
  increased use of pesticides in, 4,
    97–98
  intensification of, 4, 97–98,
    127–128
all-wheeling, 210–213, 216
Anderson, Benedict, 94, 94n
animals, villagers' views,
  back door experience of birds,
    161–163, 174–175, 177–79. *See
    also* back door
  cruelty of, 189–190, 192–195,
    198–201, 205, 222. *See also* na-
    ture, villagers' views
  equality and hierarchy of humans
    and, 154, 190–192, 199–200,
    202, 229, 231
  in the fox hunt, 182–209. *See also*
    fox hunting; nature, nurturing in,
    218–222
  possibility of talking to, 162,
    179
  social motives in, 143–144,
    218–222
anomie, 150

Aquinas, Thomas, 132, 132n, 133
Aristotle, 121, 130–132, 132n,
  133
ascription
  defined, 32
  tensions with achievement, 32–33,
    40–42, 187
  See also achievement; class; social
    mobility
aviaries, 161–163
Axworth, adjacent village of, 18

back door,
  and "foreground" experience of na-
    ture, 163–164, 178, 181, 210–
    212, 228
  and all-wheeling, 210–212, 228
  cultural conflict with front door
    style, 70–71
  defined, 52
  illustrated, 51–65
  See also front door; class conflicts;
    classes, cultural differences
Bakhtin, Mikhail, 59n
Baldwin, Stanley, 94
Barringham, nearby village of,
  14
Bartley, adjacent village of, 16
Beeching, Lord, 22
Blythe, Ronald, 115
Bourdieu, Pierre, 52
Burch, William, 228
Butler Act, 29

Callicles, 7
change-ringing, 227, 234–235
Chicago School, 88
Childerley
    building stock, 12–13
    meaning of name, 11
    description of, 27–28
    landscape and physical description,
        3, 11–13
    location of, 4
    number of households, 3
    parallels with United States, 15
    population size, 4
    pronounciation of name, 11
    settlement history, 11
Chodorow, Nancy, 224
Church of England, 14
class, community assessment
    comparisons with national figures,
        45–49
    criteria for, 43–45
    methods used to determine, 43
    models used, class differences in,
        44–45
    tables of, 46–48
class, international comparisons, 29,
    32–33
class, moral ambiguity of. See moral
    ambiguity of class
class, villagers' views
    "bloodless revolution," 37–38
    conflict, 65–76, 108–114. See also
        class conflicts
    consciousness of, 27–29, 33–50
    continuing importance of, in
        Childerley, 33–36
    decline in Victorian civilities of,
        38–39, 81–83
    historical changes in structure of,
        33–42, 81–84
    rural-urban comparisons in continu-
        ing importance of, 35–36
    terminology for, 28, 34–45, 76

See also class, community assess-
    ment; class conflicts
class conflicts
    cultural factors, 70
    deference, 14, 74–75
    derision, 75
    envy, 75
    gentrification, 15, 65–70, 108–114,
        231
    housing segregation, 15–16
    violence in, 65–66
    working class resistance, 73–74
    use of country identity in, 108–
        114, 241
    See also country and class
classes, cultural differences
    and experience of nature, 29, 161–
        164, 166–181, 185, 203, 212,
        218, 228–229. See also nature,
        villagers' views
    back door versus front door,
        51–76. See also back door; front
        door
    danger of over-drawing cultural
        contrasts, 63–65
    origin of contrasts in social organi-
        zation, 62–63. See also reflection
        theory
class in British society, 28–33, 49–50,
    239. See also Oxford Group; Essex
    Group
class structure of Childerley, 15, 42–49
class in British politics, 29–30, 32n,
    40n
Cobbett, William, 244n
Cohen, Anthony, 103
collective conscience
    defined, 7, 138
    relationship to generalized other
        and the me, 138–139. See also
        generalized other; me, the
    contrast with natural conscience,
        143–147, 166, 228, 240

conflict with natural conscience,
153–157
rejection of, 140–147, 153–157,
166, 228, 240–241. *See also*
moral ambiguity of class; social
interest, problem of
recognition of by villagers', 142–
143, 150
See also natural conscience
community
academic views on prevalence of in
countryside, 86–90
as *gemeinschaft*, 87–90, 93–95, 101
contradiction with market, 80–81
opposition to *gesellschaft*, 87–90
villagers' views on prevalence of in
countryside, 36, 86, 90–101,
115–116. *See also* rural-urban
continuum
"Community," the, 19, 63–65, 216
commuting. *See* counterurbanization;
employment
Cosgrove, Denis, 172
council housing. *See* housing
counterurbanization
in Britain, 20–23, 67–68
international comparisons, 21
country, distinctiveness of. *See* rural-
urban continuum
country life, villagers' views
as close to nature, 29, 84, 86,
90–91, 96–98, 101, 123–129,
136–38
decline in, 96–101, 115–116
greater sense of community in, 86,
89–101
country, cultural significance, 3–4, 9
country identity
as expression of natural conscience
and natural me, 7–8, 151, 155,
228, 239. *See also* natural conscience; natural me; natural
other

as source of moral security, 7–8,
29, 84, 86–87, 115–116, 119,
151–153. *See also* moral ambiguity of class
chauvinism of, 241
measures used by residents to determine, 103–105
moral security of, due to affiliation
with nature, 7–8, 119–120, 129,
136–138, 146, 151, 228, 239. *See
also* nature, idea of; pastoralism
opposition to urban identity,
101–105
terminology for, 86, 101, 107–108
See also country and class; identity
country and class
class differences in conceptions of
country life, 70–76, 105–106
class differences in granting of
country identity, 105–106
country as alternative language for
class, 105–108
country as alternative language for
material acquisitiveness, 110–
115, 241
country as more morally secure
source of identity than, 7–8,
86–87, 105–108, 114–116, 119,
146, 150–151. *See also* moral ambiguity of class
country as positional good,
108–114
See also class conflicts
"country people." *See* country
identity
Cowley, Abraham, epigraph, 85
cruelty, moral problem of. *See* nature, villagers' views

Daoism, 122, 135
Darwin, Charles, 165
development pressures. *See* counterurbanization

Dewey, Richard, 89
Disraeli, Benjamin, 52n
Doyle, Sir Arthur Conan, 244n
drinking habits, in village. See pubs
    and pub life
dualism. See nature, idea of
Durkheim, Emile, 7, 62, 100, 138,
    142, 150, 164, 166

economic conservatism, 80–81,
    188–189
employment
    commuting, 13–15, 20–23
    importance of local contacts for
        working class, 69
    in agriculture, 13–15, 69–70, 91
    non-agricultural village work, 13
Engels, Friedrich, 165–166, 229–
    230, 231–232n
environmental movement, 4, 6,
    146–147
Erikson, Kai, 100, 240
Essex Group, survey on class by,
    31–32, 42, 49, 77
established villages, 14–15
ethnography. See methods
European Community, 97
exurbs
    character of, 4
    definition of, 21
    growth of, 20–23
    meaning of, 6
    question of, 8, 245
    settlement patterns in, 14–16
    See also counterurbanization

false-consciousness, critique of theory
    of, 142–143
family life, 212–213, 223
Fleming, Patricia, 59
fox hunting

as a sport, description, 182, 185,
    206
protests against, 182–185, 196–197
See also Wild Mammals Protection
    Bill; fox hunting, villagers' views
fox hunting, villagers' views
    conservative detractors of, 200–
        202, 209
    conservative supporters of, 186–
        192, 209
    cruelty of, 189–192, 194–202,
        205–209, 222
    eroticism of, 198
    ideological significance of, 209,
        230, 237
    left and left-leaning detractors of,
        192–199, 209, 231
    working class detractors of,
        203–209
    working class supporters of,
        207–208
    See also nature, experience of
front door
    and "background" experience of na-
        ture, 163–164, 178, 181, 228.
        See also nature, experience of
    cultural conflict with back door
        style, 70–71. See also class con-
        flicts
    defined, 52
    illustrated, 51–65
    See also back door
Frye, Northrop, 234n

gardens, class differences in styles,
    175–178, 230
Geertz, Clifford, 186
gender
    danger of overdrawing contrasts in
        natural experience, 222–223
    differences in work and economic
        power, 212–213

influence of author's gender on evidence, 223
influence of family roles and economic power on outlooks, 212–215, 218–221
male aggressiveness, villagers' views, 214, 217–218
militaristic values among village men, 214, 216–218, 229
nurturing values among village men, 220–222
nurturing values among village women, 218–222, 229
physical capacities for outdoor work of village men and women compared, 214–215
relation to experience of nature, 212–224, 228–229
representativeness of Childerley in relations of, 223
roles in family, 212–213
theories of difference, 223–224
See also nature, experience of; nature, villagers' views
generalized other
concept introduced, 138–139
problem of reflection in natural other, 164–166, 224, 229–230, 237–240
villagers' critiques of, 140–143, 149–151, 228
villagers' resistance to, 153–157, 240
See also collective conscience; me, the; natural other
gentrification. See class conflicts
Gibbs, J. Arthur
epigraph, 3
quoted, 20
Gilligan, Carol, 224
Glacken, Clarence, 6, 121
Goffman, Erving, 53, 54n

Goldthorpe, John, 30, 32
Griswold, Wendy, 90
group-egalitarianism, 59–62

Halsey, A.H., 29
Hampshire, County of
housing prices in, 66
location of Childerley in, 10
physical description, 11
rural-urban interface in, 14–16, 21.
See also counterurbanization
Hampshire County Planning Department, 15
Harper, Sarah, 14–15, 21
Hart, John Fraser, 21
Harwinton, nearby city of, 19
hedgerows, loss in Childerley, 97–98, 100
Hegel, Georg Wilhelm Friedrich, 87
Hillery, George, 89
Hirsch, Fred, 108
Hobbes, Thomas, 165
Hobsbawm, Eric, 30
Horace, Roman poet, 6, 119
housing
constraints on choice, 22–23, 48, 67–68, 108–114
council housing, 13–15, 67–68
percentage rented, 68
prices, 13–14, 21, 66
segregation, 15–16
tied cottages, 12–15, 67, 245n, 248
See also counterurbanization; class conflicts
Howkins, Alun, 9
Hunter, Albert, 23

idealism, materialist critique of, 120
identity
class as source of, 7, 27–50, 76–84, 240. See also class, community assessment; class, villagers' views

identity (*continued*)
    country as source of. *See* country
        identity
    crisis of, 28–29, 50, 84, 86, 114,
        150, 157, 163
    gender as source of, 50, 240
    nature as source of, 8, 23, 29, 84,
        119, 137–140, 147–150, 153,
        157, 163, 227. *See also* natural
        me
    race and ethnicity as source of,
        49–50, 240
    religion as source of, 50, 240
ideology. *See* reflection theory; reso-
    nance
interests. *See* social interests

James, William, 139n
Johnson, Mark, 231

Kerckhoff, Alan, 32–33

Labour Party, decline of, 30, 32n
Lakoff, George, 233
landscape
    changes in Childerley, 97–98, 100
    class differences in perception of,
        166–175, 211–212, 228. *See also*
        classes, cultural differences
    cultural differences in perception
        of, 9–10, 166–175, 211–212,
        228
    Hampshire Downs, history of,
        11–12
    meaning of Childerley's, 3–4
    perception of and social power,
        172
    status implications of, 167–168,
        170–171, 231. *See also* positional
        goods
    villagers' perceptions of, 97–98,
        166–175

    See also privacy
Lao Tzu, 122
Lévi-Strauss, Claude, 232, 238n
Lipset, Seymour Martin, 32
London
    economic and cultural influence of,
        3–4, 13, 21, 66, 244, 245
    perceptions of, 3–4, 94–95,
        244–245
Lovejoy, Arthur, 8
Luhmann, Nicholas, 234n

Mackinder, Sir Halford, 22
Major, John, 30
Malthus, Thomas, 165
Marx, Karl, 62, 87, 142, 165–166,
    166n, 231, 231n
Marx, Leo, 125
materialism, moral problem of, 8, 78,
    84, 138, 140, 143–147, 149,
    156–157. *See also* moral ambiguity
    of class
Mauss, Marcel, 164, 166
McNamara, M. P. Kevin, 186
me, the, 138–139, 148, 150, 157,
    228. *See also* collective conscience;
    generalized other; natural me
Mead, George Herbert, 138–139,
    142, 150
methods
    communication problems in field-
        work, 248–249
    consent, how obtained, 245
    critiques of ethnography, 242–243
    ethical problems of fieldwork, 243–
        244, 247–249
    influence of author's identity on, 8,
        33, 77, 221, 223, 243
    influence of author's skills and
        background on, 8
    informally gathered information,
        247

interviewing techniques, 246–247
introductions to villagers, how ob-
    tained, 245–246
littoral truth, 243
number of interviews, 246
percentage of quoted material
    taped, 247
period of study, 4
rationale for location of study, 8,
    244–245
rationale for use of ethnography in
    study, 242
recording of evidence, 246–247
use of villagers' reponses to au-
    thors' interpretations, 186, 230
use of in-depth interviewing, 246
use of pseudonyms, 243–244
villagers' impressions of author, 33,
    77, 221, 223, 243, 247–249
metropolitan villages, 14–15
Mill, John Stuart, 121, 228
moral ambiguity of class
    and reference problem of reflec-
        tion theory, 230–231
    concept introduced, 7, 28–29, 50
    defined, 78
    use of country identity and country
        life to resolve, 7–8, 86–87, 105–
        108, 114–116, 119, 146–147,
        150–151, 154–156, 163, 227–
        228, 239–241. See also country
        and class
    use of natural conscience to re-
        solve, 7–8, 146–147, 149–151,
        154–156, 163, 227–228, 239–
        241. See also natural conscience
    villagers views, 76–84, 86–87
    See also social interests, problem of
morality and nature. See natural con-
    science; natural me; natural other;
    nature, idea of; nature, villagers'
    views; pastoralism

Naipaul, V.S., epigraph, 11
natural conscience
    concept introduced, 7–8, 138–140
    contradictions villagers experience
        with collective conscience,
        153–157
    defined, 7, 151
    God as a basis for, 156–157
    resonance with collective con-
        science, 227–241
    villagers' descriptions of, 143–157
    See also natural other; natural me;
        collective conscience; resonance;
        nature, moral security of
natural other
    and problem of social interests,
        143–147, 150–153, 157, 229–
        230, 237–241. See also reso-
        nance; nature, moral security of;
        social interests, problem of
    concept described, 143–147
    correspondences with social ex-
        perience, 181, 209, 212–213,
        224
    defined, 147
    God as a manner of, 157
    ideological significance of, 229–
        230, 237–241. See also reso-
        nance
    limits in adaptability, 239–241
    problem of social reflection in,
        164–166, 228–229, 237–239. See
        also reflection theory; resonance
    social criticism of, 240–241
    term introduced, 140
    variety of forms of, 151–153, 157,
        228, 239
    See also natural conscience; natural
        me; generalized other; nature,
        idea of; nature, villagers' views
natural me
    concept described, 147–150

natural me (*continued*)
  country identity as version of, 148,
    150, 228, 239–241. *See also*
    country identity
  defined, 148
  experienced as free from problem
    of social interests, 148, 150, 153,
    157, 228, 239–241. *See also* so-
    cial interests, problem of; moral
    ambiguity of class; nature, moral
    security of
  problem of solipsism in, 149
  term introduced, 140
  See also natural conscience; natural
    other; me, the
natural identity. *See* natural me
nature, idea of
  ancient views of, 121–122,
    130–133
  and sociology, 4
  Aristotelian views of, 121, 130–
    131, 132
  boundary problem in, 6, 8–10,
    120–129, 136
  Christian views of, 132–133
  complexity, 8, 120–136
  cross-cultural comparisons in per-
    ception, 6, 9–10, 122, 134–136
  cultural reach of, 4, 6
  holism defined, 121
  holistic conceptions, 121–122
  Platonic views of, 130–131
  problem of dualism in, 120–122,
    125, 133, 135–136, 147, 153
  reference problem in, 122, 125,
    136
  relevance problem in, 121–122,
    125, 133, 136, 138, 239, 241
  relevance for morality introduced, 4
  separatism defined, 121
  separatist conceptions, 121–122
  social importance, 4–6, 119–120,
    150–151

variability of, 8, 239
  See also pastoralism; nature, villag-
    ers' views
nature, moral security of, 8, 23, 29,
    84, 119–120, 136, 148, 150,
    153, 157, 228, 239–241
nature, villagers' views
  awareness of contradictions in idea
    of, 136, 151
  boundary problem in idea of, 123–
    129, 136, 227
  countryside as distinct from,
    151–153
  cruelty in, 130, 189–192, 194–199,
    200–202, 205–209, 222, 237
  design in, 133
  Eastern aspects in, 134–136
  goodness and, 130–131, 136
  greater reality of, 146–147
  hierarchy in, 190–192, 199–200,
    202, 229, 231
  use of pastoral gradient in ideas of,
    123–129, 136, 147–153, 239–
    240. *See also* pastoralism
  theological aspects, 125, 129–130,
    132–134, 136, 144–145, 195,
    199
  See also natural conscience; nature,
    experience of; nature, idea of
nature, experience of
  relation to class experience, 29,
    161–181, 185, 203–212, 218,
    228–229
  relation to gender experience,
    210–224, 228–229
  relation to political values, 182–
    209, 212, 218, 228–229
  See also nature, villagers' views
Newby, Howard, 15, 75

Oxford Group, survey on class by,
    30–32, 42, 45–49

Pahl, Ray, 21, 89
pastoralism,
    as solution to contradictions of dual-
        ism, 125, 129, 136, 147
    concept introduced, 9–10, 23
    criticisms of, 125–126
    defined, 125
    positive and negative uses of,
        125–126
    villagers' use of, 123–129, 136,
        147–153, 239–240
    See also nature, idea of; nature, vil-
        lagers' views
Perinbayagam, R. S., 142
Perkin, Harold, 30
plants, villagers' perceptions of, 127,
    175–179
Plato, 130–131, 133
politics, villagers' values
    conservatism, 13, 16–20, 80–84,
        186–192, 200–203, 209
    Green, 19
    left and left-leaning, 17–19, 192–
        199, 205, 209
    relation to experience of nature,
        182–209, 212, 218, 228–229
    working class, 203–209
    See also Labour Party, decline of;
        Thatcher, Margaret
pollution, villagers' views, 145
positional goods, 108–114, 170, 231
Postman, Neil, 234n
poverty, in village, 70
Priestly, J.B., 29
privacy, 172–174, 228, 231
property values. See housing
prototypes. See reason
pubs and pub life, 27–28, 58–59,
    61–63

R.S.P.C.A. (Royal Society for the Pre-
    vention of Cruelty to Animals),
    196–197

race and ethnicity
    as source of identity in Britain,
        49–50
    as source of rural gemeinschaft in
        Childerley, 94–95
    chauvinism, 241
    undermining of, 240
reason, theories of
    experiential realism, 233
    prototypes, 233–236
    role of physical and bodily experi-
        ence, 233
    traditional view, 232–233
    See also reflection theory; reso-
        nance
Redfield, Robert, 88–89
reflection theory
    and class-based cultural differ-
        ences, 62
    as product of social kinship,
        164
    "conjurer's trick," 165–166,
        229–230
    correspondences between social
        and natural experience, 161–
        224, 228–229
    critique of, 166, 230–239
    explained, 164–166
    ideological reinforcement and,
        165–166, 229–230, 234
    materialist explanation, 165–166
    rationalism problem in, 230
    reference problem in, 230
    separateness of natural and general-
        ized others, problem of, 166,
        228–229, 234
    sociocentrism in, 230–232
Registrar General, survey on class by,
    45–46
relativism
    nominalism, problem of, 240
    social solipsism, 231, 238
    See also reflection theory

religion
  and experience of nature, 125,
    129–130, 132–134, 136, 144–
    145, 195, 199
  decline as source of identity, 50
  undermining of, 240
residence time by families, class differences, 68
resonance
  change in understanding through,
    237–238
  change-ringing metaphor for,
    234–239
  concept pirated from Northrop
    Frye, 234n
  defined, 234, 239
  dependence on more than social ex-
    perience, 234, 236–238
  greater importance of social experi-
    ence in, 238
  ideological reinforcement through,
    238–241
  intuitive quality of ideological corre-
    spondences, 166, 230, 236–241
Rosch, Eleanor, 233
Rousseau, Jean Jacques
  and pastoralism, 125–126
  epigraph, 137
rural identity. See country identity
rural-urban continuum
  academic views on reality of,
    87–90
  villagers' views on reality of,
    90–101
rural-urban interface, 14–15, 21. See
  also counterurbanization
Russell, Anthony, 21

Saxons, influence on Childerley's land-
  scape, 11
Sayers, Dorothy, 227
Schwartz, Barry, 231, 233
Scott, James, 73, 142

Shelley, Percy, 244n
Simmel, Georg, 87
Skirmish, the
  as a sport, described, 60
  gender and, 214, 214n
  group-egalitarianism and, 60–61
social mobility
  absolute mobility, 31–33
  absolute mobility defined, 31
  continuing ascriptive constraints
    on, 39–42
  historical patterns of, 30–33
  relative mobility or social fluidity,
    31–33
  relative mobility or social fluidity
    defined, 31
  See also achievement; ascription;
    class, community assessment;
    class, villagers' views; class con-
    flicts
social interest, problem of, 7–8, 84,
  138, 140–141, 142–148, 153, 163,
  166, 227–229, 239–241. See also
  materialism, moral problem of;
  moral ambiguity of class; reflection
  theory; resonance
sociology of knowledge. See reason,
  theories of; reflection theory; resonance
spirits and ghosts, 179–181
St. Mary Bourne, nearby village of,
  65–66, 74
Stacey, Margaret, 89
status conservatism, 80–81, 187, 189,
  200

Tennyson, Alfred, 227
Thatcher, Margaret
  quoted, 30
  villagers' views of, 81, 189, 193,
    196, 200, 203–205
  See also politics, villagers' values
Thomas, William I., 86

tied cottages. *See* housing
Tönnies, Ferdinand, 87–89, 93, 97

uniform villages, 14–16
urban ecology, lack of concern for,
    241

village life, image of, 11–12

Weber, Max, 43, 87, 232
Weigert, Andrew, 139

Weiner, Martin, 40
Wild Mammals Protection Bill, 186
Wilde, Oscar, 184
wilderness, 9–10, 240
Williams, Raymond, 8, 52, 100, 101,
    166
Winford, nearby market town of, 17
Wirth, Louis, 88–89
Wordsworth, William, epigraph,
    161
Wright, Erik Olin, 45